T0323316

Financial Deregulation

Financial Deregulation

A Historical Perspective

Edited by

ALEXIS DRACH AND YOUSSEF CASSIS

OXFORD
UNIVERSITY PRESS

OXFORD
UNIVERSITY PRESS

Great Clarendon Street, Oxford, OX2 6DP,
United Kingdom

Oxford University Press is a department of the University of Oxford.
It furthers the University's objective of excellence in research, scholarship,
and education by publishing worldwide. Oxford is a registered trade mark of
Oxford University Press in the UK and in certain other countries

First Edition published in 2021

Impression: 1

Published in the United States of America by Oxford University Press
198 Madison Avenue, New York, NY 10016, United States of America

British Library Cataloguing in Publication Data
Data available

Library of Congress Control Number: 2021936809

ISBN 978–0–19–885695–5

DOI: 10.1093/oso/9780198856955.001.0001

Printed and bound by
CPI Group (UK) Ltd, Croydon, CR0 4YY

Contents

Foreword
A Swing of the Pendulum?

Youssef Cassis

The history of financial regulation and deregulation—the two are of course closely linked—is often couched in terms of swings of the pendulum, also labelled regulatory cycles. State regulations are introduced in the wake of financial crises in order to prevent the speculative excesses that led to their outbreak; they are progressively removed as a new financial boom engulfs the memories of the previous crisis; and regulations are again introduced following a subsequent, and inevitable, financial shock. From this perspective, the balance swung towards regulation in the 1930s, towards deregulation in the 1980s, and again towards regulation in the 2010s.

While there have obviously been periods of more intense regulatory tightening or loosening in modern financial history, such a framework is not entirely satisfactory to understand, in a historical perspective, the deregulations of the 1980s, which are discussed in this book. The story is more complex. There are differences between countries, not least between the United States and Europe. There are different types and indeed definitions of regulation: from the all-encompassing notion of state intervention in financial affairs to the more specific forms of financial regulation, including supervision, and self-regulation. Moreover, financial crises are not always followed by a battery of regulatory measures, and consequently, deregulation doesn't always mean the removal of regulatory measures introduced after a crisis. And whatever they may have in common, financial regulation and deregulation always take place within a specific economic, political, and cultural context.

What have been the relationships between financial regulation and deregulation over the last 150 years? Three moments should be considered: the pre-1914 years, the Great Depression, and the late twentieth century.

It is actually difficult to identify any wave of deregulation before the 1980s. Before 1914, and even 1929, there was not so much to deregulate, as the banking and more generally the financial systems had remained very lightly regulated. However one defines deregulation, the only movement bearing some resemblance is the liberalization of company laws and the introduction of limited liability in the second third of the nineteenth century, which greatly facilitated the establishment of joint stock banks in most European countries. However, this was not so much the deregulation of a regulated banking system as the removal of legal obstacles, inherited from a pre-industrial age, to the development of banking companies. Once established, the 'new banks' were very lightly if at all regulated. The fact that the big banks were deposit banks in Britain and France and universal banks in Germany was not the result of any regulation but the continuation of national experiences and traditions, though some restrictions on the investment banking activities of commercial banks were introduced in Sweden in 1911. The major exception was of course the United States where from an early stage banks were more regulated than in Europe, with in particular, the legal ban on interstate branch banking.

The financial markets were somewhat more regulated. In France, in the official Paris Bourse, stockbrokers (the *agents de change*) were appointed by the government and their number was limited by law. However, there was also a free market, the *coulisse*, which was open to everyone. The complex relationships between the two markets required state regulation, in particular concerning the type of stocks in which the *coulisse* was allowed to operate. In Germany, tight controls were introduced by the 1896 law in order to curb speculation: forward transactions were limited, and entirely prohibited on the securities of mining and manufacturing companies. Self-regulation prevailed on the London Stock Exchange. The separation of the functions of broker and jobber, a unique feature of the London Stock Exchange, came under threat in the 1890s but was maintained by the Management Committee in 1908, and further strengthened by the decision to impose fixed commissions in 1912—a victory for the small brokers and jobbers against the bigger firms, including foreign banks, which favoured deregulation. Similarly, the New York Stock Exchange was self-regulated, though with different rules, notably very restrictive membership criteria, a specialization in the stocks of large companies with a solid reputation, and the obligation for members to charge a minimum one-eighth per cent (0.125%) commission on all transactions, whatever their amount.

These are only a few examples intended to emphasize, on the one hand the nature of the first wave of financial liberalization in the mid to late nineteenth century, which marked the passage from a pre-industrial to an industrial age and concerned the entire corporate sector rather than the financial sector proper; and on the other hand the limits of the regulatory measures in place before 1914 or even 1929. There was of course some degree of state interference in financial affairs, if only because of the very nature of financial transactions and their interactions with monetary policy. Government controls increased during the First World War, but there was no call for financial deregulation during the 1920s, whose excesses were fuelled by the absence of regulation, including new financial instruments, rather than deregulation.

The regulatory framework established in the wake of the Great Depression is usually regarded as an exemplary case of lesson-drawing from a financial crisis: it combined banking regulation (banking Acts were passed in most countries), the regulation of the financial markets, and a new monetary order (the Bretton Woods system), resulting in the financial stability of the Golden Age. However, the regulatory responses to the financial crises of the Great Depression varied considerably between countries, and did not form a coherent whole.

The most severe measures were taken in the United States within the framework of the New Deal, in particular the Glass-Steagall Act of 1933 (which separated commercial banking from investment banking), the Securities Exchange Act of 1934 (which created the Securities and Exchange Commission), and the Banking Act of 1935 (which reformed the Federal Reserve System). The Glass-Steagall Act did change the shape of American banking. And yet it was dictated by political as much as by economic reasons, and it is doubtful that it addressed the main causes of the banking crises that broke out between 1930 and 1933. Most of the small banks that failed during these years (nearly 10,000) were only commercial banks, and they failed because of the depression, their fragility, and the failure of the Federal Reserve to come to their aid. Conversely, the large New York and other major cities' banks, which had securities affiliates, survived the crisis. On the other end, the introduction of the federal deposit insurance, in other words the government commitment to make banks safer to depositors, could justify a measure limiting risk taking.

In Europe, banking legislations were introduced in most countries, with the exception of Britain, but in most cases their effects remained limited. Germany did not abolish universal banking, even though it experienced the most severe banking crisis of the Great Depression. The banking law of December 1934, enacted under the Nazis, attributed the crisis to individual failings rather than to any shortcoming of the system. In effect, it strengthened bank supervision and introduced some restrictions on long-term deposits and on banks' representation on the supervisory boards of other companies. But even though universal banking survived, the government considerably strengthened its hold over financial institutions. Austria and Switzerland did not ban universal banking either, Belgium and Italy, on the other hand, did. Yet all four countries experienced severe banking crises. In France, the Vichy government introduced a law in 1941, upheld and completed in 1944, which controlled and regulated banking activities that until then had been opened to any newcomer. It also made a clear separation between an investment and a deposit bank, but such a separation had actually been in existence since the late nineteenth century. It was known as the 'doctrine Henri Germain', from the name of the founder and then chairman of the Crédit Lyonnais who, following the 1882 banking crisis, laid down this unwritten rule.

As far as European countries were concerned, state intervention in banking affairs was as much a result of the Depression as a consequence of the economic and political context of the Thirties and, even more, the Second World War. Britain is a case in point. From an informal regulatory framework, mainly based on the personal suasion of the Bank of England's Governor, it emerged from the war with a nationalized central bank and clearing banks still in the private sector but under the Treasury's and the Bank of England's strict control—as Keynes put it, in no need to be nationalized as in actual fact they had already been so. The London Stock Exchange was tightly regulated by the authorities; options, considered highly speculative, were reintroduced in 1958 only, after an interruption of 19 years. In France, most of the financial sector came under state control after Liberation. The Bank of France was nationalized, together with the four big deposit banks and all major insurance companies—though the *banques d'affaires* (investment banks), in the first place Paribas, remained in private hands. The state's grip ended up stifling the Parisian capital market, not only when it came to foreign issues, but also for issues by French companies. The Paris Bourse went through a 'long depression' that lasted until the 1980s.

The 'lessons' from the Great Depression must thus be put in perspective. The Bretton Woods system of fixed exchange rates, established in 1944, and the regulations which characterized the third quarter of the twentieth century, were the result of an exceptional historical period marked by two world wars, a devastating economic crisis, massive political upheavals, and shifts in ideological outlooks— the 'Thirty Years War' of the twentieth century.

The financial deregulations of the 1980s and 1990s cannot be simply seen as a reversal of the order inherited from the Great Depression—even though they culminated with the abrogation of Glass-Steagall Act in 1999. In many cases, they put an end to regulations dating back from the nineteenth century.

One of the first measures was the abolition by the Securities and Exchange Commission of fixed commissions in the New York Stock Exchange from 1 May 1975. The measure was made necessary by the growing part played by institutional investors in stock-market transactions; and they led to the disappearance of numerous small brokers. London followed with 'Big Bang' on 27 October 1986—in fact a reform of the London Stock Exchange, the result of an agreement in 1983 between the government and the Exchange, copying what had been done in New York in 1975, and abolishing fixed commissions, as well as the age-old separation between brokers and jobbers. Banks were also permitted to buy member firms, bringing about the disappearance of almost all the leading brokerage houses. In Paris, fixed commissions for bond issues and brokerage involving large sums were almost completely eliminated, the separation between commercial and investment banking came to an end, and the monopoly of the *agents de change* was finally abolished in 1992. Interestingly, deregulation was the answer to the Japanese banking crisis of 1997. A series of measures dubbed the 'Big Bang' were implemented between 1998 and 2001. They abolished, amongst others, the barriers separating banking activities, securities transactions and insurance; and they liberalized foreign exchange transactions.

The United States, which had made the first move by reforming the stock exchange in 1975, also relaxed its banking legislation. Regulation Q (introduced in 1933, which set a maximum rate that banks could pay on savings deposits) was phased out in 1980, and the savings and loans association deregulated in 1982—ushering in a crisis that devastated the industry. In 1994 (with the Riegle-Neal Interstate Banking and Efficiency Act), banks were allowed to set up networks of branches throughout the country. The abolition of the Glass Steagall Act in 1999, with the Financial Modernization Act, was a major break with the regulations of the 1930s. However, it only concerned the United States. The British clearing banks had become universal banks without any legislation and the German banks had never ceased to be so. But it had an enormous symbolic value, as it was justified by the need for greater concentration among the various intermediaries in the world of finance.

Another important feature of the deregulations of the 1980s was that financial innovations remained very lightly if at all regulated. A large chunk of the derivatives contracts, those traded 'over the counter' rather than in an organized market, were entirely unregulated. Hedge funds were also unregulated: they were able to escape the legal constraints on public offerings by being registered offshore or by making private offerings; and they escaped the constraints on investment companies by, in particular, having 'qualified' investors (with assets of $5 million or more).

From a long-term historical perspective, the deregulations of the 1980s and 1990s were a new historical phenomenon. They were dictated by the increased competition between financial markets following the abolition of exchange controls—itself a deregulatory measure; by financial innovation, with the constant arrival of new financial products, and the transformation of banking and financial practices; and by the growing influence of a neoliberal view of the economy and of society. At the same time, as the markets liberalized, new regulatory and supervisory frameworks were set up to ensure that they functioned properly, mainly at national, but also at international level—like the Basel Accords on banks' solvability ratios, as discussed, in particular, in the chapters on the United States, the United Kingdom, and Germany. The ambiguities deriving from the fact that deregulation came together with the rise of prudential regulation are one of the themes of this book, and are highlighted in the Introduction. Analysing the regulatory that followed the Global Financial Crisis in a historical perspective would require another book. Interestingly, however, as suggested in Chapter 9 in the case of the European Union, they have little to do with the 'financial repression' of the golden age.

There is little doubt that the financial liberalization of the late twentieth century bears part of the responsibility for the outbreak of the Global Financial Crisis. However, in order to properly understand the phenomenon, it is essential to consider its specificity, which is more perceptible in its differences than its often deceptive similarities with historical parallels. The historical approach to financial deregulation taken in this book is a step in this direction.

List of Figures

List of Tables

Contributors' bio

Forrest Capie is Professor Emeritus of Economic History at the Cass Business School City, University of London. After a doctorate at the London School of Economics (LSE) and a teaching fellowship there, he taught at the University of Warwick and the University of Leeds. He was a British Academy Fellow at the National Bureau in New York and a Visiting Professor at the University of Aix-Marseille, and the LSE, and a Visiting Scholar at the IMF. He was Head of Department of Banking and Finance at City (1989–92); editor of the *Economic History Review* (1993–99); a member of the Academic Advisory Council of the Institute of Economic Affairs in London (2000–); and an advisor to the Shadow Chancellor of the Exchequer (1997–2004). He has written widely on the history of money and banking and on commercial policy. He wrote the commissioned history of the Bank of England (Cambridge University Press, 2010). His latest book, *Money over Two Centuries*, was published by Oxford University Press in 2012.

Youssef Cassis is Professor at the Robert Schuman Centre for Advanced Studies, European University Institute, Florence, and Director of the ERC funded research project MERCATOR, 'The Memory of Financial Crises: Financial Actors and Global Risk'. He was Professor of Economic History at the European University Institute (2011–19). His work mainly focuses on banking and financial history, as well as business history more generally. His most recent books include *Crises and Opportunities: The Shaping of Modern Finance* (Oxford University Press, 2011), and, with Philip Cottrell, *Private Banking in Europe: Rise, Retreat and Resurgence* (Oxford University Press, 2015). He has also recently co-edited *The Oxford Handbook of Banking and Financial History* (Oxford University Press, 2016, with Richard Grossman and Catherine Schenk). He was a long serving member of the Academic Advisory Council of the European Association for Banking and Financial History (EBHA) and past President of the European Business History Association (2005–07).

João Rafael Cunha is a lecturer in the School of Economics and Finance at the University of St Andrews. Previously, he was a Research Fellow at the University of Cambridge, a Max Weber Fellow at the European University Institute and a Marie Curie Research Fellow at the London School of Economics. His research focuses on financial regulation, banking, political economy, law and economics, and economic history.

Alexis Drach is Research Associate at Glasgow University. He holds a PhD in history from the European University Institute in Florence. His interests lie in the history of banking regulation and supervision, banks' internationalization, European integration, globalization, and expertise. He is part of the ERC-funded project EURECON, 'The Making of a Lopsided Union: European Economic Integration, 1957–1992', where he works on British and French banks and European integration between 1957 and 1992. He is also a research fellow in the ERC-funded project MERCATOR: 'The Memory of Financial Crises: Financial Actors and Global Risk'. His publications include 'Reluctant Europeans? British and French Commercial Banks and the Common Market in Banking (1977–1992)' in

Enterprise and Society and 'From Gentlemanly Capitalism to Lobbying Capitalism: The City and the EEC, 1972–1992' in the *Financial History Review*.

Olivier Feiertag is Professor of Economic and Social History at Paris 1 Panthéon-Sorbonne University. He recently published: *Bank Al-Maghrib 1959–2016: The Emergence of a Central Bank* (Paris/Rabat, Le Cherche Midi, 2016); 'Le sens de la mondialisation: surveillance bancaire et globalisation financière' (with Alexis Drach), *Monde*(s), 13/2018, pp. 133–54.

Eiji Hotori is Professor of Japanese Economic History at Yokohama National University since April 2006. He is also a councillor of the Socio-Economic History Society in Tokyo. He received his PhD in Economics from the University of Tokyo. His research interests are in the domestic and comparative history of commercial banking, financial elites, and banking supervision. Recently his paper 'The Formalization of Banking Supervision in Japan and Sweden' (joint work with Mikael Wendschlag) was published in the *Social Science Japan Journal* 22 (2). In addition, he has published mostly in domestic journals such as *The Review of Monetary and Financial Studies*, *Journal of Political Economy & Economic History and Socio-Economic History*. His English working papers have been online in EABH Paper series (European Association of Banking History). He serves as an associate member of the editorial board of the Japan Society of Monetary Economics.

Christoph Kaserer is a full Professor of Finance at Technische Universität München (TUM). His area of expertise is corporate finance, banking, and asset management. Christoph published his research in leading international academic journals. Recently his paper 'Does Contingent Capital Induce Excessive Risk Taking' (joint work with Tobias Berg) was awarded with the best paper award 2015 in *The Journal of Financial Intermediation*. Christoph is a member of the group of economic advisors to the European Securities Markets Authority (ESMA) and also active as an expert for the German Government as well as for public and private institutions. He is an Associate of the London/Oxford-based economic consulting firm OXERA. Together with Deutsche Börse he developed the German Entrepreneurial Index (GEX©) as well as the DAXplus© Family Index. He is also an official court surveyor in financial market issues and is repeatedly invited to parliamentary hearings as an expert witness. In 2005 he was awarded with the 'Initiativpreis der Stiftung Industrieforschung'. Before joining TUM, he was appointed as Full Professor of Financial Management and Accounting at Université de Fribourg, Switzerland, in 1999. He was the Dean of TUM School of Management (2005–10). According to recently published university rankings TUM School of Management is the top management school in Germany.

Giandomenico Piluso, FRHistS, received his PhD at Bocconi University and is currently Associate Professor of Economic History at the University of Torino. He has been a visiting fellow at Nuffield College, University of Oxford, in 2015 and Jean Monnet Fellow at the Robert Schuman Centre for Advanced Studies, European University Institute (Florence) (2016–17). His research mainly focuses on financial and business history topics paying specific attention to institutions and élites. Amongst his latest publications is 'Adjusting to financial instability in the interwar period. Italian financial élites, international cooperation and domestic regulation, 1919–1939', in Y. Cassis and G. Telesca (eds), *Financial Elites and European Banking: Historical Perspectives*, Oxford, Oxford University Press, 2018.

Agnieszka Smoleńska is a visiting fellow with the Robert Schuman Centre for Advanced studies at the European University Institute (EUI) and a senior EU affairs analyst at Polityka Insight. She completed her PhD in EU cross-border banking regulation at the EUI in 2020. She holds a BA in European Social and Political Studies from University College London and an MA in European Interdisciplinary Studies from the College of Europe (Natolin). In the past she worked at the European Commission and the European Parliament and has cooperated with Transparency International, the World Bank and Florence School of Banking and Finance. Her research interests span EU financial regulation and Economic and Monetary Union (EMU), as well as differentiated integration in finance.

1

Introduction

Alexis Drach

During the Bretton Woods era, the financial system was characterized, according to some scholars, by 'financial repression',[1] meaning an overly regulated system, as opposed to today's financial system. What has changed since that period? Did competition between financial regulators lead to a 'race to the bottom' in regulation? Is deregulation responsible for the recurring financial crises which seem to have characterized the international financial system since the 1980s?[2] These questions invite us to examine what kind of change exactly deregulation was. Was it the removal of a regulation, or rather an enactment of more liberal regulations? What were the respective influence of domestic and external factors in these changes? What were the specific steps and objectives of these reforms? While there are several studies giving some historical perspective on financial regulation in various countries since the 1970s, very few have focused on the various dimensions of deregulation in the two decades or so following the end of the Bretton Woods system. In order to address these questions, this book examines, in a comparative perspective, the national and international circumstances of deregulation. Because of the contributors' main area of expertise, this book primarily focuses on banking deregulation. However, it also addresses other areas of the financial sector such as the securities industry and insurance. It delves into a major yet still poorly understood change in the political economy of global finance, and endeavours to better explain current issues by looking at the complex national and international pathways of banking deregulation.

A wave of liberalization swept the end of the twentieth century. Most developed countries have passed various measures to liberalize and 'modernize' the financial markets. Each country had its agenda, but most of them have experienced, to a different extent, a change in regulatory regime. Interest rates paid on deposits have been liberalized, competition has been favoured, traditional barriers between insurance, banking, and financial market activities, have been removed,

---

[1] Gianni Toniolo and Eugene N. White, 'The Evolution of the Financial Stability Mandate: From Its Origins to the Present Day', *NBER Working Paper* no. 20844 (2015); Stefano Battilossi and Jaime Reis, eds, *State and Financial Systems in Europe and the USA: Historical Perspectives on Regulation and Supervision in the Nineteenth and Twentieth Centuries* (Farnham, England; Burlington, VT, 2010), p. 9.

[2] Barry J. Eichengreen, *Financial Crises: And What to Do about Them* (Oxford: Oxford University Press, 2002).

Alexis Drach, *Introduction* In: *Financial Deregulation: A Historical Perspective*. Edited by: Alexis Drach and Youssef Cassis, Oxford University Press (2021). © Alexis Drach and Youssef Cassis. DOI: 10.1093/oso/9780198856955.003.0001

together with exchange controls. Access to domestic markets by foreign financial institutions has been facilitated through reciprocal agreements or an open-door approach in order to attract foreign investors. However, this movement towards a more liberal regulatory regime was neither linear nor simple.

Historians have not examined this change thoroughly yet, because of the difficulty to access archival material for recent periods. Although some political scientists and historians have considered it, no detailed historical study has been made on this question. Yet the changes that our financial system has undergone in the last decades of the twentieth century have often been depicted as a major transformation. Rajan and Zingales have shed light on a 'great reversal' in the level of financial development in most countries, which retrieved and eventually surpassed their 1913 levels of financial development only towards the end of the twentieth century, and gave an important role to financial liberalization in this change.[3] Some studies have put to the fore the importance of the 1970s and of globalization in this transformation, such as Ferguson et al.'s *Shock of the Global,*[4] which stresses the impact of various international events on most countries. Others have emphasized the role of a new political economy philosophy, such as Abdelal's *Capital Rules,*[5] claiming that it was not the United States, but the European Community, and particularly France, who favoured the liberalization of capital flows. The authors of the collective book edited by Stefano Battilossi and Jaime Reis on *State and Financial Systems in Europe and the USA in the Nineteenth and Twentieth Century*[6] have highlighted the transition from a state-led to a market-led financial system during the last 30 years of the twentieth century. However, few studies focus on the specificity of the post-Bretton Woods era and on the question of deregulation in a historical and comparative perspective.

On the other hand, a quick glance at financial regulation over the last decades, at the amount of paper it produces, at its complexity, at the number of people involved, and at the resources invested in it, is enough to say that, somehow, there is *more* regulation today than ever before. This is even more true since the 2007–08 Global Financial Crisis. In the new system, financial regulation has taken unprecedented importance. This point has been raised by several political scientists, such as Steven Vogel, in *Freer Markets, More Rules,*[7] who argued that there was *reregulation* more than *deregulation,* and that it was a state-led process. The changes in question are indeed complex, different from one country to

---

[3] Raghuram Rajan and Luigi Zingales, 'The Great Reversals: The Politics of Financial Development in the Twentieth Century'. *Journal of Financial Economics* 69, no. 1 (July 2003): 5–50.

[4] Niall Ferguson et al., eds, *The Shock of the Global: The 1970s in Perspective* (Cambridge, Mass.: Harvard University Press, 2010).

[5] Rawi Abdelal, *Capital Rules: The Construction of Global Finance* (Cambridge, Mass.: Harvard University Press, 2007).

[6] Battilossi and Reis, *State and Financial Systems.*

[7] Steven Kent Vogel, *Freer Markets, More Rules: Regulatory Reform in Advanced Industrial Countries* (Ithaca, NY: Cornell University Press, 1996).

another, and somewhat contradictory, with for instance the rise of banking supervision which counterbalanced the removal of some previously existing barriers, and thus justify the in-depth analysis of a historical approach. As more archival material is becoming available, a better understanding of the fundamental changes in the regulatory environment towards the end of the twentieth century is now possible.

Why 'Deregulation?'

If the financial sector is so regulated today, why should we be talking about deregulation at all? Why was this word ever used? A short answer would be that deregulation was a word used by the people involved in the period considered, particularly in the 1980s and 1990s. For historians, this fact is crucial. In particular, the phrase deregulation is found frequently in US archival sources, but also in archival material coming from other countries or of international organizations such as the Bank for International Settlements. In French archives, for instance, the word '*libéralisation*' is often found in records in French, while records in English use 'liberalization' and 'deregulation' somewhat indifferently. In addition, even if deregulation came with new regulations, its political meaning was closely associated with the removal or reduction of state intervention in the financial sector. Deregulation, in this perspective, is not considered here as a concept, even though there certainly was some conceptual thinking on deregulation in economics at the time.[8] In this book, deregulation is primarily considered as a word which became popular, together with liberalization, in the financial and regulatory spheres, in the 1980s. Furthermore, the period under study indeed saw the actual *removal* of many regulations: exchange controls, interest rates regulations, restrictions on inflows or outflows of capital, are just a few areas where many previously existing rules were simply revoked. To some extent, therefore, there was deregulation.[9] However, this trend happened differently, and to a different extent, in different countries, and was compensated by the introduction of other regulations.

Financial deregulation has already received substantial consideration in various academic areas, often in a single country perspective. The United States has attracted most attention, not only because it is the biggest financial power, but

---

[8] For an analysis of the impact of new economic theories on the evolution of banking regulation, see for instance: Sophie Harnay and Laurence Scialom, 'The Influence of the Economic Approaches to Regulation on Banking Regulations: A Short History of Banking Regulations', *Cambridge Journal of Economics* 40, no. 2 (1 March 2016): 401–26.

[9] For a contemporaneous account of the deregulatoy changes going on in the 1980s and early 1990s in several countries in the banking sector, see Itzhak Swary and Barry Topf, *Global Financial Deregulation: Commercial Banking at the Crossroads* (Cambridge, Mass.: B. Blackwell, 1991).

also because its deregulation trend has been the most explicit and because it is where the deregulation movement started. Calomiris pays particular attention to the branching restrictions which long existed in the United States and argues that such restrictions on the geographic activities of banks, together with other restrictions on their functional diversification, have been inefficient and costly. Calomiris situates the US bank deregulation of the 1980s and 1990s in a longer term historical perspective, and stressed three particular factors of deregulation: an alignment of the goals of vested interests with deregulation and an open support of regulatory agencies, as what he calls 'regulatory rents' declined; a competitive pressure from abroad and from the US non-bank financial sector which pushed regulators to take measures enabling banks to survive; and political entrepreneurship.[10] A more recent account of US financial deregulation is Krippner's influential book in the historical sociology of financialization: *Capitalizing on Crisis: the Political Origins of the Rise of Finance*.[11] Krippner puts forward two important drivers of deregulation in the financial markets in the United States: the 1960s and 1970s' social tensions resulting from the scarcity of capital, whereby deregulation appeared to policymakers as a way to avoid difficult political choices concerning to the allocation of resources to different areas, such as housing, industry, large corporations or small businesses; and the 1980s need to finance the fiscal deficit of the government. In all these circumstances, Krippner stresses the *unplanned* character of financialization, which resulted from these deregulation moves. A similar point has been made for the French case: in the context of high interest rates and public deficit, deregulation served to reduce the cost of financing the French state (see Chapter 7, this volume).[12] In this edited volume, the contributions on Japan and Italy also point to similar motives. Reducing the cost of public debt appear to have been an important factor, although not the only one, of financial deregulation.

Regulation has long been portrayed in terms of public and private interests. Scholars have for instance pointed to the role of interest groups in regulation and deregulation. In particular, regulation has been described as a place where rival interest groups compete for influence in order to appropriate rents.[13] As the financial sector can be a source of revenue for governments, financial regulation

[10] Charles W. Calomiris, *U.S. Bank Deregulation in Historical Perspective* (New York: Cambridge University Press, 2000).

[11] Greta R. Krippner, *Capitalizing on Crisis: The Political Origins of the Rise of Finance* (Cambridge, Mass.; London: Harvard University Press, 2012).

[12] See also Laure Quennouëlle-Corre, 'Les réformes financières de 1982 à 1985', *Vingtième Siècle. Revue d'histoire* 138, no. 2 (April 2018): pp. 65–78.

[13] Randall S. Kroszner and Philip E. Strahan, 'What Drives Deregulation? Economics and Politics of the Relaxation of Bank Branching Restrictions', *The Quarterly Journal of Economics* 114, no. 4 (1999): pp. 1437–67; Stefano Battilossi and Jaime Reis, *State and Financial Systems*, p. 3.

can have a key political interest.[14] Approaches using an interest groups perspective have been particularly used to explain deregulatory moves in the United States, in particular concerning the geographical restrictions on banking.[15]

More recently, a large number of studies have reconsidered deregulation and regulation though the lenses of the Global Financial Crisis. Many works scrutinize the regulatory changes which occurred after the crisis, while others look at the origins of the crisis. There has been much debate over the laxity of existing regulation in the discussions on the origins of the Global Financial Crisis. Barth, Caprio, and Levine have been particularly straightforward in stressing the 'colossal failure of financial regulation', in particular—but not only—in the United States, where the authors argue that there has been an 'excessive focus on deregulation'.[16] In his recent account of the global financial crisis, Tooze also stresses the role played by a 'forty-years deregulatory push'.[17] Using a 'varieties of capitalism' perspective to compare British and German approaches to financial regulation, Zimmermann depicts two distinct models, the Germans being much supportive of tighter financial regulation in international forums, and the British being categorically opposed to it.[18] For the British case, Zimmermann argues that deregulation interwove closely with the restructuring of the welfare state.[19] The extent to which the regulatory paradigm has changed in the wake of the crisis is also widely discussed. According to Helleiner et al., the post-crisis changes are not structural, but ad hoc and incremental at best.[20] That question is also addressed in the specific context of the European Union (see Chapter 9, this volume). Another area which is receiving increasing attention in the political economy of financial regulation is its complexity. Avgoulease and Donald have paid particular attention to the role of knowledge.[21] In her contribution to their edited volume, Plato-Shinar argues in particular that the complexity of financial regulation makes it more likely to induce regulatory capture than other sectors.[22]

[14] Kroszner and Strahan, 'What Drives Deregulation?', p. 1439; Battilossi and Reis, *State and Financial Systems*, p. 9.

[15] Kroszner and Strahan, 'What Drives Deregulation?'

[16] James R. Barth, Gerard Caprio, and Ross Levine, *Guardians of Finance: Making Regulators Work for Us* (Cambridge, Mass.: MIT Press, 2012), pp. 3 and 91.

[17] Adam Tooze, *Crashed: How a Decade of Financial Crises Changed the World* (London: Allen Lane, 2018), p. 67.

[18] Hubert Zimmermann, 'Varieties of Global Financial Governance? British and German Approaches to Financial Market Regulation', in *Global Finance in Crisis: The Politics of International Regulatory Change*, edited by Eric Helleiner, Stefano Pagliari, and Hubert Zimmermann (Routledge, 2010), p. 121.

[19] Zimmermann, 'Varieties', p. 135.

[20] Helleiner, Pagliari, and Zimmermann, *Global Finance in Crisis*.

[21] Emilios Avgouleas and David C. Donald, eds, *The Political Economy of Financial Regulation* (Cambridge: Cambridge University Press, 2019).

[22] Ruth Plato-Shinar, 'The Role of Political Economy in Designing Banking Regulation: The Israeli Bank Fees Reform as a Test Case', in *The Political Economy of Financial Regulation*, edited by Emilios Avgouleas and David C. Donald (Cambridge: Cambrdge University Press, 2019), p. 212.

The case of 'Regulatory Capture by Sophistication'[23] interestingly questions the increase of statutory regulation that compensated deregulation in the end of the twentieth century in financial sector: is a system with more statutory regulations necessarily more regulated, or can increasing complexity lead to a less regulated system, despite the amount of regulatory burden?

Central banks have received much attention in the literature on the history of regulation, and are important actors in the different chapters of this book. In particular, the last decades of the twentieth century have been portrayed as a period of increased power of central banks, associated with the rise of central bank independence. This period is sometimes referred to as that of the second central banking revolution.[24] Central banks have also been key players in deregulation. In her review of the recent history of central banks and of their response to the global financial crisis, however, Han points to the fact that deregulation was more a Western phenomenon, while Asian countries kept a strong government-led economy profile. She also notes that banking supervision grew at the same time as deregulation was occurring, and that central banks have come to focus much more on financial stability.[25]

Central banking is also an area where the influence of economists and economic ideas on economic policies has been put to the fore. In a comparative study of central bank governors between 1950 and 2000, Wendschlag showed the rising role of economics in their profile, together with an increase in the level of education.[26] In his overview of central banking in the twentieth century, Singleton acknowledges the role of many economists in supporting central bank independence and liberalization.[27] Prominent figures of central banking have been studied, some of them being for instance described as committed ordoliberals, such as the last governor of the Bundesbank, Hans Tietmeyer.[28] Scholars have also scrutinized how the evolution of central banks' statistical tools in the 1970s paved the way for the 1980s changes in monetary policy which would

---

[23] Hendrik Hakenes and Isabel Schnabel, 'Regulatory Capture by Sophistication', *CEPR Discussion Papers* (London: Centre for Economic Policy Research, August 2014), https://cepr.org/active/publications/discussion_papers/dp.php?dpno=10100.

[24] John Singleton, *Central Banking in the Twentieth Century* (Cambridge: Cambridge University Press, 2011).

[25] Miao Han, *Central Bank Regulation and the Financial Crisis: A Comparative Analysis* (Houndmills, Basingstoke; New York: 2015).

[26] Mikael Wendschlag, 'The Central Bank Elites—Transformations between 1950 to 2000', in *Financial Elites and European Banking: Historical Perspectives*, edited by Youssef Cassis and Giuseppe Telesca (Oxford: Oxford University Press, 2017), pp. 182–208; Mitchel Y. Abolafia, 'Central Banking and the Triumph of Technical Rationality', in *The Oxford Handbook of the Sociology of Finance*, edited by Karin Knorr Cetina and Alex Preda (Oxford: Oxford University Press, 2012), pp. 94–112.

[27] Singleton, *Central Banking in the Twentieth Century*, pp. 204, 224.

[28] Kenneth Dyson, 'Hans Tietmeyer, Ethical Ordo-Liberalism, and the Architecture of EMU: Getting the Fundamentals Right', in *Architects of the Euro: Intellectuals in the Making of European Monetary Union*, edited by Kenneth Dyson and Ivo Maes (Oxford University Press, 2016), pp. 138–69.

go together with deregulation.[29] At any rate, changes in policies, ideas, statistics, went hand in hand.

Deregulation and Neoliberalism

While this book is not focused on the history of ideas, the advent of neoliberalism is often associated with some form of deregulation or liberalization. It is beyond the scope of this book to review the literature on neoliberalism. However, the large number of publications using this word calls for a few considerations on the links between both trends. In his 1979 seminal work on the birth of biopolitics, Michel Foucault analysed a political stream of thought seeking how 'not to govern too much'.[30] The art of limiting government power is an essential element, in Foucault's perspective, in the history of liberalism. In this framework, the market becomes the site of the formation of truth, and not just a jurisdiction.[31] Foucault contextualized the ongoing changes in the 1970s thinking in political economy, going back to the eighteenth century as well as to more recent changes with the case of German ordoliberalism. Today the word neoliberalism is closely associated with Reagan and Thatcher in politics, and Hayek and Friedman in economics.[32] However, most specialists recognize the complexity and diversity of forms of neoliberalism, suggesting that there are many neoliberalisms.[33] Intellectual history has shown the long way for pro market advocates to regain mainstream status in economics—from the 1920s to the 1970s.[34] In academic spheres, the refoundation of liberalism was meant to lead to something clearly different from nineteenth century laissez-faire. Pro market advocates recognized, to a various extent from one economist to another, the need for rules to insure the proper functioning of markets.[35] In neoliberalism studies, the phrase deregulation is therefore often criticized on the same grounds as mentioned earlier, namely that what is usually associated with deregulation actually implied new regulations,

---

[29] Olivier Feiertag, 'L'École de la Banque de France: statistiques monétaires et greffe économétrique à la Banque de France (1970–1990)', in *Mesurer la monnaie*, edited by Feiertag, pp. 13–26.

[30] Michel Foucault, *The Birth of Biopolitics* (New York: Palgrave Macmillan, 2008), p. 13.

[31] Ibid., p. 30.

[32] For a general historical approach of neoliberalism, see David Harvey, *A Brief History of Neoliberalism* (Cary: Oxford University Press, 2005).

[33] Angus Burgin, *The Great Persuasion: Reinventing Free Markets since the Depression* (Cambridge, Mass.: Harvard University Press, 2012); Daniel Stedman Jones, *Masters of the Universe: Hayek, Friedman, and the Birth of Neoliberal Politics* (Princeton: Princeton University Press, 2012); Quinn Slobodian, *Globalists: The End of Empire and the Birth of Neoliberalism* (Cambridge, Mass.; London: Harvard University Press, 2018).

[34] Burgin, *The Great Persuasion*; Ola Innset, *Reinventing Liberalism. The Politics, Philosophy and Economics of Early Neoliberalism (1920–1947)* (Cham: Springer, 2020).

[35] Ibid.

and could go along with an explosion of regulation.[36] Furthermore, recent studies have put to the fore the relationship between neoliberal thinkers and globalization, and the role of Europe and the 'Geneva school' in this process, next to well-known other centres such as Chicago and Frankfurt.[37] By shedding light on the regulatory practices of the financial sector and how they evolved from the 1970s to the 1990s, and by paying attention to the technical details and not only to ideas and high politics, this book brings a contribution to the literature on neoliberalism and complements its intellectual dimension.

Deregulation and Prudential Supervision

The period under study saw the development of prudential supervision. In Chapter 6, Kaserer provides quantitative evidence showing that, in Germany, the resources allocated to banking supervision have increased compared to the size of the German banking sector, particularly after 1988. In Chapter 3, Capie makes a similar point for the staff employed in banking supervision in the United Kingdom, where banking supervision and regulation had long been informal and where the advent of statutory regulation actually coincided with the last decades of the twentieth century usually associated with deregulation. The staff employed in banking supervision actually grew steadily in many countries since the 1970s.[38] Except in the United States where it was already well developed, banking supervision often grew from a few dozen (or less) employees in the 1970s to several thousand today.[39] This growth sometimes simply reflected that of the banking and financial sector. Even more so, in the United States, banking supervisory staff shrunk compared to total Federal Reserve employees at least from the mid-1990s until the mid 2000s.[40] Still, according to Howard Davies, there was one regulator for every three banks in the United States in 1935, whereas there were three regulators for every bank by the global financial crisis.[41]

---

[36] Manuel A. Aalbers, 'Regulated Deregulation,' in *The Handbook of Neoliberalism*, edited by Simon Springer, Kean Birch, and Julie MacLeavy (New York, NY: Routledge, Taylor & Francis Group, 2016), pp. 563–73.

[37] Slobodian, *Globalists*.

[38] Alexis Drach, 'La prudence en bonne et due forme: supervision et regulation bancaires internationales à l'aube de l'èreglobale,' *Entreprises et histoire* 92, no. 3 (December 2018): pp. 92–105.

[39] United States Congress Senate Committee on Banking, Housing, and Urban Affairs, *1980 Budgets of the Federal Bank Regulatory Agencies: Hearing Before the Committee on Banking, Housing, and Urban Affairs, United States Senate* (Washington: US Government Printing Office, 1980); Drach, 'La prudence'.

[40] Thomas M. Eisenbach, David O. Lucca, and Robert M. Townsend, 'The Economics of Bank Supervision', *Federal Reserve Bank of New York Staff Reports* no. 769 (March 2016).

[41] Howard Davies, *Can Financial Markets Be Controlled?* (Cambridge, UK; Malden, MA: Polity Press, 2015), p. 71.

Banking supervision is sometimes presented as the control of banks' compliance to regulation, regulation being the overall legal framework in which banks operate.[42] This view is a bit of a simplification, however, as banking supervision, to some extent, has its own logic.[43] In the period considered, although it had changed over time and evolved along different national traditions, banking supervision usually involved checking the accounts of banks, discussing with the banks' management, and on-site inspections. It was mostly concerned with *prudential* issues, that is ensuring the safety and soundness of individual banks, and thereby protecting the depositors. Regulation, on the other hand, could have other purposes, and long had monetary purposes in addition to prudential ones. This distinction between monetary and prudential matters in regulation was often put forward in the discussions of early years of the Basel Committee on Banking Supervision, where delegates from the Group of Ten countries, Luxembourg and Switzerland exchanged about their own national supervisory system.[44] This was particularly the case in Italy and France.[45] As monetary policies increasingly relied on market mechanisms towards the end of the twentieth century, and as deregulation and globalization increased the risks run by individual banks and by the financial system as a whole, banking regulation in general focused more on prudential matters. Another important characteristic

[42] Duncan R. Wood, *Governing Global Banking: The Basel Committee and the Politics of Financial Globalisation* (Aldershot: Ashgate, 2005), p. 6.

[43] There are now numerous publications on the history of banking supervision. See for instance: Eugene Nelson White, *The Comptroller and the Transformation of American Banking, 1960–1990* (Washington, D.C.: Comptroller of the Currency, 1992); Eugene N. White, 'Lessons from the History of Bank Examination and Supervision in the United States, 1863–2008', in *Financial Market Regulation in the Wake of Financial Crises: The Historical Experience* (Roma, Italy: Banca d'Italia, 2009), pp. 15–44; Richard S. Grossman, 'The Emergence of Central Banks and Banking Supervision in Comparative Perspective', in *State and Financial Systems*, edited by Battilossi Reis (Abingdon: Taylor & Francis), pp. 123–39; Charles Albert Eric Goodhart, *The Basel Committee on Banking Supervision: A History of the Early Years, 1974–1997* (Cambridge; New York; Melbourne: Cambridge University Press, 2011); Eiji Hotori, 'A History of Prudential Bank Supervision in Japan: Organization, Institutions and Function, 1873–1942', *Economia* 62, no. 2 (November 2011): pp. 29–41; Thibaud Giddey, *Histoire de la régulation des banquesen Suisse (1914–1972)* (Genève: Droz, 2019); Catherine R. Schenk, 'Summer in the City: Banking Failures of 1974 and the Development of International Banking Supervision', *English Historical Review* 129, no. 540 (January 2014): pp. 1129–56; Kris James Mitchener and Matthew Jaremski, 'The Evolution of Bank Supervisory Institutions: Evidence from American States', *The Journal of Economic History* 75, no. 3 (September 2015): pp. 819–59; Olivier Feiertag and Alexis Drach, 'Le Sens de La Mondialisation: Surveillance Bancaire et Globalisation Financière du XXe au XXIe Siècle', *Monde(s)* 13, no. 1 (May 2018): pp. 133–54; Alexis Drach, 'A Globalization Laboratory: European Banking Regulation and Global Capitalism in the 1970s and Early 1980s', *European Review of History: Revue Européenned'histoire* 26, no. 4 (4 July 2019): pp. 658–78; Mikael Wendschlag and Eiji Hotori, 'The Formalization of Banking Supervision: A Comparison between Japan and Sweden', *EABH Papers* 18, no. 3 (2018).

[44] The Group of Ten gathered Belgium, Canada, France, Germany, Italy, Japan, the Netherlands, Sweden, the United Kingdom, and the United States.

[45] For Italy, this was for instance discussed during an early meeting of the Basel Committee on Banking Supervision; see Bank for International Settlements Archives (BISA), 1.3a(3) F, First meeting of the Basel Committee, 6 and 7 February 1975. For France, see Eric Monnet, *Controlling Credit: Central Banking and the Planned Economy in Postwar France, 1948–1973* (Cambridge: Cambridge University Press, 2018).

of banking supervision at the time is that it was focused on the individual bank, and not on the financial system as a whole. Systemic considerations and macroprudential regulation only developed in the late 1990s, although they had been discussed since the late 1970s.[46]

There has been a parallel trend, if not a trade-off, between prudential supervision and deregulation in the late twentieth century. Several scholars and practitioners have noted this two-sided trend.[47] Ribavoka argues that there was little need for supervision before liberalization, because interest rates and credit allocation were often under government control, competition was limited, and in some cases banks were publicly owned.[48] This double movement was actually perfectly perceived by regulators at the time. Robert Shumway, director of banking supervision at the Federal Deposit Insurance Corporation and member of the Basel Committee on Banking Supervision between 1984 and 1986, wrote in 1987: 'Continued deregulation of the banking industry, while both necessary and beneficial, increases the potential level of risk in banking operations. Nevertheless, deregulation is not incompatible with increased supervision. Rather, by introducing new risks and increasing those risks already present, deregulation will contribute to a need for increased supervision.'[49] In France, the vice-director of the Banking Commission, Thoraval, also noted in 1993 the coexistence of deregulatory and prudential measures, and therefore preferred the word liberalization.[50] In fact, the rise of banking supervision largely explains why the 'deregulation' trend is so ambiguous. As the contributions to this volume show, some rules were indeed removed, while others, in particular in the field of prudential supervision, were introduced or reinforced. Overall, banks and other financial institutions became freer, as they could extend their activities geographically and functionally, but they became also more closely inspected by authorities. Surveillance and freedom to operate went hand in hand. In this perspective, the evolution of banking and financial regulation in the last decade of the twentieth century coincides relatively well with what studies on neoliberalism claim neoliberalism is: not a total fall-back of the state but a change in its attitude, or even a reinforced presence, so as to ensure the proper functioning of market mechanisms.

---

[46] Piet Clement, 'The Term "Macroprudential:" Origins and Evolution', BIS Quarterly Review (March 2010), pp. 59–67; Alexis Drach, 'Supervisors against Regulation? The Basel Committee and Country Risk Before the International Debt Crisis (1976–1982)', Financial History Review (forthcoming).

[47] Davies, 'Financial Markets'; Elina Ribakova, 'Liberalization, Prudential Supervision, and Capital Requirements; The Policy Trade-Offs', IMF Working Paper (July 2005).

[48] Ribakova, 'Liberalization', p. 3.

[49] Robert V. Shumway, 'The Compatability of Deregulation and Increased Supervision', Annual Review of Banking Law 6 (1987): pp. 247–51.

[50] Pierre-Yves Thoraval, 'La déréglementation du système bancaire français est-elle optimale?', Revue d'économie financière 27, no. 4 (1993): pp. 221–30.

The 1970s also saw the development of *international* banking supervision, with the establishment of a group of EEC supervisors in 1972, and, at the level of the Group of Ten countries, of the Basel Committee on Banking Supervision in late 1974.[51] The Basel Committee was established after a series of failures, in particular of the German Herstatt bank whose closure had caused upheavals in international banking markets, and of Franklin National in the United States.[52] The Basel Committee became much famous for its successive agreements on banks' capital adequacy ratio, known as Basel I (1988), Basel II (2004), and Basel III (from 2010 on). However, its initial mandate was not about setting standards for large international banks, but to foster cooperation in the field of banking supervision and exchange on best practices.[53] The Basel Committee was created by the central bank governors of the Group of Ten countries, who met at the Bank for International Settlements, in Basel. As competition increased between international banks from various countries, the role of the Committee to foster the supervision of international banking activities was complemented by another mandate: that of creating a level playing field between large international banks. In political science, the 1988 Basel I agreement has been largely portrayed as a move imposed by the United States and, to a lesser extent, the United Kingdom, to force other countries to raise their banks' capital adequacy and enable US American banks to compete on equal footing with banks from these other countries. Although this view exaggerates the role of the United States and downplays that of the European Economic Community which had started a similar capital convergence exercise earlier, competitive considerations were critical in the Basel I and subsequent Basel agreements.[54] And at any rate, banking supervision could not be conceived at the national level only from that moment on.

Deregulation, Globalization, and Competition

This book focuses on a group of countries which, even though they represented the biggest financial powers of their time, were not the only actors in the global

---

[51] Goodhart, *Basel Committee*; Schenk, 'Summer in the City'; Emmanuel Mourlon-Druol, 'Banking Union in Historical Perspective: The Initiative of the European Commission in the 1960s–1970s', *JCMS: Journal of Common Market Studies* 54, no. 4 (January 2016): pp. 913–27; Drach, 'A Globalization Laboratory'.

[52] Emmanuel Mourlon-Druol, '"Trust Is Good, Control Is Better": The 1974 Herstatt Bank Crisis and Its Implications for International Regulatory Reform', *Business History* 57, no. 2 (February 2015): pp. 311–34.

[53] Christopher Kobrak and Michael Troege, 'From Basel to Bailouts: Forty Years of International Attempts to Bolster Bank Safety', *Financial History Review* 22, no. 2 (August 2015): pp. 133–56; Drach, 'A Globalization Laboratory'.

[54] Drach, 'A Globalization Laboratory'.

regulatory scene, and certainly did not represent the entire world. While a complete review of other countries is beyond the scope of this book, the 1970s and 1980s worldwide financial landscape is important to take into account. The 1970s came with the end of the Bretton Woods system and the advent of floating in the international monetary system.[55] Shortly after the final act of the breakdown of the system in 1973, the first oil shock was another decisive blow to the international financial system. The accumulation of dollars in oil exporting countries were deposited in Western and Japanese banks which 'recycled' them by lending to various countries, mostly through the Eurodollar markets. This led to an international lending boom in the 1970s. This boom came to a halt when, in the early 1980s, the international debt crisis threatened the largest banks of the world, in particular in the United States where banks were particularly exposed to Latin American, Eastern European, and other indebted developing countries.[56] The crisis triggered an active role of the IMF to prevent from a default in developing countries, which would have threatened the international banking system, through convincing banks to continue lending.[57] Throughout the 1980s, more than 50 countries entered into debt rescheduling procedures.[58] As is well known today, part of the conditions for this continuation of financial flows from Western and Japanese banks to developing countries was liberalization and structural reforms. At their June 1985 meeting in Tokyo, finance ministers and central bank governors from the Group of Ten countries issued a statement: 'We also recognize the need to deregulate further capital markets and liberalize capital movements, as well as to provide financing on appropriate terms to developing countries which, despite adjustment efforts, lack sufficient access to financial markets.'[59] The 1980s trend of deregulation was also partly circumstantial, in the sense that it resulted from the very peculiar international debt situation running through the entire decade, and itself resulting from the 1970s upheavals in the international financial system.[60]

---

[55] Harold James, *International Monetary Cooperation since Bretton Woods* (Washington, DC; New York: International Monetary Fund; Oxford University Press, 1996).

[56] Robert Devlin, *Debt and Crisis in Latin America: The Supply Side of the Story* (Princeton, NJ: Princeton University Press, 1989); James, *International Monetary Cooperation*; Fritz Bartel, 'Fugitive Leverage: Commercial Banks, Sovereign Debt, and Cold War Crisis in Poland, 1980–1982', *Enterprise & Society* 18, no. 1 (March 2017): pp. 72–107; Sebastian Alvarez, 'The Mexican Debt Crisis Redux: International Interbank Markets and Financial Crisis, 1977–1982', *Financial History Review* 22, no. 1 (April 2015): pp. 79–105; Carlo Edoardo Altamura, *European Banks and the Rise of International Finance: The Post-Bretton Woods Era* (London, New York: Routledge, Taylor & Francis Group, 2017). Emmanuel Mourlon-Druol, 'The Role of a Creditor in the Making of a Debt Crisis: The French Government's Financial Support for Poland, between Cold War Interests and Economic Constraints, 1958–1981', *Financial History Review* 27, no. 1 (April 2020): pp. 73–94.

[57] James, *International Monetary Cooperation*.   [58] Altamura, *European Banks*, p. 196.

[59] Federal Reserve Bank of New York archives (FRBNYA), *central files*, box 198389, '*Communiqué of the Ministers and Governors of the Group of Ten, Tokyo, June 21, 1985*', p. 3.

[60] Altamura, *European Banks*.

In the context of internationalizing financial activities, competition was increasing in two forms: between different national financial systems, and between banks and non-bank financial institutions. Increased competition pushed financial institutions to design new financial instruments. This new competitive environment at the international level became a major motive behind the Basel exercise to find an agreement on common capital adequacy ratios for international banks in 1988 (Basel I).[61] As already noted, the Basel Committee progressively became a tool for creating a level playing field in international banking.[62] Regulatory competition also existed in the context of the competition between international financial centres in the Group of Ten countries. This was for instance visible in the deregulatory measures enacted to promote Paris as financial centre, but also in Germany, even though this country had otherwise been less involved with deregulation.[63] For example, in 1990 the German government passed the Financial Market Promotion Act, abolishing the stock duty tax and liberalizing investment funds, while the Bundesbank was changing its policy to stimulate the money market and the first derivatives exchange was being established (see Chapter 6 by Kaserer).

Another important dimension of regulatory competition in a worldwide context was the rise of offshore financial centres. These financial centres, although very diverse from one another, often developed in the afterwar period or in the 1970s after adopting regulations favourable to banks and created competitive deregulatory pressures.[64] That was for instance the case in the United States, where the creation of International Banking Facilities (IBFs) in New York, discussed since the mid-1970s and enacted in late 1981, was a direct response to the development of offshore centres.[65] IBFs were not a physical location, but a separation in banks' accounts enabling them to book some operations which were previously booked in offshore centres. IBFs established a free trade zone in New York. They combined several regulatory advantages: they exempted banks from Federal Reserve interest rates restrictions related to regulation Q, from reserve

---

[61] Goodhart, *The Basel Committee*; Drach, 'A Globalization Laboratory'.

[62] Ethan B. Kapstein, *Governing the Global Economy: International Finance and the State* (Cambridge, Mass.; London, England: Harvard University Press, 1994); Wood, *Governing Global Banking*; David Andrew Singer, *Regulating Capital: Setting Standards for the International Financial System* (Ithaca, NY: Cornell University Press, 2010).

[63] Youssef Cassis, *Capitals of Capital: A History of International Financial Centres, 1780–2005* (Geneva: Pictet, 2005).

[64] On offshore centres, see for instance: Vanessa Ogle, 'Archipelago Capitalism: Tax Havens, Offshore Money, and the State, 1950s–1970s'. *The American Historical Review* 122, no. 5 (1 December 2017): pp. 1431–58; Catherine Schenk, 'The Origins of the Asia Dollar Market 1968–1986: Regulatory Competition and Complementarity in Singapore and Hong Kong.' *Financial History Review* 27, no. 1 (April 2020): pp. 17–44; Emmanuel Mourlon-Druol, 'The Rise of International Financial Centres after the Breakdown of Bretton Woods. The Case of Bahrain, 1966–1986.' *Monde(s)* 13, no. 1 (4 June 2018): pp. 49–66.

[65] FRBNYA, central files, box 615781, note on *International Banking Facilities*, 15 October 1981.

requirements related to regulation D, and from New York state and local taxes.[66] The project had a marked New York character. It emanated from big New York banks, and was supported by New York based trade associations, New York congressmen and senators, New York State and City governments. They were resisted by non-New York bankers and trade associations, some senators and congressmen outside New York, and most foreign bankers.[67] The Federal Reserve itself was quite reluctant initially because it feared losing control of its monetary policy. However, it eventually accepted the idea, and IBF became operational from December 1981 on.[68] They were meant to have an impact in particular on the Caribbean zone, which was operating in the same time zone and was closely linked to US activities.

In order to limit gaps in the international surveillance of banks, offshore centres became widely discussed at the Basel Committee on Banking Supervision from 1977 on. The Committee made a distinction between those offshore centres which were only booking centres, such as the Bahamas or the Cayman Islands, and those where actual transactions were made, such as Hong Kong, Singapore, or Bahrein, which were real international financial centres.[69] In a 1978 report to the central bank governors of the Group of Ten countries, the Basel Committee stated that the most frequent characteristics offshore centres were that most operations were conducted in a currency different from the domestic currency, that clients were not residents in these countries, and that the control of banks in these territories was light or inexistent.[70] Offshore centres also had light fiscal requirements and very liberal corporate law, exempted banks from monetary regulations, and enabled them to work 24 hours a day because of their geographic location. In some cases, like for the Bahamas and Cayman Islands, absolute banking secrecy rules were in place:[71] a pro-business environment was not only about light regulation, but more about regulatory structures protecting banking

---

[66] FRBNYA, central files, box 615781, 'International Banking Facilities in the United States', Mark Lindbloom and Dr P. Hayek, fall 1980.

[67] FRBNYA, central files, box 615781, 'International Banking Facilities in the United States', Mark Lindbloom and Dr P. Hayek, fall 1980, p. 5.

[68] FRBNYA, central files, box 615781, 'Offshore financial centers—The next twenty years. Remarks by H. David Willey, Vice President, Federal Reserve Bank of New York at the Third International Banking Conference of the Association of International Banks in the Bahamas, Nassau, The Bahamas, March 16, 1981'.

[69] Catherine Schenk, *Hong Kong as an International Financial Centre: Emergence and Development, 1945-1965* (London: Routledge, 2001); Catherine R. Schenk, 'The Dissolution of a Monetary Union: The Case of Malaysia and Singapore 1963-1974', *The Journal of Imperial and Commonwealth History* 41, no. 3 (September 2013): pp. 496-522; Emmanuel Mourlon-Druol, 'The Rise of International Financial Centres after the Breakdown of Bretton Woods', *Monde(s)* 13, no. 1 (June 2018): pp. 49-66.

[70] Bank for International Settlements Archives (BISA), 1.3a(3) 1978/8, BS/78/2 f: 'Problèmes posés aux autorités de contrôle bancaire des pays du Groupe des Dix et de Suisse par l'existence de centres financiers offshore dans d'autres pays', July 1978.

[71] BFA, 1749200912/304, 'Informal record of the joint meeting between the Basle Committee on Banking Regulations and Supervisory Practices and supervisory representatives from ten offshore centres held at the BIS on 29th, 30th and 31st October 1980'.

interests. In 1979, the Basel Committee organized an international conference of banking supervisors, where they invited delegates from offshore centres. From 1980 on, it regularly organized joint meetings with regulators from these places. The first meeting in October 1980 gathered delegates from the Bahamas, Bahrein, Cayman Islands, Guernsey, Hong Kong, Jersey, Lebanon, Netherlands Antilles, Panama, and Singapore.[72] The second one gathered the same countries except Panama, plus Barbados, Cyprus, Gibraltar, the Isle of Man, and Vanuatu.[73] Most of these discussions aimed at enabling at least informal cooperation between the G10 countries offshore centres. Their regulatory implications were limited, however. At any rate, these contacts revealed the issue of regulatory competition for attracting banking activities, and the possibilities for banks to escape national regulation through booking part of their operations offshore, which was another incentive for deregulating at home.

Deregulation and Innovation

Deregulation and innovation bore a mutually reinforcing relationship: some innovations resulted from deregulatory measures, and these innovations exerted a pressure in other countries to take similar deregulatory moves, while these innovative activities undermined domestic control. For example, the removal of British and Japanese exchange controls in 1979 and 1980 constituted an important accelerator in the development of innovations. However, deregulation was not the only factor of innovation: the rise of inflation in the 1970s, the high volatility of interest rates and exchange rates, the early 1980s debt crisis and fall in oil prices, the competition from the non-bank financial sector, the development of new technologies were all contributing to the rise of innovation. In addition, a new regime of innovation was being established, where innovation was becoming a permanent feature of the financial system, because banks and financial institutions started to introduce innovation in their business model and to hire specialists dedicated to devising new products. Innovation was not resulting from deregulation only but was exerting a pressure for more deregulation.

The Bank for International Settlements followed closely the rise in innovation and its links with both a regime-change in regulation and the wider context. In April 1986, the Bank for International Settlements published a study conducted by experts from the Group of Ten countries on recent innovations in international banking. In 270 pages, it analysed the various aspects of financial innovation,

---

[72] Ibid.
[73] BFA, 1749200912/357, BS/82/86, 'Informal record of the joint meeting between the Basle Committee on Banking Regulations and Supervisory Practices and supervisory representatives from ten offshore centres held at the BIS on 28th October 1982'.

with a particular interest in off-balance sheet instruments. It highlighted the deep mutation of banking and financial systems and the interconnexion of the observed changes with deregulation, globalization, and innovation. The development of new instruments in banking activities, in particular of note issuance facilities, currency and interest rate swaps, foreign currency and interest rate options, and forward rate agreements experienced a sharp grow in the first half of the 1980s. Deregulatory measures were also bringing domestic and international financial markets closer together. For instance, the US euro-markets and domestic markets became more integrated after the deregulation on interest rates ceilings and the establishment of IBFs in the early 1980s.[74] In Japan, Germany, France, and the Netherlands, the authorities relaxed national regulations controlling the variety of new instruments available for non-dollar borrowing, thereby facilitating the spread of innovations from dollar-denominated markets, where most innovations originated.[75] Regulation and deregulation also favoured the global integration of financial markets by fostering the international diversification strategies of the institutionally managed funds, such as pension funds, insurance companies, unit trust or mutual funds.[76] For instance, the Employee Retirement Income Security Act in 1974 in the USA, requiring pension funds to prudently diversify their investment, had a major impact the level of institutional investment because it was followed by an increase in foreign investment.[77] Likewise, British pension funds' holding of foreign securities grew steadily after the abolition of exchange controls in the United Kingdom in 1979, which facilitated foreign investment from the United Kingdom.[78] In Italy and Japan, unit trusts, insurance companies, and pension funds were allowed to invest an increasing share of their assets abroad from 1980 on.[79]

The Book's Contribution to the Debate on Deregulation

This book gathers contributions on different countries, using different approaches, but also reflecting diverging opinions of scholars on deregulation. We considered this diversity of cases and of views as a welcome element of discussion which brought much to the reflexion on deregulation. In particular, the authors of the chapters on Britain and Germany present these two countries as less concerned by deregulation. In the first case, the long tradition of informal regulation, even during the Bretton Woods system, makes it difficult to portray

---

[74] Euro-Currency Standing Committee, 'Recent innovations in international banking (Cross Report)', Bank for International Settlements, April 1986, p. 149.
[75] Ibid., p. 157.   [76] Ibid., p. 155.   [77] Ibid., p. 155.   [78] Ibid., p. 156.
[79] Ibid., p. 156.

the last decades of the twentieth century as a deregulation era, as they were also the beginning of statutory regulation. Capie also question the fact that the 1986 'Big Bang' was really a deregulatory move, as what it brought to an end was more self-regulating clubs (Chapter 3).[80] In the case of Germany, the banking regulation system was liberalized earlier, and there was less to deregulate, except in the capital market sector, where deregulatory moves also occurred.

Cunha adopts a regulatory cycle view of the financial sector in the United States, a new cycle of looser regulation having replaced the tight regulation period which started in the Great Depression. He argues that in the United States, the system shifted from a stable but poorly competitive one to a competitive but unstable one. Branch banking was particularly restricted in the United States, which led the country to have many banks, but few branches. Reviewing the removal of regulations on deposit interest rate, branch banking, and separation between commercial and investment banks, Cunha portrays a massive shift away from a state led to a market led financial system. He analyses how the separation between banking, insurance activities, and securities activities faded from the 1980s on. He also shows that liberalization occurred in the real estate lending area. Cunha reviews several rationale for deregulation which have been put forward in the literature: the fight against inflation, which was the main reason for the repeal of Regulation Q, the ideological shift to the right, and market pressure. Financial deregulation in the US had several impacts. It led to an increase in non-interest income, a concentration of the banking industry, an increased reliance on the national deposit insurance scheme which created moral hazard problems, the practice of 'too-big-to-fail' resolution doctrine. It also enabled banks to access new markets, such as the subprime loans market which played an important role in the global financial crisis. Deregulation did not stop in the end of the 1990s but continued until the crisis. Lastly, Cunha makes a comparison with Canada, whose financial system has been more stable. While in Canada universal banking led to bigger banks, in the United States the move towards universal banking led to shadow banking.

Capie provides a long-term perspective on the history of banking regulation in the United Kingdom from the nineteenth century to the twenty-first century. He contrasts the second half of the twentieth century with a wave of deregulation that swept the United Kingdom from the 1830s onwards, with the end of usury laws, the authorization of limited liability or the relaxation of bank share prices. Capie argues that deregulation occurred in the nineteenth century, but that since the Second World War, regulation has only been increasing. He also points that, contrary to what is commonly thought, financial stability in the United Kingdom

---

[80] For a historical analysis of Big Bang, see Christopher Bellringer and Ranald Michie, 'Big Bang in the City of London: An Intentional Revolution or an Accident?', *Financial History Review* 21, no. 2 (2014): pp. 111–37.

came with a deregulated system. What brought this to an end was the Second World War, which led British banks to hold large amounts of government debt, and to a change in the business climate. Strict liquidity and cash ratio were in use. Some controls which had been established during the war were maintained. By the 1950s, directives and ceilings were introduced to direct credit to specific sectors. Other measures were also used to contain lending, like in other countries. Capie also stresses the rise of banking supervision from the 1970s, and the fact that there are now more people than ever overseeing banking activities. He also challenges the view that the famous 1986 'Big Bang' usually associated with deregulation really was a deregulatory move, as it was more about abolishing clubs, which were self-regulation bodies, and as the bureaucratic burden on British banks continued to rise in the 1980s. Overall Capie highlights the unusual character of statutory regulation in the banking sector in the United Kingdom, which had long been informally or self-regulated. He further argues that increased regulation of the late twentieth century did not prevent the Global Financial Crisis. He finally briefly shows that a similar story happened in the insurance sector.

In the fourth chapter, Hotori argues that the US pressure on Japan to deregulate its financial system was not as overwhelming as commonly thought, and stresses that there were domestic reasons for deregulation in Japan. In particular, he underlines the role of fiscal reasons in the deregulatory trend: the ratio of government bonds to GDP rose sharply after the first oil shock, from 7.6% in 1974 to 25.4% in 1979. Under pressure from securities companies, the Ministry of finance liberalized the financial sector, removing in particular the barriers between banking and securities activities. If the pressure of the United States was strong in the 1980s, liberalization had started in the late 1960s and early 1970s in the wake of an administrative shift away from the conventional rigid regulatory system, and carried on in the 1990s while the US pressure was not central any more: it was then more the sluggish economic growth which drove financial liberalization. Hotori focuses on three areas where deregulation can be observed: the separation between banking and securities businesses, the regulation of deposit interest rates, and the liberalization of financial markets. The Japanese approach to deregulation was described as 'gradualist'.

In the fifth chapter, Drach scrutinizes the role of European integration in the liberalization of the financial sector. Financial liberalization was meant to promote financial integration which, in the 1980s, was seen as lagging behind commercial integration. The plans for financial integration, although they were not implemented before the 1980s, date back to the very beginnings of European political integration. Drach analyses in particular the construction of a common market in banking and the liberalization of capital flows in the European Community, and finally addresses other areas of the financial sector, such as insurance and securities activities. The advent of the mutual recognition principle played an important role in unlocking progress in European financial regulation, as it gave the Commission the opportunity to establish the freedom of establishment and the freedom to provide services throughout the Community without having to go through a total harmonization of regulations. Mutual recognition was as a liberalization step not necessitating the removal or addition of regulations, but simply circumventing existing national regulations. Harmonization occurred in particular in the field of banking supervision, and was not necessarily an increase in regulation, but a way to remove obstacles to integration. Drach argues that the European integration process played important role in the liberalization of financial services in the Community and that it added a further push for liberalization on EEC member states. In the Community, liberalization had two main motives: deepening the common market and making monetary cooperation/integration work better.

The case of Germany, analysed by Kaserer, looks like that of the United Kingdom, despite the two countries' different financial history. Both countries were quite liberal by the 1970s, and regulation tended to increase in the end of the century, although not in the capital markets. In Germany, capital movements were liberalized in the 1960s, and deposit interest rates in 1967. The Herstatt failure in 1974 triggered a shift in the regulatory landscape, as regulation tended to increase afterwards. Kaserer also reviews international standards governing capital adequacy (Basel I and Basel II). He argues that Basel I and II were not necessarily tighter regulations than those preexisting in Germany, but that they increased the regulatory burden and perimeter of banking supervision. He makes a similar case for Europe, stating that international European activities have become much easier while at the same time the regulatory burden has increased. Kaserer particularly stresses the increased complexity of banking regulation. He further makes a thorough analysis of the importance of banking supervision compared to the size of the banking sector and concludes that banking supervision has substantially increased. The growth of banking supervision really started after 1988. On the other hand, Kaserer depicts a different story for capital market regulation, where he identifies a clear liberalizing trend from the 1990s, when German authorities passed several measures to promote and develop the German capital market. He also particularly stresses the role of European integration in this process.

Feiertag analyses the case of France, which has sometimes been portrayed as paradoxically at the forefront of financial liberalization. Feiertag argues that public debt was the major motive behind French financial deregulation, and that the state, and not the market, had the leading role in this process. Between 1978 and 1985, the level of public debt doubled and the debt service burden was multiplied by 3.6. This rise was not limited to France and was linked to the rise in real interest rates in the wake of disinflation policies. However, in the context of the arrival of the left in 1981 France, the rise of public debt was at the core of a political battle between two visions of economic policy: that of continuation of the French social model even at the cost of high public debt, and that of reduction of public debt at all cost. Using archival material from the entourage of François Mitterand, Feiertag shows that the key players of French economic policy were very anxious about public debt issues from 1983, both because of a real concern about these high levels of indebtedness and because the opposition was massively using the argument of public debt to attack the socialist government. In this context, the liberalization of the financial sector appeared as a way to soften the constraint on French economic policy and autonomy, as it aimed to reduce the cost of debt by dynamizing the French financial markets.

Piluso (Chapter 8) analyses the case of Italy. He argues that, contrary to a commonly held view, financial deregulation was not a political agenda of the government and parliament. The Bank of Italy was the main driver of what is portrayed as a 'sea-change' in financial regulation and monetary policy. The origins of this change are to be found in the perceived inefficiency of previously existing regulations in the face of weak economic growth, inability to deal with macroeconomic turmoil episodes, stagflation, and currency instability. The system of 'rationed private sector credit' dating back from the 1930s was progressively dismantled. The causes of the change were not only domestic, however. It was also an adjustment to the international regulatory landscape. In particular, the European framework proved particularly influential, and became the main driver of financial liberalization in the 1980s. For a long time the cornerstone of the credit system was the state backed bond market, which heavily depended on macroeconomic stability. When inflation started to rise in the mid-1960s it threatened this system and triggered much pessimism. The turning point in regulation occurred with the arrival of Baffi at the Bank of Italy in 1975, even though the changes were very progressively introduced. Like for other countries, government borrowing played an important role too. The rationale for financial liberalization evolved from escaping inefficiency in the 1970s to EEC regulatory convergence in the 1980s, and was more an attempt to reorganize allocative mechanisms in order to restore economic growth than a political plan for radical deregulation.

Analysing the post-crisis reforms in the financial sector in the European Union, Smoleńska stresses the peculiarity of the EU context, characterized by the challenging 'dilemma between preserving market openness associated with EU integration without compromising financial stability'. She identifies a change of regulatory regime since the Global Financial Crisis, but not a return to the 'financial repression' era, as liberal market openness continues to characterize EU regulation. Smoleńska argues that it was not just lax regulation which caused the specific European banking crisis, but a lack of cross-border supervision matching cross-border activities of banks. The crisis in the European Union triggered a fragmentation in banking markets which further aggravated the crisis. This fragmentation was the result of an incomplete regulatory framework. Smoleńska identifies five stages in post-Global Financial Crisis regulatory reform: a calibration of EU state aid rules to the banking sector (2008–10), a first EU institutional reform with the establishment of the European Banking Authority in 2010, a substantive bank regulation reform between 2010 and 2014 with the enactment of the Capital Requirement Directive IV and the Bank Recovery and Resolution Directive, the Banking Union and second institutional reform between 2013 and 2018, and a second substantive bank regulation reform with the adoption of the Capital Requirement Directive V and of the Bank Recovery and Resolution Directive 2 between 2016 and 2019. A new regime was introduced and its main characteristics were the increased discretionary powers of authorities, the public interest concerns imposed on bank management, and a reinforced attention to cross-border entities. The new regulatory and supervisory apparatus are now so intrusive that they blur the traditional boundaries between regulation and corporate governance. A high degree of discretion and a hybrid, public–private governance are now central to the new system, but are very different and much more nuanced than those in place in many European countries until the 1970s.

Conclusion: The Deregulation Trends in the 1980s

In a broad perspective, banking deregulation, and more generally financial deregulation, revolved around four main areas: market access by foreign institutions (or access to other countries from domestic institutions), interest rates, capital flows, and the blurring of boundaries between spheres of activities, such as insurance, securities, and banking.[81] The contributions to this book show the importance of the relaxation of existing rules on interest rates paid on deposits in the United States and Japan (Chapters 2 and 4). With the removal of such regulations, banks could freely compete to attract depositors. The liberalization of capital flows was another critical element: as shown in Chapter 5, it was critical in the European integration context, where it was also pivotal for all financial activities, banking, insurance, or capital market activities, and for monetary integration. The blurring of the boundaries between fields of activities such as banking, insurance, and capital market was another structural change of financial systems and was facilitated both by deregulatory measures and innovation.[82]

---

[81] BFA, 1749200912/265, '5th International Conference of Banking Supervisor'.
[82] Euro-Currency Standing Committee, 'Cross Report'.

Deregulation also had country-specific or region-specific features. That was for instance the case of the gradual lift of the restrictions on branch banking in the United States (Chapter 2), where previously many banks were prevented from opening branches in other states. In the European Economic Community, the framework for monetary cooperation, in particular from 1979 on with the European Monetary System, was another regional specificity. The chapters on France, Italy, and the European Economic Community particularly stress the role of European monetary affairs in pushing towards liberalization. In his recent book on central banking in postwar France, Monnet makes a parallel between the end of credit controls in Europe and convergence of central banks' policies, which were at least partially related to the project and constraints of European monetary cooperation.[83] In Japan, deregulation was also partly the result—although less than commonly thought, as Hotori shows—of external pressure exerted by the United States (Chapter 4).

Looking at the different contributions to this volume, four elements of the deregulatory process keep coming at the forefront: fiscal issues, monetary issues, international pressure, and low economic growth. Several states encountered fiscal issues, in particular in the 1980s, and in Italy, Japan, France, and the United States, financial deregulation was implemented in order to limit the price of public (and private) debt. This point has already been made for some individual countries.[84] The contributions to this volume give this point further weight, but also show that it was not the only driver of deregulation. Another important motive for the liberalization of banking and financial markets was the evolution of monetary policy, often in the wake of the fight against inflation. In France and several other European countries, for instance, the credit system was under strict control until the 1970s, but the central bank progressively gave the market a more important role in the allocation of credit.[85] A first movement of liberalization had actually happened in the early 1970s, but the monetary and financial upheavals of the decade brought it to an end. At the European Economic Community level, monetary considerations had a critical role in furthering liberalization of capital movements, along with common market concerns (Chapter 5). International factors, such as European integration or globalization, also exerted a pressure on other countries to liberalize their financial sector, either for competitive reasons or for harmonization reasons. Lastly, financial liberalization was also often seen by policymakers as a way to support sluggish economic growth, as is particularly

---

[83] Monnet, *Controlling Credit*, pp. 271–3.

[84] In particular, on the United States: Krippner, *Capitalizing on Crisis*; on France: Quennouëlle-Corre, 'Les réformes financières de 1982 à 1985'; on the United Kingdom: Sahil Jai Dutta, 'Sovereign Debt Management and the Globalization of Finance: Recasting the City of London's "Big Bang"', *Competition & Change* 22, no. 1 (February 2018): pp. 3–22.

[85] Monnet, *Controlling Credit*, pp. 270–1.

illustrated in this volume by the contributions on Japan (Chapter 4) or Italy (Chapter 8).

The deregulation trends examined in this book spanned from the 1970s to the 1990s, with a sharp acceleration in the 1980s. They were the national and international variants of a change in regulatory regime towards a more market-oriented system. Some regulations were indeed revoked. However, this alleviation of state control went hand in hand with a dramatic increase in prudential supervision, and therefore of surveillance. The new liberal order paradoxically involved a very active and intrusive role of authorities in financial institutions' affairs. The 1980s were particularly central in the deregulation trends, because many countries took deregulatory measures at the same time. In that perspective, the United States played a leading role, but in Europe the European Economic Community, pursuing its monetary and economic integration programme, was also instrumental, particularly after the relaunch of the integration process in the mid-1980s. The 1980s were also a decade where new political tools were experimented after the failed attempts of the 1970s to fight inflation and relaunch economic growth. To some extent, the deep change in economic forces, marked by low economic growth, high inflation, accelerating globalization, and technological change, combined with new political tools to produce a new regulatory regime.

2

The Advent of a New Banking System in the US

Financial Deregulation in the 1980s

João Rafael Cunha

Introduction

The 1980s was one of the most eventful and consequential decades in the development of the US financial system.[1] During this decade, the regulatory framework established in response to the Great Depression started to be dismantled. These regulatory changes were a key driving force behind the transformation of the banking sector.[2] Moreover, the end of the decade saw the most serious banking crisis since the Great Depression. This pattern of deregulation and crises, which started in the 1980s, has continued until the present. Thus, it is worth study this period in greater detail and the consequences it has had for the US banking and financial system.

In this chapter, I will argue that the deregulatory process that occurred in the 1980s changed the profile of the US banking system from a not very competitive and stable system to a competitive, but unstable system.

The banking sector is marked by a peculiar feature. Greater competition may be good for efficiency, but bad for financial stability.[3] In the 1980s, there was a clear change in the profile of the US banking system in the 1980s. In this decade, the US banking sector went from one end of the competition–stability trade-off (stable, but not very competitive) to the other (competitive, but unstable).

Between the Great Depression to the 1980s, the US banking regulators favoured stability. During this period, the US banking system was characterized by low competition and stability.

---

[1] This chapter was prepared for *Financial Deregulation: A Historical Perspective*, Oxford University Press. I am grateful to Maria-Chiara Iannino and the editors for insightful comments and suggestions. All remaining mistakes are mine.

[2] Allen N. Berger et al., 'The Transformation of the US Banking Industry: What a Long, Strange Trip It's Been', *Brookings Papers on Economic Activity* 1995/2 (1995): pp. 55–218.

[3] Franklin Allen and Douglas Gale, 'Competition and Financial Stability', *Journal of Money, Credit and Banking* 36, no. 3 (2004): pp. 453–80.

João Rafael Cunha, *The Advent of a New Banking System in the US: Financial Deregulation in the 1980s* In: *Financial Deregulation: A Historical Perspective*. Edited by: Alexis Drach and Youssef Cassis, Oxford University Press (2021).
© Alexis Drach and Youssef Cassis. DOI: 10.1093/oso/9780198856955.003.0002

Since the 1980s, banking regulators have favoured competition. For this purpose, they deregulated this industry. As a consequence, this sector has become more competitive, but also more unstable. As we can see in Table 2.1 from White,[4] in the four decades from 1940 to 1979, there were a total of 246 bank failures and 134 million dollars in deposit insurance losses. The decade from 1980 to 1989 alone dwarfed this numbers with 1086 bank failures and 22,961 million dollars in deposit insurance losses. These numbers are more than 4 and 171 times greater than the ones observed in the previous four decades combined.

This deregulatory process was achieved by loosening and repealing regulation in several areas of the banking sector. The 1980s saw a loosening of the restrictions on business areas in which commercial banks could be involved. They also witnessed the repeal of Regulation Q, the interest rate ceiling on deposits. Moreover, there was a gradual lift of the restrictions on branch banking and real estate lending.

The main argument proposed here links to the idea of the financial regulatory cycle proposed by Rajan; Coffee Jr.[5] They suggest that financial regulation moves in a cyclical manner. According to them, periods of loose regulation are followed by times of tight financial regulation, which then revert back to looser regulation. These regulatory changes continue in a cyclical manner.

In my argument, I am referring to a long type of cycle. A type of Kondratiev regulatory cycle. In this long regulatory cycle, the 1980s started a new period of looser regulation. This new phase followed the previous period of tighter regulation that lasted from the Great Depression to the 1980s.

As the largest economy in the world and the global superpower of the time, the US conducted most of its economic policy without much influence from the rest

Table 2.1 Bank failures and deposit insurance losses, 1940–99

Decade	Number of bank failures	Deposit insurance losses ($ million)
1940–49	99	6
1950–59	28	3
1960–69	43	8
1970–79	76	117
1980–89	1086	22,961
1990–99	509	13,769

Source: White[6]

---

[4] Lawrence J. White, 'Bank Regulation in the United States: Understanding the Lessons of the 1980s and 1990s', *Japan and the World Economy* 14, no. 2 (2002): pp. 137–54.

[5] Raghuram G. Rajan, 'The Credit Crisis and Cycle-Proof Regulation', *Federal Reserve Bank of St. Louis Review* 91, no. 5 (2009): pp. 397–402; John C. Coffee Jr, 'Political Economy of Dodd-Frank: Why Financial Reform Tends to be Frustrated and Systemic Risk Perpetuated', *Cornell L. Rev.* 97 (2011): p. 1019.

[6] White, 'Bank Regulation in the United States: Understanding the Lessons of the 1980s and 1990s'.

of the world. However, there was one aspect in which coordination with other large economies affected US banking regulation. The Basel Accords attempted to regulate banking practices at an international level. In 1988, Basel I created a set of rules to establish capital adequacy. However, it may have contributed to the growth of securitization and, thus, the 2007–08 financial crisis.[7]

There are several explanations proposed as the main reason for the deregulatory process that occurred in the US financial sector in the 1980s. The main one is usually attributed to the prevailing economic conditions following the end of the post-WWII 'Golden Age' prosperity.[8] Political reasons[9] and pressure from the industry[10] are also other notable reasons to justify the financial deregulation of this decade.

The next section of this chapter will elaborate on the regulatory changes that liberalized the banking sector in the US in the 1980s. In the third section I will focus on the consequences of the deregulatory process. The fourth section presents a comparison between the US and Canadian banking systems. The fifth section concludes.

The Liberalization of the US Financial Sector in the 1980s

In the 1980s, several of the regulatory constraints imposed on the financial sector were loosened. Most of the regulations that were lifted had their origin in the regulatory response to the Great Depression. These changes represented a tectonic shift in the level of restrictions financial firms faced. This represented a shift along the financial regulatory cycle from a period of high regulatory constraints on financial firms to a period of looser regulation.

Regulatory Background

Until the 1980s, commercial banking in the US was a protected industry. Through the McFadden Act of 1927, the federal government prohibited interstate branch

---

[7] Shadow Financial Regulatory Committee, *The Basel's Committee New Capital Adequacy Framework, Statement Number 156, September 27* (Shadow Financial Regulatory Committee, 1999); Markus K. Brunnermeier, 'Deciphering the Liquidity and Credit Crunch 2007–2008', *Journal of Economic perspectives* 23, no. 1 (2009): pp. 77–100.

[8] Matthew Sherman, *A Short History of Financial Deregulation in the United States* (Washington, DC: Center for Economic Policy Research, 2009).

[9] Greta R. Krippner, *Capitalizing on Crisis: The Political Origins of the Rise of Finance* (Harvard University Press, 2011); Christopher Hare and Keith T. Poole, 'The Polarization of Contemporary American Politics', *Polity* 46, no. 3 (2014): pp. 411–29.

[10] Douglas D. Evanoff et al., 'Financial Industry Deregulation in the 1980s', *Federal Reserve Bank of Chicago, Economic Perspectives* 9, no. 5 (1985): pp. 3–5.

banking, thus, protecting banks from out-of-state competition. Moreover, most states also imposed restrictions on intrastate banking.

Following the Great Depression, the Glass-Steagall Act of 1933 separated commercial and investment banking. This allowed regulators to more tightly regulate commercial banks, while also shielding them from competition from other financial institutions. Additionally, Regulation Q imposed an interest rate ceiling on deposits, which restricted price competition between commercial banks.

Nationwide branch banking was de facto prohibited in the US. The Douglas amendment to the Bank Holding Company Act of 1956 forbade holding firms from acquiring banks outside the state where it was headquartered unless the state of the bank being acquired explicitly allowed this type of acquisitions in their law. As we can see in Table 2.2, no state allowed it until 1978. Additionally, most states also restricted within-state bank branching.[11] Thus, making the US a country where nationwide branch banking was banned. Figure 2.1 provides supporting evidence to this point. It shows that in 1980, there were many banks, but few branches.

Table 2.2 Year of deregulation of restrictions on geographical expansion, by state—year in which a state entered into an interstate banking agreement with other states

State	Year	State	Year	State	Year
Alabama	1987	Kentucky	1984	North Dakota	1991
Alaska	1982	Louisiana	1987	Ohio	1985
Arizona	1986	Maine	1978	Oklahoma	1987
Arkansas	1989	Maryland	1985	Oregon	1986
California	1987	Massachusetts	1983	Pennsylvania	1986
Colorado	1988	Michigan	1986	Rhode Island	1984
Connecticut	1983	Minnesota	1986	South Carolina	1986
Delaware	1988	Mississippi	1988	South Dakota	1988
DC	1985	Missouri	1986	Tennessee	1985
Florida	1985	Montana	1993	Texas	1987
Georgia	1985	Nebraska	1990	Utah	1984
Hawaii	1997	Nevada	1985	Vermont	1988
Idaho	1985	New Hampshire	1987	Virginia	1985
Illinois	1986	New Jersey	1986	Washington	1987
Indiana	1986	New Mexico	1989	West Virginia	1988
Iowa	1991	New York	1982	Wisconsin	1987
Kansas	1992	North Carolina	1985	Wyoming	1987

Source: Stiroh and Strahan[12]

[11] Randall S. Kroszner and Philip E. Strahan, 'What Drives Deregulation? Economics and Politics of the Relaxation of Bank Branching Restrictions', *The Quarterly Journal of Economics* 114, no. 4 (1999): pp. 1437–67.
[12] Kevin J. Stiroh and Philip E. Strahan, 'Competitive Dynamics of Deregulation: Evidence from US Banking', *Journal of Money, Credit, and Banking* 35, no. 5 (2003): 801–28.

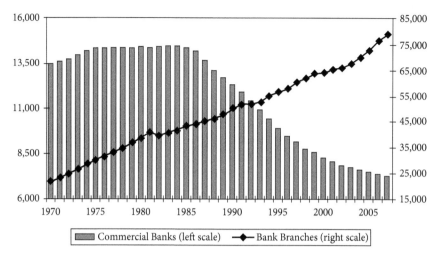

Figure 2.1 Number of commercial banks and commercial bank branch offices in the US between 1970 and 2007.

Source: DeYoung and Rice[13]

Just before the start of the 1980s, over 95% of commercial banks were community banks. These were banks that held less than $1 billion in assets (2006 dollars). These banks were able to exist, because the restriction on branch banking heavily protected them from competition from larger nationwide banks.[14]

New Business Areas

One of the cornerstones of the Glass–Steagall Act of 1933 was the separation of commercial and investment banking. The 1980s witness the erosion of this separation, despite the fact that this Act was only formerly repealed in 1999 with the Gramm–Leach–Bliley Act. In 1984, the Federal Deposit Insurance Corporation ruled that insured non-member banks could establish or acquire subsidiaries that were engaged in securities activities.[15]

Additionally, in 1986, the Federal Reserve reinterpreted the Glass–Steagall separation between commercial and investment banks. The Fed established that a bank could receive up to 5% of its gross revenues from investment banking services. To support their new interpretation, the Fed argued that the Glass–Steagall Act

---

[13] Robert DeYoung and Tara Rice, 'How Do Banks Make Money? The Fallacies of Fee Income', *Economic Perspectives-Federal Reserve Bank of Chicago* 28, no. 4 (2004): p. 34

[14] Robert DeYoung, 'Banking in the United States', in *The Oxford Handbook of Banking* (Citeseer, 2010), pp. 777–806.

[15] Federal Deposit Insurance Corporation, *Annual Report of the Federal Deposit Insurance Corporation* (Federal Deposit Insurance Corporation, 1984).

did not precisely define what 'engaged principally' meant. Thus, the amount to which commercial banks were involved in other activities was open to interpretation. In the following year, the Fed pushed this rationale further by allowing several banks to be involved in securities underwriting.[16]

In this same year of 1987, Alan Greenspan was appointed Chairman of the Federal Reserve. Under his tenure, the Fed continued to reinterpret the Glass–Steagall Act. This time, it allowed commercial banks to operate 'Section 20' subsidiaries to underwrite corporate securities as long as they did not exceed 10% of gross revenues.[17] Section 20 of the Glass–Steagall Act prohibited member banks of the Federal Reserve System from being affiliated with any firm that was 'engaged principally' in securities underwriting. The Fed chose to not interpret this as a total prohibiting against the underwriting of securities by commercial banks and relaxed the existing restrictions.

Later on, in 1989, the Fed started relaxing the restrictions from the Glass–Steagall Act that banned banks from underwriting corporate securities themselves.[18] This was due to the competitive pressure US commercial banks faced from their European counterparts and non-bank financial institutions.[19]

Following these developments, many states started allowing state-chartered banks to participate in securities underwriting, securities brokerage, real estate development, insurance underwriting and insurance brokerage. By the end of the decade, only seven states prohibited state-chartered banks from doing securities brokerage and 29 allowed them to engage in securities underwriting. Twenty-five states permitted their banks to enter into real estate development and six allowed banks to underwrite insurance beyond credit life insurance.[20]

Branch Banking

Nationwide branch banking was not fully allowed in the US. The McFadden Act of 1927 had prohibited interstate branching. This lasted until the Riegle-Neal Interstate Banking and Branching Efficiency Act of 1994. Kane[21] explains that the status quo of not allowing nationwide branch banking was the best for regulators due to economic and political incentives.

---

[16] Sherman, *A Short History of Financial Deregulation in the United States*.

[17] Sherman, *A Short History of Financial Deregulation in the United States*; DeYoung, 'Banking in the United States'.

[18] DeYoung, 'Banking in the United States'.

[19] Charles W. Calomiris, *US Bank Deregulation in Historical Perspective* (Cambridge University Press, 2000).

[20] Lee Davison, 'Banking Legislation and Regulation', in *History of the 1980s: Lessons for the Future*, Vol. I (Federal Deposit Insurance Corporation, 1997).

[21] Edward J. Kane, 'De Jure Interstate Banking: Why Only Now?', *Journal of Money, Credit and Banking* 28, no. 2 (1996): pp. 141–61.

However, a nationwide banking system began being established in the 1980s. This happened because branch banking restrictions were gradually removed throughout the 1980s. The Garn-St Germain Depository Institutions Act of 1982 amended the Banking Holding Act to permit any bank holding firm to acquire failed banks or thrifts regardless of the state where they were headquartered. This created a manner for banks to enter another states where they would normally not be able to receive a charter.[22]

Shortly afterwards, the Office of the Comptroller allowed nationally chartered banks to branch without restrictions in states where savings institutions were not subjected to branching restrictions. This introduced statewide bank branching in several states, most of them located in the south.[23]

Throughout the 1980s, most states relaxed their laws prohibiting interstate banking and branch banking. States circumvented the McFadden Act by establishing bilateral and multilateral agreements that allowed banks to acquire their counterparts from any other state participating in the agreement. This allowed banks to cross state lines through multi-bank holding firms.[24] As we can see in Table 2.2, by 1993, only Hawaii did not permitted the entrance of banks from all other states. Additionally, most states changed their laws to allow branch banking. By 1990, only the Colorado still completely prohibited branch banking.[25]

All these factors led to the creation of a de facto nationwide banking system in this decade. Figure 2.1 shows that this deregulatory process was followed by an increase in the number of branches.

According to Kerr and Nanda,[26] the lift of branch banking restrictions led to an increase in competition in other industries. This happened because entrepreneurship grew remarkably after this reform. They argue that the lift of restrictions on branch banking reduced the distortions in the banking sector due to the limited competition. This, in turn, democratized access to loans for entrepreneurship and, thus, increased competition in other areas of the economy.

Interest Rate Relaxation

One of the most important regulatory changes in the 1980s was the relaxation of the ceiling on interest rates. The Depository Institutions Deregulation and

---

[22] Kroszner and Strahan, 'What Drives Deregulation? Economics and Politics of the Relaxation of Bank Branching Restrictions'.

[23] Stiroh and Strahan, 'Competitive Dynamics of Deregulation: Evidence from US Banking'.

[24] DeYoung, 'Banking in the United States'.

[25] Michael D. Bordo, Hugh Rockoff, and Angela Redish, 'The US Banking System from a Northern Exposure: Stability versus Efficiency', *The Journal of Economic History* 54, no. 2 (1994): pp. 325–41.

[26] William R. Kerr and Ramana Nanda, 'Democratizing Entry: Banking Deregulations, Financing Constraints, and Entrepreneurship', *Journal of Financial Economics* 94, no. 1 (2009): pp. 124–49.

Monetary Control Act of 1980 established the Depository Institutions Deregulation Committee (DIDC), who was required to gradually phase-out Regulation Q. Moreover, it also allowed commercial banks and thrifts to offer money market deposit accounts (MMDAs). Later, the Garn-St Germain Depository Institutions Act of 1982 required the DIDC to abolish any remaining Regulation Q differentials by 1984.

Regulation Q set interest rate ceilings on deposits. It was established in 1933 as part of the response to the Great Depression. It was meant to increase lending to local communities by reducing the balance small banks held at large ones, increase bank profits by restricting competition for deposits, and increase the liquidity of the banking system.[27]

As the post-war high growth rate economic climate was dying off, interest rate ceilings became a problem in a high inflation and high interest rate climate. As Figure 2.2 shows, from 1966 until 1986, market interest rates rose sharply with Treasury bills rising above the ceiling rates on deposits. This meant that as inflation became endemic in the 1970s, savings in banks lost value in real terms. Thus, consumers were moving away from deposits that offered low interest rates in an economy with high inflation. In this economic environment, as Figure 2.3 shows,

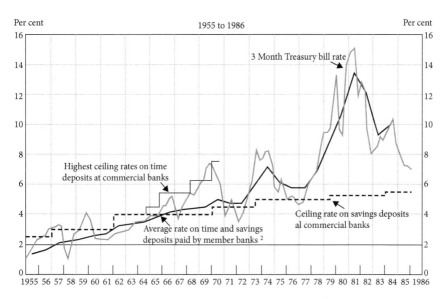

Figure 2.2 Interest rates and the ceiling rates on time and savings deposits.
Source: Gilbert[28]

[27] R. Alton Gilbert, 'Requiem for Regulation Q: What It Did and Why It Passed Away', *Federal Reserve Bank of St. Louis Review* 68 (1986): 22–37.
[28] Gilbert, 'Requiem for Regulation Q: What It Did and Why It Passed Away'.

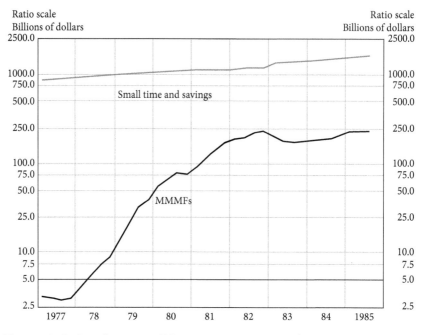

Figure 2.3 Savings deposits at all depository institutions and investments on money market mutual funds.

Source: Gilbert[29]

money market mutual funds continued to grow and were becoming an alternative that paid higher interest rates compared to deposits at commercial banks.

Regulation Q failed its original aims of increasing profits and reducing the balance banks held at other banks. Thus, Congress repealed Regulation Q. This measure quickly produced results. As we can see in Table 2.3, in this period, checkable deposits started growing rapidly after all depository institutions were allowed to offer these type of accounts in 1981. Additionally, Table 2.4, shows that, in the same period, the share of small time and savings deposits plus money market deposit account at commercial banks increased from around 40% of the overall market to over 50% in 1985.

Real Estate Lending

The 1980s also saw the liberalization of regulation governing real estate lending. The Garn–St Germain Depository Institutions Act of 1982 removed statutory

---

[29] Ibid.

Table 2.3 Checkable deposits

Year	Amount at all depository institutions (billions of dollars)	Percentage at commercial banks
1978	5.3	46.9
1979	14.5	74.1
1980	21.8	76
1981	65.7	81.4
1982	90.4	79.2
1983	121.2	74.9
1984	139.2	72.9
1985	159	71

Source: Gilbert[30]

Table 2.4 Time deposits at commercial banks as a percentage of deposits at all depository institutions

Year	Small time deposits	Small time and savings deposits plus MMDAs
1978	36.6	40.7
1979	36	40.1
1980	38.6	41.4
1981	40.9	42.5
1982	43.8	44.4
1983	44.7	48
1984	44.3	48.7
1985	43.7	50.7

Source: Gilbert[31]

restrictions on real estate lending by national banks. These restrictions included maximum loan-to-value ratios for real estate loans and set aggregate limits on real estate limits.

Additionally, this act gave the Comptroller of the Currency the authority to set these rules in the future. This agency proposed no limitations on real estate loans, because it believed that they were hampering the ability of the banks to response to changes in the real estate market. Moreover, it also believed that this choice should be the prerogative of the bank management team.[32]

Later in the decade, the Alternative Mortgage Transactions Parity Act of 1982 removed the restrictions on classes of mortgages with exotic features, such as adjustable rates and interest only mortgages.[33] These type of loans had teaser

[30] Gilbert, 'Requiem for Regulation Q: What It Did and Why It Passed Away'.
[31] Ibid.
[32] Davison, 'Banking Legislation and Regulation'.
[33] Sherman, *A Short History of Financial Deregulation in the United States*.

rates, which were very low to non-existent in the first years and then ballooned to very high interest rates. Lenders usually targeted low income, high risk borrowers with low credit ratings for these types of loans, thus giving rise to the subprime loans. These consumers often did not fully understand the financial contract into which they had entered. These type of loans became one of the main financial arrangements used to inflate the real estate bubble of the early 2000s that was at the root of the financial crisis of 2007–08.[34]

Entry

In 1980, the Office of the Comptroller changed its policy to award a bank char-ter.[35] The OCC started emphasizing more on the organizing group and its operat-ing plan rather than the ability of a region to support a bank. This new policy led to an increase in the number of bank charters granted due to an increase in the percentage of approved bank applications. The number of new national bank charters issued increased by around 75% from 1980 to 1984. This was fuelled by an increase in the average percentage of approved new bank applications per year from 58% in the 1970s to 89% in the 1980s.[36]

Deposit Insurance

During the 1980s, the main regulatory goal was to increase competition. However, as the stability competition trade-off suggests, as competition increases, the sta-bility of the financial system may decrease.[37] This increase in instability was clear. The 1980s witnessed the highest number of bank and thrift failures since the Great Depression. To try to mitigate this problem, regulators used deposit insur-ance to prevent bank runs following the rationale of Diamond and Dybvig.[38] The Depository Institutions Deregulation and Monetary Control Act of 1980 increased the deposit insurance limit from $40,000 to $100,000.

Avoiding bank runs and credit-flow disruptions through the use of deposit insurance can be an expensive business. Hanc[39] estimates that the cost of dealing with the S&L crisis was $160.1 billion, of which $132.1 billion is the estimated

---

[34] Brunnermeier, 'Deciphering the Liquidity and Credit Crunch 2007–2008'.

[35] Davison, 'Banking Legislation and Regulation'.

[36] Eugene N. White, *The Comptroller and the Transformation of American Banking, 1960–1990* (DIANE Publishing, 1992); Davison, 'Banking Legislation and Regulation'.

[37] Allen and Gale, 'Competition and Financial Stability'.

[38] Douglas W. Diamond and Philip H. Dybvig, 'Bank Runs, Deposit Insurance, and Liquidity', *Journal of Political Economy* 91, no. 3 (1983): pp. 401–19.

[39] George Hanc, 'The Banking Crises of the 1980s and Early 1990s: Summary and Implications', *FDIC Banking Rev.* 11 (1998): p. 1.

figure supported by the taxpayers. The author suggests that these figures may have been smaller if there were penalties or costs to tame risky behaviour. He mentions risk-based premiums and capital requirements as examples of penalties or costs that would have reduced risky taking. Capital requirements were eventually adopted exactly to address this issue.

This preference to achieve short-term stability though deposit insurance led to a moral hazard problem. Given that the deposit insurance scheme assumes the losses of the depositors, depositors have no incentives to monitor bank risk. This allows managers to take on more risk. Additionally, they are able to raise an amount of funds that is frequently not commensurate with the risk of the endeavours. This may lead to a misallocation of resources and, thus, increase the likelihood of failures.

Pyle[40] argues that the deposit insurance scheme in place in the US was one of the causes of the S&L crisis. He states that this scheme was unsound because it led to moral hazard. Additionally, he claims that it increased the cost of the crisis.

Failure Resolution: The Rise of the 'Too-Big-to-Fail' Doctrine

This preference of the regulators for short-term stability over market discipline has also been evident in the manner they resolved troubled financial institutions. In 1984, Continental Illinois was the first large bank rescued in the United States. This introduced the 'too-big-to-fail' doctrine in the United States. To salvage the troubled institution, regulators prepared a $4.5 billion rescue plan for the bank. Continental Illinois was the seventh largest bank in the US with over $40 billion in assets.[41]

Through the extensive use of deposit insurance and 'too-big-to-fail', policymakers gave bankers an implicit guarantee subsidy. Effectively, the government and its agencies were implicitly guaranteeing deposits and debts of the banks. This means that depositors and lenders don't have any incentive to monitor to whom they borrow their money. Thus, bankers were able to raise more funds than they would normally do for the level of risk they were taking. This, then, led to a misallocation of financial resources and may contribute to an increase in the long-term instability of the banking system.

Forbearance was an alternative way to deal with troubled financial institutions that was introduced in the 1980s. It was inaugurated with the Net Worth Certificate Program that was a part of the Garn-St Germain Act of 1982. This

[40] David H. Pyle, 'The US Savings and Loan Crisis', *Handbooks in Operations Research and Management Science* 9 (1995), pp. 1105–25.
[41] Hanc, 'The Banking Crises of the 1980s and Early 1990s: Summary and Implications'.

allowed insured depository institutions to operate without meeting the the regulatory standards of safety and soundness. Forbearance was applied at the discretion of the regulators on a case-by-case basis.[42]

This forbearance policy permitted bank regulators to allow several banks that later failed to operate with minimal capital for a long period of time. The Federal Savings and Loan Insurance Corporation (FSLIC) was the most permissive agency regarding this policy. This very tolerant attitude led to an increase of the costs of thrift failures throughout the 1980s.[43]

This policy of forbearance was highly criticized by Romer and Weingast.[44] They argue that by keeping institutions in business, it allowed them to gamble for resurrection. This, in turn, meant that the cost of resolution of troubled financial institutions increased.

Capital Requirements and Basel I

With the reduction of competitive barriers in the banking industry throughout the 1980s, regulators believed that a reasonable level of capital was necessary to sustain the soundness and safety of the banking system.[45] Capital requirements were expected to induce prudent behaviour and give banks a buffer in case they faced financial troubles in an increasingly competitive banking system.[46] They were meant to be a cushion for unforeseen losses and a protection for depositors, which would increase the confidence of the public in banks.

Capital requirements became increasingly a more important topic in the regulatory agenda in the US as capital levels in the largest banks steadily declined throughout the 1970s. This topic became a very contentious one. There was a lot of debate over what types of capital to include and how to weight them. The guidelines on capital ratios were decided by the main three national regulatory bodies, the Federal Reserve (Fed), Federal Deposit Insurance Corporation (FDIC), and The Office of the Comptroller of the Currency (OCC), However, the guidelines they adopted were not uniform.[47]

---

[42] Davison, 'Banking Legislation and Regulation'; Hanc, 'The Banking Crises of the 1980s and Early 1990s: Summary and Implications'.

[43] Hanc, 'The Banking Crises of the 1980s and early 1990s: Summary and Implications'.

[44] Thomas Romer and Barry R. Weingast, 'Political Foundations of the Thrift Debacle', in *Politics and Economics in the Eighties* (University of Chicago Press, 1991): pp. 175–214.

[45] Christopher Kobrak and Michael Troege, 'From Basel to Bailouts: Forty Years of International Attempts to Bolster Bank Safety', *Financial History Review* 22, no. 2 (2015): pp. 133–56.

[46] Thomas F. Hellmann, Kevin C. Murdock, and Joseph E. Stiglitz, 'Liberalization, Moral Hazard in Banking, and Prudential Regulation: Are Capital Requirements Enough?', *American Economic Review* 90, no. 1 (2000): pp. 147–65.

[47] Davison, 'Banking Legislation and Regulation'.

Recognizing the benefits of international coordination, national authorities started working on a common set of principles regarding capital adequacy.[48] This was done by the Basel Committee on Banking Regulations and Supervisory Practices, a committee of G10 banking authorities. In 1988, the Basel Committee reached an agreement on a general set of guidelines for bank capital adequacy, usually known as Basel I.

Basel I defined standard capital, set risk weights and credit conversions for off-balance sheet exposures. Moreover, it also established standards to compute the agreed measure of capital adequacy. This was a risk-based capital ratio intended to reflect the riskiness of the portfolio of a bank. This measure was a refined version of an equity-to-assets ratio. The risk weights for each item were devised somewhat arbitrarily. In the end, the Committee agreed on a minimum risk-based total capital ratio of 8%.[49]

The Shadow Financial Regulatory Committee[50] credits Basel I as being an important factor in the fast growth of securitization, because it gave banks an incentive to shed assets that had a high risk weight and replace them with tranches of those pooled assets that carried a lower risk coefficient in the calculations of the risk-weighted capital ratios. Brunnermeier[51] also suggests that Basel I was responsible for the increase in popularity of securitized and structured products. This increase in securitization has been linked with the financial instability witnessed in 2007–08.[52] Moreover, Berger et al.[53] point out that given that banks did not have to hold capital against off-balance sheet items, these capital requirements gave banks incentives to shift items into off-balance sheet activities.

Rationale for Deregulation

There are several explanations that have been proposed as the main reason for the financial deregulation that occurred in the US during the 1980s. Sherman[54]

[48] Alexis Drach, 'A Globalization Laboratory: European Banking Regulation and Global Capitalism in the 1970s and Early 1980s', *European Review of History: Revue européenne d'histoire* 26, no. 4 (2019): pp. 658–78.

[49] Bank for International Settlements Committee on Banking Regulations and Supervisory Practices, *International Convergence of Capital Measurement and Capital Standards* (Bank for International Settlements, 1988); James R. Barth, Gerard Caprio, and Ross Levine, *Rethinking Bank Regulation: Till Angels Govern* (Cambridge University Press, 2008); Michael B. Gordy and Erik A. Heitfield, 'Risk-Based Regulatory Capital and Basel II', in *The Oxford Handbook of Banking* (Oxford University Press, 2010).

[50] Shadow Financial Regulatory Committee, *The Basel's Committee New Capital Adequacy Framework, Statement Number 156, September 27.*

[51] Brunnermeier, 'Deciphering the Liquidity and Credit Crunch 2007–2008'.

[52] Andreas Lehnert, 'Residential Mortgages', in *Oxford Handbook of Banking*, Citeseer (2009); David Marques-Ibanez and Martin Scheicher, 'Securitisation: Instruments and Implications', in Allen N. Berger et al., *The Oxford Handbook of Banking* (2010): pp. 530–55.

[53] Berger et al., 'The Transformation of the US Banking Industry: What a Long, Strange Trip It's Been'.

[54] Sherman, *A Short History of Financial Deregulation in the United States.*

identifies the inflation observed in the 1970s as the main reason for the need to repeal Regulation Q. The post WWII 'Golden Age' period had witnessed economic growth and stability. However, the 1970s were a decade of great economic turmoil with the end of the Bretton Woods system, the oil shocks, and slower economic growth. These events and the policies followed by the Fed were the causes of the great increase in inflation seen in this decade. This economic turmoil laid the foundations for the repeal of Regulation Q.

Evanoff et al.[55] identifies that in the 1980s there were market pressures and an impetus for change in the financial industry. This pressure was motivated by the combination of tight financial regulation and adverse economic conditions that severally limited the profit opportunities of financial institutions.

Krippner[56] argues that the deregulation of the US financial markets in the 1980s was an attempt to depoliticize the allocation of the limited resources in the economy. This would make the markets, rather than politicians, responsible for any unsatisfactory outcomes. She asserts that this happened because in the 1970s there was a growing lack of confidence in the ability of the government to manage the economy. This was due to the increase in wealth inequality, government budget deficits, and inflation.

Finally, Hare and Poole[57] state that there has been a significant shift to the right in US politics starting in the 1980s. Ronald Reagan won the presidential election of 1980 with an economic motto of less government interference in the economy. This victory was part of a greater ideological shift in the economic policies followed in the US since then. This new ideology firmly established itself in US politics during the 1980s under the leadership of Presidents Reagan and Bush.

Consequences and Legacy of the 1980s Deregulation

The consequences of the deregulatory process of the 1980s have been long-lasting. The regulatory changes of this decade gave momentum to a process of deregulation that has continued in the following decades. These regulatory changes have moved the US financial sector from a highly regulated one to a more loosely regulated sector. This represented a move along the financial regulatory cycle.

Increase in Non-Interest Income

As Figure 2.4 shows, the share of non-interest income as a percentage of aggregate operating income of US commercial banks gradually increased throughout

[55] Evanoff et al., 'Financial Industry Deregulation in the 1980s'.
[56] Krippner, *Capitalizing on Crisis: The Political Origins of the Rise of Finance*.
[57] Hare and Poole, 'The Polarization of Contemporary American Politics'.

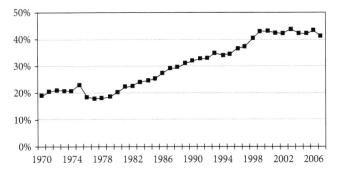

Figure 2.4 Aggregate non-interest income as a percentage of aggregate operating income of US commercial banks, 1970–2007.

Source: DeYoung and Rice[58]

the 1980s and 1990s. The main reasons for this change were the ability to expand to other financial services that generate non-interest income, the repeal of Regulation Q and the growth of 'originate-and-distribute' business model.[59] Moreover, Stiroh[60] shows that 39% of the net operating revenue (net interest income plus non-interest income) in 1986 was from non-interest sources. This value increased to 48.2% in 1996 and 53.2 in 2006.

The gradual loosening of the restrictions on the separation of commercial and investment banking allowed commercial banks to enter into non-traditional lines of businesses that produce non-interest income. These areas include securities brokerage, securities underwriting, and insurance sales.

Moreover, the removal of Regulation Q meant that banks were not always allowed to pay market interest rates on deposits. However, banks compensated this competitive restrictions by competing on the products market. They offered depository services (e.g. certified check, overdraft protection, safe deposit boxes) for free or below costs. As a result, they were earning more in interest income than they would in a free market. Once Regulation Q was repealed, banks started offering market rates for deposits and charging fees for depository services that were previously provided for free.[61]

In the traditional originate-to-hold banking business model, banks originate loans and keep them until maturity in their balance sheets. In the originate-to-distribute business model, banks instead originate the loans, but, then, repackage them and sell them to investors. This means that the interest income is transferred

[58] DeYoung and Rice, 'How Do Banks Make Money? The Fallacies of Fee Income'.

[59] DeYoung, 'Banking in the United States'.

[60] Kevin J. Stiroh, 'Diversification in Banking', in *The Oxford Handbook of Banking* (2010): pp. 146–71.

[61] DeYoung, 'Banking in the United States'.

to these investors together with the risk. In this latter model, banks generate income from fees and from selling the loans.

DeYoung and Roland[62] argue that the rise in non-interest income has substantially changed the risk-return profile of US commercial banks. They show that non-deposit fee income at commercial banks is linked with greater revenue volatility, higher operating leverage, and higher earnings volatility. The originate-to-hold model generates a greater interest income and is based on a long-term relationship between the lender and the borrower. The fees generated by originating and distributing loans are a non-repeated transaction. Thus, these fees respond to developments in interest rates and the housing market. These factors make them more volatile. Additionally, other sources of non-deposit fees are equally volatile. Fees from brokerage are usually linked to the value of assets. They have, thus, an undiversifiable risk due to market fluctuations.

DeYoung and Rice[63] corroborate these results. They found that marginal increases in non-interest income are associated with a worsening of the risk-return trade-off for commercial banks.

Concentration

In the US, there has been a sharp decline in the number of commercial banks. As Figure 2.5, the number of commercial banks in the US dropped from about 14,000 in 1984 to 4652 in 2019. This trend was clearly started in the 1980s. As we can see in Table 2.5, the number of US commercial banks decreased from 12,463

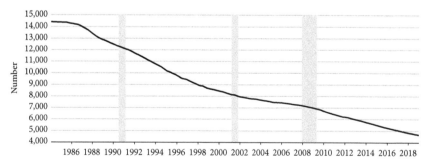

Figure 2.5   Commercial banks in the US.

Source: https://fred.stlouisfed.org/[64]

[62] Robert DeYoung and Karin P. Roland, 'Product Mix and Earnings Volatility at Commercial Banks: Evidence from a Degree of Total Leverage Model', *Journal of Financial Intermediation* 10, no. 1 (2001): pp. 54–84.

[63] Robert DeYoung and Tara Rice, 'Noninterest Income and Financial Performance at US Commercial Banks', *Financial Review* 39, no. 1 (2004): pp. 101–27.

[64] https://fred.stlouisfed.org/

Table 2.5 Number of US commercial banks

	1979	1994
Total number of banking organizations	12,463	7926
Small banks	10,014	5636

Source: Berger et al.[65]

in 1979 to 7926 in 1994. This reduction came mostly from the reduction of the number of small banks.

Moreover, following the deregulatory process of the 1980s, there was a wave of mergers and acquisitions of commercial banks. This decade also witnessed the liberalization of antitrust policy towards banks.[66] Excluding acquisitions orchestrated by the FDIC to find a solution for failing banks, there were around 3500 bank mergers in the 1980s and almost 5000 in the 1990s.[67] This increased the size and geographical reach of US commercial banks, while reducing the overall number of banks.

Furthermore, regulators closed more than 1500 insolvent banks in the late 1980s and early 1990s. This was the largest number of bank failures in the US since the Great Depression.[68]

This increased concentration, however, appears to have had some positive results. DeYoung and Rice[69] found that increases in the size of US commercial banks up to $500 million improved their risk-return trade-off. This means that their expected returns increased while their volatility decreased. However, increases beyond $500 million were associated with the common risk-return trade-off, meaning as returns increased, so did risk.

Deposit Insurance

In the aftermath of the financial crisis of 2007–08, there was a lot of discussions about the incentives faced by bankers and the policies that led to moral hazard.[70] Most of these distorted incentives and moral hazard originated in the 1980s. While the national deposit insurance scheme was not established in the 1980s,[71]

---

[65] Berger et al., 'The Transformation of the US Banking Industry: What a Long, Strange Trip It's Been'.
[66] Berger et al., 'The Transformation of the US Banking Industry: What a Long, Strange Trip It's Been'.
[67] DeYoung, 'Banking in the United States'.   [68] Ibid.
[69] DeYoung and Rice, 'How Do Banks Make Money? The Fallacies of Fee Income'.
[70] Charles Calomiris, *Banking Crises and the Rules of the Game*, tech. rep. (National Bureau of Economic Research, 2009).
[71] Charles W. Calomiris and Eugene N. White, 'The Origins of Federal Deposit Insurance', in *The Regulated Economy: A Historical Approach to Political Economy* (University of Chicago Press, 1994): pp. 145–88.

it was in this decade that it became one of the main tools to achieve financial stability in the short term.

This reliance on deposit insurance to be an important tool to achieve short-term financial stability in the banking sector has continued beyond the 1980s. In 2008, as part of the response to the ongoing financial crisis, the Emergency Economic Stabilization Act increased deposit insurance from $100.000 to $250.000.

The choice to have deposit insurance has created a moral hazard problem in the banking sector. It removed the incentives depositors had to monitor bank risk. Thus, it has led to greater risk-taking by banks and a misallocation of resources.

Failure Resolution: The 'Too-Big-to-Fail' Doctrine

The 'too-big-to-fail' doctrine instituted in the 1980s set the blueprint for the resolution of troubled financial institutions until the present. The 1990s saw it being used to rescue Long-Term Capital Management. It was once again one of the main policy tools used to deal with troubled financial institutions during the 2007–08 financial crisis, when most large financial institutions received aid from the federal government or from a financial regulator.

The use of the 'too-big-to-fail' doctrine has created an implicit guarantee for banks. This has in turn reduced lender monitoring and allowed banks to take excessive risk. Thus, this policy has contributed to the instability observed in the financial system since the 1980s.

Further Real Estate Lending Deregulation

The deregulatory trend of the 1980s repealed the restrictions on teaser rates. The lift of this restriction allowed banks to enter the subprime loans market. This gave banks a new market with consumers that previously were not accessible. These type of subprime loans became one of the main financial arrangements used to inflate the real estate bubble of the early 2000s.[72]

The loose regulation of the real estate lending market was one of the main causes of the 2007–08 financial crisis.[73] This point was achieve because regulators continued the trend started in the 1980s towards deregulation in this market. Examples of this continuing deregulation include the Housing and Community Development Act of 1992 and the American Dream Downpayment Act passed in 2003.[74]

---

[72] Brunnermeier, 'Deciphering the Liquidity and Credit Crunch 2007–2008'   [73] Ibid.
[74] Joao R. Cunha, 'The Making of Financial Regulation: Voting on Financial Regulation in the U.S. Congress', *University of St Andrews Working Paper Series* (2020).

Derivatives Investment

Derivatives products did not receive much attention from regulators throughout the 1980s. This is an example of a deregulated market reached by regulatory omission. This attitude towards loose regulation in the derivatives market continued throughout the 1990s. Brooksley Born was the Chair of the Commodity Futures Trading Commission (CFTC) between 1996 and 1999. During her tenure, she attempted to introduce regulation to tame the over the counter (OTC) derivatives market. However, this was opposed by Alan Greenspan (then Federal Reserve chairman), Robert Rubin and Lawrence Summers (Treasury Secretaries during her tenure).

Born lost this political battle. In 2000, after she left the CFTC, the Commodity Futures Modernization Act of 2000 was implemented. It did not allow the CFTC to have functional regulation powers in the over the counter derivatives market. It allow this institution only to supervise this market. Born[75] believes that the deregulation of the financial markets was one of the major causes of the 2007–08 crisis.

This outcome was not surprising to at least one experienced investor who witnessed the lack of regulatory action in this market in the 1980s. In 1982, Warren Buffett sent a letter to congressman John Dingell warning him about the dangers of a growing, but deregulated derivatives market. He compared the deregulated market in derivatives to gambling, because of the 'large prize versus a small entry fee'.[76]

Moreover, he also stated that 'the net effect of high-volume futures markets in stock indices is likely to be overwhelmingly detrimental to the security-buying public and, therefore, in the long run to capital markets generally'.[77]

Monetary and Fiscal Policies

The goals of financial deregulation in the 1980s aligned with the goals of fiscal and monetary policies. Krippner[78] argues that they all tried to leave the economic outcomes more to the markets and less to the state.

The postwar abundance of the 1950s meant that fiscal policymakers did not have to make tough choices during this period, because the rapid economic growth of the postwar allowed everybody to be better off. With the end of the postwar abundance, policymakers had to again choose who their policies would favour. However, after the initial wave of financial deregulation, there was an

---

[75] Brooksley Born, 'Deregulation: A Major Cause of the Financial Crisis', *Harv. L. &Pol'y Rev.* 5 (2011): p. 231.

[76] Robert Lenzner and Stephen S. Johnson, *Buffett Tried to Block Derivatives Back in 1982*, 2010.

[77] Lenzner and Johnson, *Buffett Tried to Block Derivatives Back in 1982*.

[78] Krippner, *Capitalizing on Crisis: The Political Origins of the Rise of Finance.*

increase of the inflows of foreign capital to the US. This allowed the government, in particular during the Reagan presidency, to run a budget deficit to satisfy the demands of the major groups in the American society, without having to make difficult policy choices. However, it came at the expense of increasing public debt.

Krippner[79] argues that the intention of letting the markets play a more important role in the economic outcomes was also clear in monetary policy. According to her, the goal of monetary policymakers in this period became to follow the market rather than to lead it. She claims that 'Greenspan's lax monetary policy was a culmination of a much longer term evolution in which policy makers gradually abdicated control over credit to the market.'

Continuing Deregulation

The trend of deregulation has continued after the 1980s. In 1994, Congress passed the Riegle-Neal Interstate Banking and Branching Efficiency Act. This repealed existing restrictions on opening bank branches across state lines.[80] In 1999, the Gramm–Leach–Bliley Act repealed the remaining barriers to the conglomeration of banking, securities, and insurance companies under the same holding company.

The early 2000s witnessed the deregulation of the derivatives and real estate lending markets. Examples of this deregulatory process include the Commodity Futures Modernization Act of 2000 and the American Dream Downpayment Act of 2003.[81]

Increasing Instability

At the same time, the US also witnessed financial turmoil with greater frequency. This is particularly true if compared with the period between the end of the Great Depression and the end of Bretton Woods. The late 1980s witnessed the S&L crisis in which around one third of the savings and loan associations in the US failed. The early 2000s saw a recession and a stock market crash linked with the collapse of the speculative dot-com bubble.

A few years later, the 2007–08 crisis started due to the collapse of the housing bubble on the heels of the subprime mortgage crisis. This crisis was the worst banking and global financial crisis since the Great Depression. It also set the US and the world for the Great Recession.

---

[79] Ibid.
[80] Cunha, 'The Making of Financial Regulation: Voting on Financial Regulation in the U.S. Congress'.
[81] Ibid.

According to Krippner,[82] this increase in financial fragility was due to the turn to the markets, which hampered policy making, introduced 'a number of fragilities into the economy', and, thus, created conditions for a financial crisis.

International Comparison: Canada

Bordo, Redish, and Rockoff[83] argue that the deregulatory movement in the US was an attempt to develop universal banks that resembled the ones created in Canada. They argue, however, that given the different starting points of this deregulatory process, the outcomes were different. In Canada, it led to bigger banks, while in the US, it led to shadow banking. The comparison between the two countries is made due to their political, cultural, and historical similarities.

Canada started the decade of the 1980s with large nationwide commercial banks. When they were allowed to merge with mortgage banks and investment dealers, commercial banks dominated the new consolidated institution, an universal bank in which the commercial bank arm was the dominant. This distinct quality of the Canadian banking system paired with tighter regulation contributed to the stability of their financial system.

The US, however, started the decade with small local commercial banks. Deregulation led to the expansion of shadow banking and a greater reliance on financial markets. This was evident in the rise of the securities markets, investment banks, and money market mutual funds.

Additionally, the authors argue that the multitude of regulators also contributed to the growing instability of the US system. They argue that this allowed the banks to shop for the most favourable regulatory environment, which led to a decline in the regulatory oversight. In Canada, however, all activities of the universal banks fell under the jurisdiction of one entity, the Office of the Superintendent of Financial Institutions. They argue that together with tougher regulation, it led to the containment of an unregulated shadow banking system, higher capital requirements, lower leverage, and less securitization.

Conclusion

In this chapter, I argued that the 1980s saw a structural change in the profile of the US financial sector. In this decade, this industry went from a not very competitive but stable one to a competitive but unstable one. This was achieved

---

[82] Krippner, *Capitalizing on Crisis: The Political Origins of the Rise of Finance*.
[83] Michael D. Bordo, Angela Redish, and Hugh Rockoff, 'Why Didn't Canada Have a Banking Crisis in 2008 (or in 1930, or 1907, or...)?', *The Economic History Review* 68, no. 1 (2015): pp. 218–43.

through a process of deregulation in several areas of the banking sector. This deregulatory process included loosening of regulation on the type of businesses in which commercial banks could be involved, repeal of Regulation Q, and lifting restrictions on branch banking and real estate lending.

The argument proposed here is associated with the idea of a regulatory cycle in the US financial sector. In this case, it links with the view of a long cycle. Before the 1980s, financial regulation was tighter since the Great Depression. The 1980s marked the turn of this cycle to a period of looser regulation.

Deregulation was an important part of the economic policy followed in the 1980s and, thus, it never left the policy and legislative agendas. This deregulatory process continued in the following decades and had a profound impact in the economic performance of the US, including in the increasing instability experienced in the banking sector.

The events in the financial sector since the 1980s can be very informative to all those involved. Borrowers must be carefully selected and regulators must require that banks only lend to those who are able to repay the loans. A stable banking system may require interest income to be the main source of operating income for banks. Policymakers must be careful so that their actions do not lead to moral hazard. Finally, a deregulated and more competitive banking system is usually also a more unstable system.

3

Financial Deregulation in the United Kingdom

Forrest Capie

In this chapter I argue that care should be taken when talking of banking deregulation in Britain in the late twentieth century. After setting out a brief framework within which a consideration of the central questions can be carried out, a short account of the course of financial regulation in the United Kingdom over the long run provides the context for a discussion of the more recent past.

The essence of that long-run story is of the dissatisfaction in the early nineteenth century with the over-bearing state—the 'old corruption' of the Mercantilist state. Usury laws capped the rate of interest that could be charged. No joint-stock banking was permitted. Banks could have no more than six partners. They were subject to unlimited liability. There followed the adoption of laissez-faire—small government, free trade and sound money. Deregulation was the theme and that is what happened in the nineteenth century. The usury laws were relaxed in 1833 and later abolished. Joint-stock banking was allowed at first outside London but then after 1833 inside London. Limited liability came later in legislation in the 1850s.

The First World War brought that to an end. As Jacob Viner put it, the war brought to an end to 'the intermission in mercantilism'.[1] The banking system in Britain, however, did remain largely untouched and thus essentially unregulated and subject only to prevailing company law until the Second World War. From that point, however, there was a relatively steady increase of actions that led to ever more supervision and regulation.

At the beginning of the 1970s following about 30 years of increasing regulation there were some reflections on the possible need for greater competition and some moves were made in that direction but then almost equally quickly reversed. Then in the mid-1980s there was a 'Big Bang' comprising a number of reforms in the financial system that were commonly presented as the beginning of the deregulation that is frequently talked about. This is the territory that is the principal focus of discussion—the late 1970s to the early 2000s. Since the financial

---

[1] Jacob Viner, *Studies in the Theory of International Trade* (New York: Harper & Brothers Publishers, 1937).

Forrest Capie, *Financial Deregulation in the United Kingdom* In: *Financial Deregulation: A Historical Perspective.* Edited by: Alexis Drach and Youssef Cassis, Oxford University Press (2021). © Alexis Drach and Youssef Cassis. DOI: 10.1093/oso/9780198856955.003.0003

crisis of 2008/09 of course there has been a veritable avalanche of new regulation. The knee-jerk response to any failing or perceived failing in the market has been to impose fresh regulations. Finally, briefly, some consideration of the insurance markets will be set out to illustrate that a similar story can be told of the wider financial markets.

The conclusion reached is that there has been little in the way of deregulation in banking in Britain in the second half of the twentieth century.[2] Regulation may be difficult to measure but what is clear is that the regulatory bureaucratic burden has risen steeply.

Regulation/Deregulation Framework

There have been two sharply contrasting theories of regulation among economists. The first is best thought of as the economist's traditional view of regulation: 'Competition when possible, regulation where necessary' as Kay and Vickers expressed it.[3] Regulation, then, seeks to identify market failures that prevent an industry from functioning competitively, and to correct for such failures. On this view it is a way of reducing market failure. That is of course a normative theory of regulation; it sets out what regulation 'ought' to do.

The principal alternative view sees regulation as in fact producing market failure—of producing monopoly profits. This approach is identified particularly with the work of George Stigler and his co-workers mostly at Chicago. Stigler defined regulation as, 'any policy which alters market outcomes by the exercise of coercive government power'.[4] He went on to ask, in a pioneering series of studies what regulation actually achieves. Whom does it benefit and whom does it harm? Over a wide range of industries he and his co-workers found that regulation was either totally ineffective or worked to the benefit of existing firms in the industry. It did not eliminate market failures. So regulation, ostensibly intended to benefit the consumer, is often encouraged by producer groups as a way of restricting competition.

But by whatever means regulation comes into being there are costs. Regulation can be analysed in the same way as any tax or trade tariff. There is movement along demand and supply curves, prices and quantities change, consumer and producer surpluses change and there are 'welfare triangles'. However the costs appear to the producer, they are likely to be passed on to the consumer but as with any tax it is impossible to know quite how they fall without a knowledge of

---

[2] There is a similar story told of Germany in this volume by Christoph Kaserer, see Chapter 6.

[3] John Kay and John Vickers, 'Regulatory Reform in Britain', *Economic Policy* 3, no. 7 (October 1988): p. 287.

[4] George J. Stigler, 'The Theory of Economic Regulation', *Bell Journal of Economics and Management Science* 2, no. 1 (Spring 1971): pp. 3–21.

the demand and supply elasticities. What is inescapable is that the imposition of any restriction will result in some combination of higher prices, lower output, and 'welfare triangles'. So a tax on output would raise prices and lower output. That would deliver revenue to the tax imposing body—a redistribution of a kind. In addition there would be losses not recouped in any form—welfare costs. But with regulation there is of course no revenue for the restriction-imposing body to distribute.

State regulation should not be confused with self-regulation. The best substitute for regulation is a concern with reputation. Something that developed early in British financial institutions was a rigorous system of internal checking and inspection. This was motivated by a desire both to have, and to present, a well-run and reliable institution that would attract new custom and reassure existing customers. It is the antithesis of *state regulation* where compliance with the rule-book takes over. The customer is not in the picture. The seller looks only to the regulator. Self-regulation is designed with the customer in mind.

For a very long time, certainly from the nineteenth century, professional bodies characterized much of British professional life, from medicine to accounting. These professional associations often had Royal Charters and were designed to inspire confidence. But they could drift into imposing restraints on trade and end up with similarities with medieval guilds. What evolved in British banking, and finance more generally, was somewhat different and is best described as 'clubs'. These were common in all areas of British finance from insurance to retail banking. Clubs generally set entry qualifications and rules of conduct. And they could be relied upon to discipline errant members and arrange the rescue of those felt to be deserving. They were driven by a desire to woo, persuade, and reassure the customer. At the same time they could carry some risk of becoming anti-competitive by presenting a barrier to entry for potential new entrants.

The Long Run

In the late twentieth century and in the twenty-first century the knee-jerk reaction to problems in almost any area of economic activity, but perhaps particularly in banking and finance, is to regulate. The opposite gradually came to be the case in the nineteenth century. In the age of mercantilism, roughly from the fifteenth century until the beginning of the nineteenth century, the state was central and regulation was extensive. It was revulsion against this that ushered in the age of laissez-faire, or the age of reform, and allowed the period of deregulation in banking that followed in the course of the nineteenth century. The first evidence of that came in the wake of the first great financial crisis of capitalism in 1825. That was a banking crisis on a huge scale at a time when the number of banks in the country was close to its peak.

Something had clearly gone wrong. The reaction was to free up the system. Joint stock banking, which had been prohibited, was then allowed albeit at a distance from London. Then a little later the joint stock banks were allowed in London. When it became clear that the Bank of England could not do its central job in the crisis of 1825 in a satisfactory fashion then the usury laws were relaxed. In the 1833 Act they were removed on key money market instruments and then further relaxed and shortly after that finally abolished. Slightly later, through a series of company law reforms between 1857 and 1862, limited liability was permitted. The 1879 Companies Act then eased the transition to limited liability. Greater freedom of corporate governance was then possible. The gold standard had been more strictly defined in 1844 but after the crisis of 1847, in which the gold standard's restraints were identified, greater flexibility was introduced. Additionally, the denomination of bank share prices had acted as a further constraint on banks attracting funds, for they had a minimum value of £100 (in rough terms that would be about £4000 at the present time.) In time this constraint too was relaxed.

And so it went on. So it was that a system that was highly regulated prior to the 1820s became one that was essentially unregulated by the 1860s. Banks were subject to Company Law but they and other firms were generally ahead of the law in their behaviour[5] (see e.g. Turner in particular for an illustration of that in relation to the Company Law Act of 1867) Banks had to produce a balance sheet but not much more. It so happened that in the period of regulation financial crises were periodic, roughly every decade. In the period following deregulation there were no longer any financial crises. Stability came with a deregulated system.

The legitimacy of the State is a reflection of the confidence or the trust that the populace has in the State. In a recent study of the politics of taxation, Daunton has argued that the necessary trust in Britain in the early nineteenth century rested on the success of early-nineteenth-century governments replacing the 'old corruption' with a fiscal constitution that emphasized probity in collection and expenditure, with full accountability and transparency.[6] This is the environment in which there is a reduced need for regulation and it applied equally to regulation in banking.[7]

An added benefit after the completion of deregulation in banking was that no bureaucracy had grown up. That removed the danger of a self-perpetuating body

---

[5] For an illustration of that in relation to the Company Law Act of 1867, see for example John D. Turner, *Banking in Crisis: The Rise and Fall of British Banking Stability, 1800 to the Present* (Cambridge: Cambridge University Press, 2014).

[6] Martin Daunton, *Trusting Leviathan: The Politics of Taxation in Britain, 1799–1914* (Cambridge: Cambridge University Press, 2001); Martin Daunton, *Just Taxes: the Politics of and Taxation in Britain, 1914–1979* (Cambridge: Cambridge University Press, 2002).

[7] For a less enthusiastic view of deregulation in the course of the nineteenth century see Kevin Dowd, 'The Evolution of Central Banking in England, 1821–90', in *Unregulated Banking. Chaos or Order?*, edited by Forrest Capie and Geoffrey E. Wood (New York: St Martin's Press, 1991): pp. 159–95.

ever-ready to introduce refinements and extensions to existing rules and regulations as at minimum a justification for its existence. Bureaucracies tend to grow. Indeed, has it ever been known for a bureaucracy to shrink in size willingly? Thus when the banking sector had been deregulated it remained that way for a long time without any threat. It would be the later twentieth century before any bureaucracy had been built up and became a factor in the growth of regulation from that point on.

Beginning of a Return to Regulation

The road back to regulation began with informal arrangements made between government or the monetary authorities and the banking sector. During the Second World War the banks had been obliged to hold government debt on their balance sheets. That was carried to such an extent that their balance sheets were completely distorted from their normal peacetime shape. Furthermore, the banks were unable to raise new capital and so their capital/asset ratios shrank. It could be argued that since they were holding 'risk-free' assets in the form of government stock, there was no problem. But after the war as they gradually restored their normal balance sheet the capital-raising constraint remained and stayed in place for two more decades. So the capital/asset ratio remained low while the composition of the balance sheet became more risky.

After the war the economic and business climate had changed. Nationalization was the order of the day and the Bank of England was among many sectors that were nationalized, in 1946. Nationalization did not reach the clearing banks but a large number of informal controls came into place. A number of what are now called, slightly confusingly, macroprudential regulations, were informally agreed. The banks had arrived at liquidity ratios of around 30% and cash ratio of around 8% by the interwar years. Soon after the war it was agreed that they would continue to adhere to these ratios. These would become burdensome by the 1960s but there was no movement tolerated.

The banks had been understandably constrained in their raising of new capital during and immediately after the war. And with government debt on their books the risks could be interpreted as being low. That was not quite the case as the price of government stock went on a long-term downward trend. Nevertheless, the Capital Issues Committee, which was established in wartime to approve new capital, was not disbanded until the 1960s. As the banks tried to move away from their wartime balance sheets to a normal structure, risk increased but as they could not raise new capital their capital asset ratios were weakened. That was a major constraint on their growth and performance.

In the course of the 1950s two other principal means of controlling bank lending were directives and ceilings. Directives were used to direct bank lending to industries/sectors that government approved of or deemed worthy of support, and away from the unworthy. Property was frowned on and exports approved of. But if these measures did not bring lending into line ceilings were imposed. Ceilings of x% of the previous period's lending would be set down (to what extent these kinds of measures could be effective was, and is, a matter of dispute; there were many ways around the first and the overdraft system might be seen to have been an obstacle to all these kinds of controls). At any rate when it became clear that the various direct controls did not achieve what was required the Bank of England was asked to come up with something better. At the end of the 1950s they then designed another measure called 'special deposits'. These were additional deposits the clearing banks were obliged to lodge with the Bank of England, with the aim of increasing the banks' liquidity ratios.

In addition to the specific bank controls hire-purchase agreements were manipulated. Indeed, hire-purchase arrangements were widely seen as the authorities' most potent monetary weapon. The terms of the agreements could be varied at short notice and were believed to have more or less immediate effects on spending. These controls were administered by the Board of Trade and not by the Bank of England.

Thus there was a whole panoply of controls in place through the 1940s, 1950s, and the 1960s. Exchange controls preventing the free movement of capital were also in place from WWII until 1979 when the Thatcher Government abolished them and capital was then free to move again.

Some Second Thoughts

The banking system that had evolved in Britain by the early twentieth century was essentially an oligopoly. The monetary authorities had quietly encouraged that structure. Five big banks dominated the system. But there were misgivings in the 1960s that the costs in terms of a lack of competition might be too high. There was too external pressure coming from the IMF. In the late 1960s when Britain's exchange rate was under pressure and devaluation was being prepared for, the IMF insisted on some control of monetary growth, seeing 'domestic credit expansion' in their terms complying with its guidelines. This was an early monetary aggregate and after a fashion a target to which Britain was obliged to adhere.

There were in any case also some beginnings of recognition that money mattered in macroeconomics and that greater control over the growth of monetary aggregates needed to be achieved. This was by no means the widespread view but rather a grudging acceptance by the authorities that the facts were overwhelming. Monetary control was also associated with a move away from direct controls that had caused dissatisfaction, towards using price, that is in the case of money, interest rates.

So it was that the Bank of England came up with its proposal for 'Competition and Credit Control' (CCC) in 1971, a proposal that the Treasury was persuaded to be the appropriate way forward. In brief the proposal was that the restraints on the banks in terms of liquidity and cash ratios would be changed/reduced, that Bank Rate would be abolished and replaced by a market-determined rate that would be called Minimum Lending Rate, a rate that could be overruled by the authorities supposedly only in extreme cases.

It so happened that the Heath Government of 1970 had embarked on an expansionary economic programme and particularly a substantial fiscal expansion. The consequence of this mix was a wild expansion of money in the early 1970s and the beginnings of an inflation that would culminate in annualized rates of close to 30% in 1975.

But before this happened the new type of reaction to warning signs was already emerging—when there were danger signals, regulate. And the Bank was asked to find a solution to what was seen as the emerging problem at the time—that is, serious inflationary pressure. They resorted to one of their previous instruments but gave it a slightly different name: 'supplementary special deposits'. This was a dressed up version of the previous special deposits. It was a return to the old controls but presented in a sufficiently complicated way as to save the Bank of England's blushes.

It could be noted here that much of the instruction to banks in the period from the 1950s to the 1980s was motivated by a desire both to direct lending and to some extent contain lending. Thereafter, it had more to do with monetary growth and more reliance was placed on control through interest rate movement.

The numbers employed in supervision in the Bank increased steadily across the 1970s firstly from the quick reversal of some of the 1971 moves, but accelerated in the second half of the decade following the more formal supervision being pursued. The continuing move to increasing bank regulation continued with the Banking Act of 1979, the first piece of statutory regulation for banking in Britain in the twentieth century.[8]

There was a secondary banking crisis in the middle of the 1970s and some of the response to that was to take a closer interest in the whole banking sector. There was too, since the joining of the EEC in 1973, some pressure from Europe to pursue greater financial regulation. Most of the sector was affected by the new legislation that was introduced in the 1979 Banking Act. This was the first statutory regulation of the banking sector in more than a century and the beginning of the more serious increase in banking regulation that would proceed over the late twentieth century.

---

[8] For a full discussion of the process over two decades that led to Act see Forrest Capie, *The Bank of England* (Cambridge: Cambridge University Press, 2010).

Big Bang in 1986

The story of deregulation that is commonly told is of the Thatcher Government that came to power in 1979 determined to free the economy of all manner of controls. The series of reforms that were made in 1986 in the financial sector and described as 'Big Bang' are often seen as central to this.

But how far can this be said to be the case? What 'Big Bang' did was remove restrictive practices and what were essentially private club-type regulations in the securities markets. A range of different financial institutions had their own committees that set the rules for membership behaviour and took responsibility for disciplining the membership. These 'clubs' were effectively abolished. In their place bodies responsible to the State replaced them. 'Big Bang' had more to do with the prohibition of clubs making their own rules for the benefit of their reputation and by extension the good of the consumer. The net outcome of the changes made in the mid-1980s was to increase the bureaucratic burden on firms. This of course penalizes the small firm more than the large and deters entry to the sector and so inhibits competition.

In any case 'Big Bang' had relatively little to do with banking, although banking did not escape. It was felt that the 1979 Banking Act was not a complete success. There needed to be wider coverage—a common feature once the bureaucratic machine begins to move. A new Banking Act was introduced in 1987 and that did affect the clearing banks, laying down as it did specific requirements on lending in relation to the balance sheet and so on.

At the same time the Financial Services Act was passed, for implementation from 1988, with detailed regulation in areas previously unregulated by the state. Bodies such as the Securities Investment Board were established and made responsible to the Secretary of State. This body in turn spawned many others responsible in similar fashion for different aspects of City life. The extent of the regulation, its detail, and prescriptive nature were completely new to the British financial sector.

Retail financial products were extensively regulated. Further bodies were established. These would authorize which individuals and organizations could do what. Rules required that 'best advice' be given and on that basis inappropriate sales could be found and firms fined years after transactions were carried out. As one author has expressed it the market became a 'caveat vendor' market.[9]

As a consequence of all this across the 1980s there was a huge increase in the statutory regulation of financial markets and the compliance burden. Again to quote Booth: 'it is unambiguously the case that the statutory regulation of financial markets increased under the Thatcher Government'.[10]

---

[9] Philip Booth, 'Thatcher: The Myth of Deregulation', *Institute of Economic Affairs Discussion Paper* 60 (2015): p. 24.
[10] Ibid., p. 31.

As far as banking was concerned that was only the beginning of more intrusive regulation. The beginnings of coordinated international regulation came in the wake of two 1974 bank failures, Bankhaus Herstatt and of Franklin National Bank. In large part due to the way in which regulatory authorities handled these failures, these relatively modestly sized banks caused considerable problems for other banks when they failed. This led to the formation of a standing committee of bank supervisors from the G10 countries; it has a permanent secretariat at the Bank for International Settlements in Basel (BIS)—hence it is also known as the Basel Committee.

This committee started to concern itself with capital regulation in 1988. The 1988 Basel Accord established a set of 'Capital Adequacy Standards' for internationally operating banks. This accord, known as Basel I, required banks to hold capital according to Basel risk-asset rules. It was recognized that risk assets were not homogeneous, but despite that recognition attention was paid only to credit risk—risk of default. Each asset held by a bank was assigned to one of five risk classes; the higher the risk, the higher the weighting, and the higher the capital required.

Some deficiencies in Basel I were recognized and, to some extent, tackled. In an amendment to Basel I, announced in 1996 and adopted by 1998, market risk—the risk of loss through changes in the market price of assets—was addressed. It is not surprising that the deficiencies of Basel I led to further change. The changes they led to were contained in Basel II. This was a 'three pillar' approach and was supposed to support the structure of banking, to ensure that banks measured their risks properly.

As is well known, the three pillars did not support the structure of banking. There was a major banking crisis over a substantial part of the world. Every writer on the subject, as a survey in Lastra and Wood shows, identifies the same principal features: perverse incentives, complacent management and shareholders, inadequate evaluation of risk, and regulatory failure so gross as in some cases deservedly to be described as incompetence.[11] Regulation had increased hugely but not only did that not prevent a financial crisis but rather contributed to one.

Insurance

What I have said thus far has concentrated on banking and largely implicitly some other financial services. But the story holds on a wider front. Take, for example, insurance.[12] British insurance was originally overseen by the Board of Trade (a government department). From 1870 onwards it was governed by the Life Insurance Acts of 1870 and 1872. As with banking what these Acts required

---

[11] Rosa Lastra and Geoffrey Wood, 'The Crisis of 2007–09: Nature, Causes, and Reactions', *Journal of International Economic Law* 13, no. 13 (2010): pp. 531–50.

[12] These paragraphs draw heavily on Booth, 'Thatcher'.

was the publication of information. There was no attempt to control what companies did. That arrangement remained in place more or less untouched for the 100 years after 1870. (The original Act ran to nine pages.) So in general, insurance was unregulated other than by contract law.

All of this changed in the early 1980s with the Insurance Companies Acts 1981 and 1982. One change was that the information asked for from companies went to the regulator rather than the public, and the regulator had the power to take action against the company. In the Financial Services and Markets Act (2000) powers were given to regulatory bodies to make new regulations with these bodies, 'only weakly accountable to parliament or to a government minister'.[13] These powers of the regulator were then extended further. Thus again an important sector of financial services experienced growing regulation in a period that is usually described as one of deregulation.

Conclusions

While much has been written and spoken about the late-twentieth-century deregulation of the financial markets, closer examination suggests a different picture. In fact the myth of deregulation in the financial sector applies widely. Charles Calomiris has demonstrated convincingly that deregulation was the opposite of the case in the US.[14] A particular example he gives was the 2004 change in the SEC net capital rules that was hailed by some as deregulation but was in fact a regulatory failure that loaded firms down with extra data collection and reporting.

The myth applies equally to Britain. In summary, the British financial system enjoyed a long period of relatively light regulation from the middle of the nineteenth century to the middle of the twentieth. But that began to change to a more heavily regulated system from the Second World War and it intensified from the 1970s. The growth of supervision and regulation from within the Bank of England began to gather pace in the 1970s. The first statutory regulation in banking came with the Banking Act of 1979.

Much is often made of the Big Bang of 1986 although this did not deal directly with banking. The 1986 change was more a change in regulation rather than a reduction; from self-regulation to regulation by agencies responsible to the state. The changes fostered increasing concentration in the sector and increased complexity. Thus, as Jaffer et al. expressed it: 'a multiplicity of different bodies, multiple levels of administration and greater complexity' led to heavier bureaucratic burdens.[15]

[13] Ibid., p. 8.
[14] Charles W. Calomiris, 'Another "Deregulation" Myth', American Enterprise Institute, *On the Issues*, 18 October 2008, https://www.aei.org/articles/another-deregulation-myth/.
[15] Sue Jaffer, Susana Knaudt, and Nicholas Morris, 'Failures of Regulation and Governance', in *Capital Failure: Rebuilding Trust in Financial Services*, edited by Nicholas Morris and David Vines (Oxford: Oxford University Press, 2014): pp. 100–26.

Then there was another Banking Act in 1987. Then the Financial Services Act implemented in 1988. With the creation of the Financial Services Authority (FSA) in 1998 regulation took off in a serious way. That institution grew from 700 employees at the start to 2750 in 2006 (before the crisis). FSA numbers reached 4000 in 2012.

Since 2008 there has been an avalanche of new financial regulation. Huge numbers of compliance people populate the financial institutions. There have been many estimates of how many are employed in compliance in some form or other in banking in the City of London. For the years soon after the 2008/09 crisis these suggest that there were close to twice as many estimates overseeing in one way or another what the bankers do as there were people working in banking. Or, speaking solely of regulators, the Bank of England's chief economist expressed it: 'In 1980 there was a regulator for roughly every 11,000 people employed in the UK financial sector. By 2011 there was one regulator for every 300 people employed in finance' (Haldane).[16] There can surely be no argument that this was not a period of deregulation but rather the reverse. The regulatory burden was growing for a long time before the financial crisis and grew even more quickly in the wake of the crisis. Yet most of those involved continue to speak of the certainty of the next crisis.

---

[16] Andrew G. Haldane, 'The Dog and the Frisbee' (speech at the Federal Reserve Bank of Kansas City's 336th economic policy symposium, 'The changing policy landscape', Jackson Hole, USA, 31 August 2012).

4

Drivers of Financial Deregulation in Japan

Eiji Hotori

Introduction

This chapter seeks to reconsider the drivers of financial deregulation in Japan in the 1980s. Historically, it is generally accepted that the Japanese deregulation process was caused (and stimulated) by pressure from the United States, with Japan's Ministry of Finance (MOF) endeavouring to oppose such external pressure. This perception was promoted by the media, particularly by Nikkei (Japan's main economic newspaper) and by NHK (Japan's national broadcasting corporation). Even today, this view is generally accepted. For example, Takita emphasized that the MOF encountered strong pressure to deregulate from the US, especially from David Mulford, the then Under Secretary for International Affairs at the US Department of Treasury (1984–92).[1] In the academic field of Economics, there is little primary theoretical or empirical research on Japan's financial deregulation process.[2] Indeed, several economic studies focus on the link between the financial deregulation and Japan's 'bubble economy' in the second half of the 1980s.[3] The most important aspect from a macroeconomics perspective, is the affect that the appreciated yen had on the Japanese economy.[4]

---

[1] Yoichi Takita, *Nichi-Beitsūkakōshō: 20-nen me no shinjitsu* (Japan–US Currency Negotiations: Truths after 20 years) (Tokyo: Nikkei Press, 2006).

[2] Japanese deregulation tends to be studied by political scientists as well as by journalists, with a primary focus on the Plaza Accord (1985) and on the political negotiations. See Yoichi Funabashi, *Tsūkaretsuretsu* (Fierce Negotiations on Currency between Japan and US) (Tokyo: Asahi Newspaper Press, 1992); NHK, ed., *Puraza-gōi* (Plaza Accord) (Tokyo: NHK Press, 1996); and Takehiko Kondo, *Puraza-gōi no kenkyū* (A Study of the Plaza Accord) (Tokyo: Toyo Keizai Press, 1999) for reference. In the US, the research interest was similar to that in Japan. See, for example, Brian Semkow, 'The American Trade Deficit with Japan: Whither the Role of Japanese Financial Deregulation and Liberalization?', *Maryland Journal of International Law* 13, no. 1 (January 1988): pp. 39–70, https://digitalcommons.law.umaryland.edu/mjil/vol13/iss1/4.

[3] See Akiyoshi Horiuchi, *Nihon keizai to kin'yūkiki* (Financial Crisis and Japanese Economy in the 1990s) (Tokyo: Iwanami Shoten Publishers, 1999); and Kunio Okina, Masaaki Shirakawa, and Shigenori Shiratsuka, 'The Asset Price Bubble and Monetary Policy:Japan's Experience in the Late 1980s and the Lessons', *IMES Discussion Paper Series*, no. 2000-E-12 (March 2000): pp. 1–69, http://www.imes.boj.or.jp/research/papers/english/00-E-12.pdf.

[4] See Kazuo Ueda, 'The Japanese Current Account Surplus and Fiscal Policy in Japan and the US', in *Government Policy towards Industry in the United States and Japan*, edited by John Shoven (New York: Cambridge University Press, 1988), ch. 6; and Hiroshi Yoshikawa, *Tenkanki no nihonkeizai* (Japanese Economy at the Turning Point) (Tokyo: Iwanami Shoten Publishers, 1997).

Eiji Hotori, *Drivers of Financial Deregulation in Japan* In: *Financial Deregulation: A Historical Perspective.*
Edited by: Alexis Drach and Youssef Cassis, Oxford University Press (2021). © Alexis Drach and Youssef Cassis.
DOI: 10.1093/oso/9780198856955.003.0004

Although US pressure did progress financial liberalization in Japan, it is noteworthy that the financial deregulation would be advantageous to both domestic customers and financial institutions. Moreover, the MOF not only held a financial regulatory role, it was also in charge of Japan's fiscal policy until the creation of the Financial Services Agency (FSA) in 1998. The MOF's double role possibly influenced the course of Japan's financial deregulation during the rapid increase in the government bond issuance from the mid-1970s. The conventional view that US pressure was the primary driver of Japan's financial deregulation can be challenged by an in-depth analysis of historical facts.

It is generally accepted that Japan's deregulation process was very gradual, the well-known 'gradualism' phenomenon.[5] Aoki stated that 'financial deregulation often is hampered by inter-bureau jurisdictional disputes' because the bureaus within the MOF were traditionally compartmentalized.[6] However, he did not explore what caused the 'gradualism', as this chapter does.

This chapter employs a narrative approach, analysing the relevant archive materials released under the 30-year rule.[7] Additionally, in the early 2000s, the MOF used their internal data to compile an official history of fiscal policy including Japan's deregulation process. Those data explain the true aim and the practical strategy of the MOF, as well of as the BOJ, at the time. In examining 'gradualism', this chapter focuses on three of the financial deregulation issues prevalent in Japan in the 1980s: (1) the barriers between the banking and the securities businesses; (2) the regulation of deposit interest rates; and (3) the liberalization of the financial market in Japan.

This chapter focuses on the deregulations regarding the systematically important financial institutions in Japan—commercial banks, long-term credit banks, trust banks, securities companies, postal savings bank, and insurance companies. In addition, we trace the deregulating processes of domestic deposit market and foreign exchange transactions including limitation of capital movement. Conversely, this chapter does not examine the deregulations of credit associations (namely Shinkin Banks), credit unions, labour banks, agricultural cooperatives and consumer finance companies because of their minor positions (especially in quantity) in the Japanese financial system.[8] Hampered by secrecy,

---

[5] Similarly, the formalization process of banking supervision was incremental, and it took approximately 50 years in Japan. See Eiji Hotori and Mikael Wendschlag, 'The Formalization of Banking Supervision in Japan and Sweden', *Social Science Japan Journal 22*, no. 2 (August 2019): pp. 211–28, doi: 10.1093/ssjj/jyz011.

[6] Masahiko Aoki, 'The Japanese Bureaucracy in Economic Administration: A Rational Regulator or Pluralist Agent?', in *Government Policy towards Industry in the United States and Japan*, edited by John Shoven (New York: Cambridge University Press, 1988), ch. 10: pp. 290–1.

[7] The materials held in the Bank of Japan (BOJ) archives (up to the late 1980s) are now available.

[8] This chapter does not also cover the regulations of the central bank. Indeed, the Bank of Japan Act of 1997 in part reflected a trend of financial deregulation in the 1990s, and the enactment of the Bank of Japan Act of 1997 incorporated the idea that monetary policy management should be

this chapter does not detail the liberalization process of call loan dealers (namely Tanshi companies) as well as the call loan market itself. In November 1997, a default on call loan took place in the interbank market for the first time in the postwar period, and the event was the catalyst of financial crisis in late 1997. Amount of outstanding call loan decreased to 22 trillion yen on 31 December 1999 from 39 trillion yen on 31 December 1997.[9]

The rest of the chapter is organized as follows. The second section provides an overview of the Japanese economy and financial system in the postwar period, focusing on Japan's financial regulation. The third to seventh sections examine the important elements of Japan's financial deregulation and liberalization from 1967 to 2001. These sections trace the processes of financial deregulation, and consider the drivers of the financial deregulation under the changing domestic and international circumstances. The eighth section reviews the fundamental attitude to financial deregulation in Japan ('gradualism'). The ninth section offers several concluding remarks.

Overview of the Japanese Economy and Financial System in the Postwar Period

Under the Bretton Woods system the Japanese financial system was rigidly regulated. For example, the interest rates paid on deposits were officially controlled, and bank-entry, branching, and exiting were strictly regulated. Specifically, the regulation which the securities business should be separated from the banking business was implemented in Japan under the US Occupation (1945–52). The barriers between the banking and the securities businesses were similar to the Glass-Steagall Act of 1933 in the US. In addition, the Diet of Japan enacted a Long-Term Credit Bank Act in June 1952, and under the direction of the government the Long-Term Credit Bank of Japan (LTCB) was newly founded in December 1952. Along with the Industrial Bank of Japan (IBJ), a mission of the bank was to provide long-term financing to major (manufacturing) industries in Japan. The business of ordinary (commercial) banks was mainly limited to short-term lending. Separation, specialization, and control represented characteristics of the financial system in postwar Japan (Table 4.1). Originally, the package of rigid financial regulations was mostly implemented in the wartime economy, and the government continued the wartime measures with minor amendments to control the unstable domestic economy in the second half of the 1940s. The rigid

independent of the government. Bank of Japan, *Nihon ginkō no kinō to gyōmu* (Functions and Operations of the Bank of Japan) (Tokyo: Yuhikaku Publishing, 2011): pp. 11, 232–44.
   [9] Yoshiaki Shikano, *Nihon no kin'yūseido* (Japanese Financial System) (Tokyo: Toyo Keizai Press, 2001): pp. 150–1, 188–91.

Table 4.1 List of major financial regulations in postwar Japan

Types	Contents of regulation	Commencement of deregulation
Bank-entry regulation	No new entry is permitted under the bank licensing system operated by the Ministry of Finance.	1998
Bank-branching regulation	Number, location, and size of a new branch is rigidly regulated by the Ministry of Finance.	1981
Control of bank exit	No exit is permitted. Instead, the Ministry of Finance coordinates a merger plan for a bank.	1971
Control of deposit interest rates	Ordinary banks are coerced into following the Bank of Japan's guidance to maintain their membership of the Japanese Bankers Association.	1985 (large time deposits), 1991 (small time deposits)
Barriers between the banking and the other financial businesses	The securities, trust, and insurance businesses should be separated from the banking business.	1983
Long-Term Credit Bank Act	Only three banks are deemed as a specialty bank for the purpose of providing long-term credit.	1998

Sources: Ministry of Finance, *Shōwazaiseishi* (Fiscal Policy in Japan 1952–73), vol. 10 (Tokyo: Toyo Keizai Press, 1991); Ministry of Finance, *Shōwazaiseishi* (Fiscal Policy in Japan 1974–88), vol. 6 (Tokyo: Toyo Keizai Press, 2003); Yoshimasa Nishimura, *Nihon no kin'yūseidokaikaku* (Financial Reforms in Japan) Tokyo: Toyo Keizai Press, 2003.

financial regulatory system enabled saving of resources for financial supervisory activities.[10]

The rigid regulated financial system fit with the time of high economic growth (1955–73). Over the period, the growth rate of gross domestic products (GDP) had been quite high level (6–13%). The financial regulation limited various sorts of competition (deposit interest rates, bank-entry, branching, etc.), and thus the financial institutions could supply necessary funds to certain borrower (mainly a manufacturing company) without concern for excessive competition. Ordinary banks played the role of intermediaries absorbing deposits from household funds.[11] Overall, the deposits growth rate exceeded the same year level of the

[10] Eiji Hotori, François Pasqualini, Stéphane Prigent, Jacques Richard, and Nicolas Praquin, 'Le juriste, le comptable et le banquier: regards croisésur la prudence' (The Judge, the Accountant and the Banker: Different Perspectives on Prudence), *Entreprises et Histoire 92* (December 2018): pp. 115–16, doi: 10.3917/eh.092.0106.

[11] Takafusa Nakamura, *The Postwar Japanese Economy: Its Development and Structure, 1937–1994* (Tokyo: University of Tokyo Press, 1995), pp. 139–42.

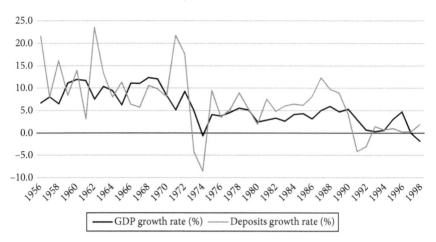

Figure 4.1 Growth rate of GDP and bank deposits in Japan, 1956–98 (fiscal year basis)

Notes: At constant prices (At market prices in calendar year of 1990).

Sources: Statistics Bureau, ed., Historical Statistics of Japan, accessed 5 June 2018, http://www.stat.go.jp/english/data/chouki/index.html.

GDP growth rate (Figure 4.1). Apparently, the rigid regulated financial system worked effectively to develop Japanese economy during the high growth period.

In 1974 Japan experienced the first minus GDP growth in the postwar period. In order to avoid a serious recession, the Japanese government began to increase its issue of bonds. Although the amount of outstanding national government bonds continued expanding, the Japanese economy shifted to the stable growth period (1974–90)—GDP growth rate was around 5%. From the 1970s the way of manufacturing companies' financing gradually shifted from the form of bank loan to bond-issuing. Over the period, deposits growth rate was slightly higher than GDP growth rate of the same year (Figure 4.1). Under such a disintermediation trend ordinary banks desired to broaden the scope of their business to securities-related business, trust business, and insurance business. Indeed, from the mid-1970s tide of financial internationalization also influenced the direction of Japanese financial reform. However, the fundamental structure of financial system in Japan had not changed until the 1990s due to awkward arrangement to coordinate interests of multiple financial sectors. Over the 1980s, many banks inevitably engaged in lending business for real estate industry and non-banking sector (finance companies) under the rigid regulated financial system. Thus, the notorious bubble economy was caused in the second half of the 1980s.

In 1990 the collapse of the bubble occurred, and the Japanese economy plunged into recession, namely 'a lost decade'. In addition to steep descent in stock prices and land prices, deposits growth rate and GDP growth rate decreased and maintained around zero in the 1990s. Many Japanese financial institutions, especially major city banks, were forced to deal with the serious non-performing loan problem. Along with resolving the non-performing loan problem, financial system reform and deregulation were assumed a role of important measure to revive the Japanese financial system as well as the Japanese economy. From 1996 a series of financial deregulations, namely the Japanese 'financial Big Bang', were implemented, and regulatory measures shifted from ex-ante regulation to ex-post regulation (supervision) to promote more competition as well as to benefit financial institutions and customers. Financial deregulation such as a liberalization of deposit interest rates was incrementally implemented before the mid-1990s, and the financial Big Bang transformed the financial structural regulations: New bank-entry as well as creation of financial holding company has been permitted for the first time since 1901 and 1945 respectively, which enabled a new competitive company to enter the traditional banking system. Instead, banking supervision occupied a more crucial role to better regulate systemically important financial institutions.

The Beginning: Liberalization of Capital Movement from 1967

In 1964 Japan joined the Organization for Economic Co-operation and Development (OECD), and the OECD member countries, especially the US, required to liberalize Japan's capital account. Aforementioned rigid regulatory regime began to change, starting with the partial liberalization of capital movements in 1967.[12] The Japanese government anticipated the challenges that would accompany this liberalization, as foreign financial institution entered its market. In response, the Director-General of the Banking Bureau of the MOF (1966–69), Satoshi Sumida, announced a new regulatory approach, namely the *Kin'yū Kōritsuka Gyōsei*.[13]

This approach is summarized as follows: (1) the reconsideration of the traditional barriers between banking and other financial businesses; (2) the promotion of competition among financial institutions; for example, the conventional branching regulation—where one new branch was permitted per year—was moderated; under the interest rates regulation, the number of branches that a bank has is crucial for the bank to collect deposits; thus, this was the first step toward the liberalization of the interest rates regulation; (3) an increase in the competitiveness of financial institutions. To enhance competitive power, the

---

[12] Liberalization of capital movements was implemented with five incremental steps until 1973 in order to protect domestic industries such as an automobile.

[13] Ministry of Finance, *Shōwazaiseishi* (Fiscal Policy in Japan 1952–73), vol. 10 (Tokyo: Toyo Keizai Press, 1991): pp. 347–52.

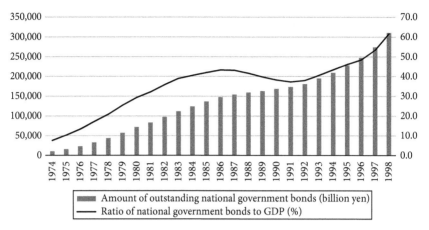

Figure 4.2 Increase of national government bonds in Japan, 1974–98

Sources: Statistics Bureau, ed., *Historical Statistics of Japan*, accessed 5 June 2018, http://www.stat.go.jp/english/data/chouki/index.html.

MOF supported several instances of bank amalgamations. For example, the Dai-ichi Bank (First Bank) was merged with the Nihon Kangyō Bank (Japan Bank for the Encouragement of Industry). This merger included no administrative guidance on the curtailment of overlapping branches which had been adopted by the MOF previously.[14] Additionally, the government created a safety-net for ordinary depositors. The Deposit Insurance Corporation of Japan was established in July 1971. This meant that the MOF would allow a bank to fail under the new regulatory regime, although an actual failure did not happen until the Hyōgo Bank failure in 1995—the first bankruptcy of a bank in postwar Japan.

These new administrative approaches demonstrate the shift from Japan's rigid regulatory regime to a less regulated system. With a prospect of liberalizing deposit interest rates, the BOJ also introduced a normative guideline on interest rate setting instead of previously adopted control measures based on the 'temporary' law (see the fifth section of this chapter).[15]

Fiscal Policy Shift and Acceleration of Financial Deregulation

From the mid-1970s the domestic trend of financial deregulation was accelerated due to the transformation of Japan's fiscal policy. In the mid-1970s, Japan's economy was affected by the international oil crisis of 1973, and in 1974 by the

---

[14] MOF, *Shōwazaiseishi*, vol. 10 (1991): pp. 443–4.
[15] Bank of Japan, *Nihon ginkōhyakunenshi* (The Bank of Japan: A History, 1882–1982), vol. 6 (Tokyo: Bank of Japan, 1986): pp. 237–8.

first experience of minus GDP growth in the postwar period. In response, the Japanese government began to increase its issue of bonds to avoid a serious recession. The ratio of national government bonds to GDP soared up from 7.6% in 1974 to 25.4% in 1979 (Figure 4.2). The rapid increase of government bonds created a new role for the MOF—that is, managing stable and smooth financing without any serious shock to the financial market. As aforementioned, the banking business and the securities business were separated in postwar Japan. During Japan's high economic growth period (1955–73), its banks developed significantly more than its securities companies because of the strict restrictions on the capital market. For instance, the amount of corporate/municipal bonds issued was carefully controlled (limited) under the Bond Joint Committee. The committee members were from the BOJ, several syndicate banks, and major securities companies.

The necessary bulk issue of bonds by the Japanese government in the mid-1970s signalled a change to the postwar situation. The large banks were expected to deal with a large amount of the government bonds, although the traditional barrier on issuing such bonds was an obstacle. However, for the major securities companies such as Nomura the situation—the prospect of increasing the government bonds issuances—meant a golden opportunity for their business, because the securities business had been monopolized since 1945.

A clear conflict of interest existed between the banks (and the government) and the securities companies. The first official coordination process took place in March 1974.[16] The Securities Bureau in the MOF considered the balance of power among Japanese financial institutions if the major banks were permitted to engage in the securities business. The Securities Bureau was particularly concerned that several major banks might monopolize the bond issue markets. In the worst case, the ordinal investors might be squeezed out of the capital market. Under objections from the securities companies, the Securities Bureau explored the possibility of selling government bonds over the bank counter. The Securities Bureau pointed out the merit in developing the circulation market of the government bonds to maintain/stabilize the bond prices.[17]

However, it was not until October 1983 that the banks were permitted to sell government bonds over the counter. There were two major reasons for this delay, with the first being legislative. The original Bank Act was enacted in 1927, and needed substantial amendments.[18] The new Bank Act was eventually enacted on

---

[16] Securities Bureau, 'Regarding the Securities Act Section 65' (March 1974), in Ministry of Finance, *Shōwazaiseishi* (Materials of Fiscal Policy in Japan 1974–88), vol. 10 (Tokyo: Toyo Keizai Press, 2002), no. 10–147. Hereinafter, we translated all titles of the materials originally written in Japanese.

[17] Securities Bureau, 'Sale of Government Bonds over the Counter of the Banks' (14 August 1975), in MOF, *Shōwazaiseishi*, vol. 10 (2002), no. 10–148.

[18] Ministry of Finance, 'Legislation for Securities Business Operated by a Bank' (15 December 1980), in MOF, *Shōwazaiseishi*, vol. 10 (2002), no. 10–152.

Table 4.2 Timeline of liberalization of the time deposit interest rates in Japan

Implementation	Size of time deposit	Fixed term
Jul. 1976	*Start consideration of liberalization of interest rates	
Oct. 1985	(more than) 1,000 million yen	3–24 months
Apr. 1986	(do.) 500 million yen	do.
Apr. 1987	(do.) 100 million yen	do.
Apr. 1988	(do.) 50 million yen	1–24 months
Oct. 1989	(do.) 10 million yen	do.
Nov. 1991	(do.) 3 million yen	3–36 months
Jun. 1993	All	All

Sources: Bank of Japan, *Nihon kin'yūnenpyō* (Chronological Table of Japanese Financial History)
Tokyo: Institute for Monetary and Economic Studies, 1995.

1 June 1981. The second reason for the delay was in relation to innovations of the financial instruments. The advent of the Money Market Fund (MMF) in the US in November 1971 made it evident that the securities companies could engage in the saving business. The Japanese securities companies requested permission to handle such bond investment funds. The MOF welcomed the suggestion, since they could issue more government bonds. However, the Japanese banks fiercely opposed the suggestion, because an MMF would damage their own deposit-taking business. Eventually, the securities companies were permitted to handle the open-type medium-term government bond investment funds in January 1980. The banks were finally permitted to engage in the government bonds businesses (including underwriting, selling, and dealing) in 1983–84.[19]

Under the fiscal demands of the MOF, the interests between a bank and a securities company were coordinated in a barter-type structure. The barriers between the banking and the securities businesses were partially removed in the 1980s: It was not until the implementation of the Financial System Reform Law in 1993 that a cross entry between banks and securities companies through subsidiaries was permitted.

Liberalization of the Deposit Interest Rates

The regulation of the deposit interest rates was liberalized in April 1967 in Germany,[20] and in the US deregulation of interest rates for large deposits in

---

[19] Ministry of Finance, 'Regarding Securities Business Operated by a Bank' (19 May 1983), in MOF, *Shōwazaiseishi*, vol. 10 (2002), no. 10–157 and Securities Bureau & Banking Bureau, 'Permission of the Government Bonds Dealing' (7 April 1984), in MOF, *Shōwazaiseishi*, vol. 10 (2002), no. 10–158.
[20] Daniel Detzer and Hansjörg Herr, 'Financial Regulation in Germany', *FESSUD Working Paper Series*, no. 55 (September 2014): p. 147, http://fessud.eu/wp-content/uploads/2013/04/Financial-Regulation-in-Germany-FESSUD-Working-Paper-55.pdf.

denominations of $100,000 took place in the late 1970s.[21] In Japan, the deposit interest rates had been controlled based on the Temporary Interest Rate Adjustment Act of 1947 (operated by the MOF in conjunction with the BOJ), and in April 1970 the regulation of the deposit interest rates was conducted by the BOJ as *a gentlemen's agreement*. The individual banks were coerced into following the BOJ's guidance to maintain their membership of the Japanese Bankers Association. The liberalization of the deposit interest rates progressed relatively slowly (Table 4.2). Regarding fixed deposit, liberalization was implemented for large time deposits (over one billion yen) in October 1985. The interest rate for medium deposits (over 10 million yen) was liberalized in October 1989. It was not until June 1993 that the interest rates for all time deposits were completely liberalized.[22] The international trend towards the liberalization of deposit interest rates did not significantly affect the process in Japan. Notably, the MOF began to consider the liberalization of the deposit interest rates in response to complaints made by the ordinary depositors. In 1976, the Banking Bureau of the MOF stated that the criticisms relating to the profiteering banking business would be alleviated if the regulation on the deposit interest rates was relaxed. The MOF was also concerned that the interest rate for small depositors would be lower (hence unfair) than for large depositors under the market mechanism if the regulation on the deposit interest rates was suspended. The MOF anticipated that the increased competition for deposit-taking would cause higher loan interest rates: such increases might damage the borrowers' activities (especially those of small-to-medium-sized enterprises).[23]

However, domestic academic opinions pushed the MOF to progress the liberalization of the deposit interest rates. In 1978, the Banking Bureau noted that Professor Komiya and Professor Kaizuka (prominent economists from the University of Tokyo) both supported suspending the regulation on the deposit interest rates. Both professors pointed out the merits to liberalizing the interest rates as follows: (1) unregulated interest rates would enhance effectiveness of monetary policy; (2) allocation of financial assets would be improved under the market principles; (3) tougher competition among banks would increase management efficiency of financial institutions. In addition, majority of domestic academic scholars including both professors suggested deregulation of government and corporate bond markets to attract large investors before deposit interest rates were fully liberalized. The MOF basically agreed to the

---

[21] Alton Gilbert, 'Requiem for Regulation Q: What It Did and Why It Passed away', *Federal Reserve Bank of St. Louis Review 68*, no. 2 (February 1986): p. 30, doi:10.20955/r.68.22–37.zge.

[22] Bank of Japan, *Nihon kin'yūnenpyō* (Chronological Table of Japanese Financial History) Tokyo: Institute for Monetary and Economic Studies, 1995, pp. 29–32.

[23] Ministry of Finance, 'Issues on Liberalization of Deposit Interest Rates' (1 July 1976), in MOF, *Shōwazaiseishi*, vol. 10 (2002), no. 10–88.

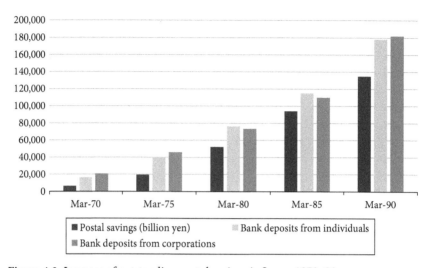

Figure 4.3 Increase of outstanding postal savings in Japan, 1970–90

Sources: Statistics Bureau, ed., Historical Statistics of Japan, accessed 5 June 2018, http://www.stat.go.jp/english/data/chouki/index.html.

liberalization-oriented opinions because of a large-scale issuance of government bonds.[24] Essentially, the course toward the liberalization of Japan's deposit interest rates was already decided before Japan encountered pressure from abroad.

Even after the liberalization of the interest rates for large time deposits, the MOF was still reluctant to suspend the regulation of the interest rates for small depositors. The critical issue was the substantial levels of post office savings: such savings were regulated by the Japanese Cabinet, rather than by the MOF. The BOJ clearly documented this issue. According to its materials,[25] the BOJ was worried that the partial introduction of market principles to post office savings might jeopardize the competition among banks. Indeed, the amount of Japanese post office savings increased rapidly in the 1980s, and the regional banks were already in severe competition with the post offices (Figure 4.3).

The majority of the ex-Directors in charge of prudential supervision from the MOF and the BOJ entered a regional bank or a regional bank II. As the president/executive director of those banks, the ex-Directors probably complained about this unfair competition condition to the MOF's active elites.[26] Yet, for the public good, post offices should be distributed nationwide without consideration for

---

[24] Banking Bureau, 'Regarding Liberalization of Deposit Interest Rates' (20 January 1978), in MOF, *Shōwazaiseishi*, vol. 10 (2002), no. 10–90.

[25] Bank of Japan, 'Regulation of Deposit Interest Rates for Small Depositors and the Postal Savings Service' (August 1985), BOJ Archives, No. 39533–5.

[26] See Eiji Hotori, 'The role of financial elites in banking supervision in Japan from 1927 to 1998', *eabh Papers*, no. 16–01 (March 2016): pp. 1–22, http://bankinghistory.org/wp-content/uploads/eabh-papers_16_01.pdf.

profitability. Additionally, post office savings were important fiscal investments and acted as the *second national budget*. On 22 May 1986, Japan's Advisory Committee for Financial Issues recommended that the liberalization of the deposit interest rates for small depositors should be progressed gradually. The committee advised that the government should carefully coordinate the interest between the banks and the post office.[27] Even the pressure from the US did not expedite the deregulation of the deposit interest rates for small depositors. The progress towards this deregulation was awkward and slow.

Increased Foreign Pressure from the 1980s

From the 1980s, American pressure in part promoted both financial liberalization and internationalization in Japan. By July 1982, at the 19th Japan–US Business Conference, the exchange rate imbalance between the yen and the US dollar was at the top of the agenda. The US expected that the liberalization of the capital market in Japan would promote a more internationally use of the yen, and would stimulate currency appreciation.[28] However, the MOF was sceptical of this economic theory. According to its internal materials, the International Finance Bureau worried about which economic policy would promote the development of the euro-yen market. Indeed, the euro-dollar market developed spontaneously not artificially. Moreover, Japan imported most of its important goods—oil, gas, wheat, corn, etc.—through dollars.[29] The internationalization of the yen appeared to be a challenging theme theoretically as well as practically.

Following the November 1983 visit of the US president, Ronald Reagan, a 'Joint Japan–US Ad Hoc Group on Yen/Dollar Exchange Rate, Financial and Capital Market Issues' was newly created. The group's first meeting took place on 23–24 February 1984. The US requests can be summarized as: (1) the liberalization of the euro-yen market; (2) the lowering of the Japanese entry barriers to foreign financial institutions; and (3) the liberalization of the deposit interest rates.[30]

The group met each month for three months, and the final report was compiled in May 1984. The report covered many financial liberalization topics, with the main points summarized as follows: (1) the US confirmed that the deposit interest

[27] Ministry of Finance, 'Report of the Advisory Committee for the Financial Issues: An Abstract' (22 May 1986), in MOF, *Shōwazaiseishi*, vol. 10 (2002), no. 10–93.

[28] Ministry of Finance, 'Summary of the 19th Japan-US Business Conference's Statement' (July 1982), in Ministry of Finance, *Shōwazaiseishi* (Materials of Fiscal Policy in Japan 1974–88), vol. 11 (Tokyo: Toyo Keizai Press, 2003), no. 11–77.

[29] International Finance Bureau, 'Questions regarding Euro-yen Market and Internationalization of Yen' (19 March 1984), in MOF, *Shōwazaiseishi*, vol. 11 (2003), no. 11–181.

[30] Ministry of Finance, 'Summary of the Working Group's First Meeting in the Joint Japan-US Ad Hoc Group on Yen/Dollar Exchange Rate' (16 March 1984), in MOF, *Shōwazaiseishi*, vol. 11 (2003), no. 11–78.

rates in Japan were gradually liberalized for all deposits, from large to small; (2) Japan agreed to eliminate the actual demand rule for the foreign currency exchange futures transactions; (3) Japan permitted the trust business, operated by foreign financial institutions, through a joint domestic enterprise; (4) Japan enlarged the scope of the entities that were permitted to issue euro-yen bonds without security to a foreign company and a regional foreign government (from a foreign government and an international organization).[31] The fourth point was also applied to domestic companies. Although Japanese companies enjoyed the resulting currency appreciation by financing from abroad, the deregulation resulted in the issue of too many Eurobonds during the bubble economy period (1985–90). Thus, the land boom was promoted by the domestic companies financed by the domestic financial institutions as well as from Eurobond markets.

Notably, Japan made several suggestions to the US. For instance, Japan proposed that the US government (the US currency authority) should purchase Japanese government bonds to promote the international use of the yen. However, the US was reluctant to accept this proposal, and declined further consideration of it.[32] This episode shows that fiscal reasons were important drivers for Japan progressing its financial deregulation.

Path to Japanese 'Financial Big Bang'

In the 1990s, the Japanese financial authorities were confronted with three difficult issues: (1) a further increase in issuing government bonds; (2) the internationalization of financial regulation; and (3) the financial crisis of 1997–98. In response to the first two issues, the Financial System Reform Law was implemented in April 1993. Moreover, a series of deregulations were implemented through the 'financial Big Bang' (1996–2001).

In September 1985, the Study Group on Japanese Financial System was organized within the Fiscal System Research Council (an advisory body to the Finance Minister). The MOF seriously recognized a trend of disintermediation and the need for financial reform (especially for conventional banking). Yet, it was not until July 1990 that the Working Party 2 of the Study Group released the report on 'New Framework of Financial System,' since the direction of the reform was transformed into a measure of expanding financial business under the bubble

---

[31] Ministry of Finance and US Department of the Treasury (USDT), 'Report of the Special Meetings Working Group in the Joint Japan-US Ad Hoc Group on Yen/Dollar Exchange Rate, Financial and Capital Market Issues' (May 1984), in MOF, *Shōwazaiseishi*, vol. 11 (2003), no. 11–83.

[32] MOF and USDT, 'Report of the Special Meetings' (May 1984), in MOF, *Shōwazaiseishi*, vol. 11 (2003), no. 11–83: chapter 4-E. The amount of Japanese government bonds held by foreign investors increased to 4360 billion yen (March 1988) from 2096 billion yen (March 1985), although the reason should be examined carefully. Bank of Japan, BOJ Time-Series Data Search, accessed 20 December 2019, http://www.stat-search.boj.or.jp/index.html.

economy. Due to a series of financial scandals in 1991 the MOF was busy for coping with them, and thus enactment of the Financial System Reform Law was postponed until June 1992. The financial reform contained a significant step of Japan's financial deregulation. Notably, an ordinary bank, a securities company, and a trust company were permitted to enter the other type of financial business through a form of subsidiary company. This meant that the barrier between banking and securities businesses was no more effective. From July 1993, most of the city banks established a subsidiary of securities business and trust business. In September 1993, four of the major securities companies established a subsidiary of trust business. From October 1993, three of the major trust companies established a subsidiary of securities business.[33] Regarding insurance business, Revision of Insurance Business Act was enacted in 1995 following long continued deliberation. Not only partial liberalization of insurance premiums setting the Act also contained important deregulation—that is, life/non-life insurance companies were permitted to operate mutual business (including the third field) through subsidiaries. Since the third field such as a cancer insurance had been mostly occupied by an American insurance company (namely American Family Life Assurance Company of Columbus), this deregulation caused confliction of interests. Following the US–Japan Framework Talks, deregulation in relation to the third field was postponed until 2001.[34]

Further financial reform was suspended during 1995 because of the *Jūsen* (housing finance company) problem and the Great Hanshin-Awaji Earthquake. In November 1996, Prime Minister Ryutaro Hashimoto directed Finance Minister to grapple with a financial reform so that Tokyo financial market could be ranked the third in the world. The principles of the reform were 'Free', 'Fair', and 'Global'. In June 1997, the MOF announced the Financial Reform Plan, following deliberation of five councils (financial system, securities and exchange, insurance, business accounting, and foreign exchange). The contents of financial deregulation and liberalization are summarized as follows: (1) brokerage fees for the purchase and sale of stocks were liberalized; along with this liberalization, shift from a licensing system to a registration system led to creation of many online securities companies; (2) insurance companies were permitted to operate banking business through subsidiaries; (3) banks and insurance companies were permitted to deal with over-the-counter investment trusts; (4) several privileges such as a financial bonds issuance for long-term credit banks were released to ordinary banks.[35]

In addition, on 5 December 1997 two important sets of bills in relation to the lifting of the ban on financial holding companies were enacted, and thus large

---

[33] Yoshimasa Nishimura, *Nihon no kin'yūseidokaikaku* (Financial Reforms in Japan) (Tokyo: Toyo Keizai Press), 2003, pp. 239–84.

[34] Nishimura, *Nihon no kin'yūseidokaikaku*, pp. 286–91.

[35] Shikano, *Nihon no kin'yūseido*, pp. 51–60.

Table 4.3 Non-performing loans of city banks in Japan (1995–2005)

	Amount of the NPLs of city banks (billion yen)	Amount of outstanding loans (billion yen)	NPLs' ratio (%)
30 Sep. 1995	13,557	275,741	4.9
30 Sep. 2000	11,883	238,682	5.0
31 Mar. 2005	6463	211,217	3.1

Notes: Originally, city banks consisted of 13 major commercial banks in Japan.

Sources: Ministry of Finance, *Kin'yūNenpō: Heisei 9-nen ban* (Annual Report of the Banking Bureau: 1997) Tokyo: Kinzai Institute for Financial Affairs, 1998; Financial Services Agency, *Kin'yūchō no ichinen: Heisei 12 jimunendo-ban* (Annual Report of the Financial Services Agency: 2000) Tokyo: Financial Services Agency, 2001; Financial Services Agency, *Kin'yūchō no ichinen: Heisei 16 jimunendo-ban* (Annual Report of the Financial Services Agency: 2004) Tokyo: Financial Services Agency, 2005.

commercial banks were prompt to organize the 'Financial Holding Company Group'. Under the US occupation policy (1945–52), the large financial combines, namely *zaibatsu* groups, were dissolved and divided into banks, securities companies, insurance companies, etc. The Antimonopoly Act of 1947 included the provision of a ban on establishment of pure holding companies so that ex-*zaibatsu* could not reorganize any type of holding company (Article 9). From the early 1990s, the ratio of non-performing loans to outstanding loans of Japanese major banks increased to 5% (Table 4.3), and stock prices including those banks dropped rapidly in 1995. The Japanese government started consideration of (re)introducing the financial holding company system to revive Japan's international competitiveness. In the US separation of commercial and investment banking prescribed in the Glass-Steagall Act was already in decline in the 1980s due to development of financial products (e.g. residential mortgage-backed security). The Financial System Research Committee of Japan addressed the reform of financial institutions during 1995–96, and on 11 June 1996 the Antimonopoly Act was revised to permit establishment of a holding company.[36] Thus, creation of the financial holding company groups was permitted in December 1997. The Financial Holding Company Group was expected to consist of commercial banks, trust banks, securities companies, and insurance companies.[37] A merger movement among financial institutions occurred around the turn of the century, and finally three largest financial groups, namely Mitsubishi UFJ Financial Group, Sumitomo Mitsui Financial Group, and Mizuho Financial Group, were established by 2005. The final step of this deregulation was

---

[36] Nishimura, *Nihon no kin'yūseidokaikaku*, pp. 354–5.
[37] Financial Services Agency, *Kin'yūchō no ichinen: Heisei 12 jimunendo-ban* (Annual Report of the Financial Services Agency: 2000) Tokyo: Financial Services Agency, 2001, pp. 33–6.

primarily promoted by market force in response to the serious non-performing loan problem.[38]

In parallel with the Japanese 'financial Big Bang', technical innovation (especially the IT revolution) taking place from the mid-1990s promoted to create a new type of financial institutions. For example, Seven Bank Ltd,[39] which was established in April 2001, concentrates on fee-based businesses through automatic teller machines (ATM) in the 7-Eleven convenience stores. The bank operates only a few branch offices for the over-the-counter services, and the business of the bank is profitable thanks to lower labour costs. Technical innovation was also an important driver to promote financial deregulation.

Review of Authorities' Posture on Japan's Financial Deregulation

The fundamental attitude to financial deregulation in Japan was the aforementioned 'gradualism'. As illustrated above, the MOF preferred to coordinate the interests of ordinary banks and other financial institutions in a deliberate manner. The Bank of Japan (BOJ) synchronized the MOF's posture. The BOJ understood that financial deregulation was an inevitable trend, and that in principle the government should progress liberalization (particularly the deregulation of the deposit interest rates) as quick as possible. However, Japan stuck to its original deregulation plan, even under strong pressure from the US. For example, the executive director of the BOJ, Reiichi Shimamoto, stressed that Japan should seek *'balanced liberalization'* without damaging its financial stability, as well as managing effective fiscal policies.[40] Although Shimamoto mentioned the importance of financial deregulation in principle, he concluded that a *'soft-landing'* shift to a liberal financial system was ideal for Japan.

The main BOJ priority appeared to be controlling the payment system as 'the bank of banks'. Following a series of joint group meetings in 1986, the BOJ documented its deregulation plan for the barrier between the banking and the securities businesses.[41] This documentation shows that the securities companies were reluctant to have a more deregulated barrier, while the banks were amenable to the prospect because they needed to cover their profits under the disintermediation trend of the 1980s. The BOJ noted that the brokerage fees for

---

[38] On 30 October 2002, the FSA announced the 'Program for Financial Revival' in order to accelerate disposal of the non-performing loans of city banks. Financial Services Agency, *Kin'yūchō no ichinen: Heisei 14 jimunendo-ban* (Annual Report of the Financial Services Agency: 2002) Tokyo: Financial Services Agency (2003): pp. 325–34.

[39] The parent companies of the bank are 7-Eleven Japan and Ito Yokado.

[40] Bank of Japan, 'Speech Drafts on the Theme of Financial Deregulation and Fiscal Policy in Japan' (January 1985), BOJ Archives, No. 39533–5.

[41] Bank of Japan, 'Reconsideration of the Barriers among Financial Businesses' (November 1986), BOJ Archives, No. 39534–23.

the purchase and sale of stocks were still regulated to maintain the profitability of the securities companies. This brokerage fee regulation impaired fair competition, because the deregulation of the deposit interest rates had already started. This unfair situation would be grounds for the banks to move further into the securities businesses (e.g. underwrite corporate bonds and deal with investment funds). Concurrently, the BOJ did not want the major city banks to enter the stock businesses, because it wanted to prevent the monopolization of the capital market. Additionally, the BOJ was opposed to the idea of the securities companies engaging in the payments business by, for example, enlarging the scope of the deposits to the Money Reserve Fund. At the time, the BOJ appeared to be conservative in its attitude to securities companies due to their speculative behaviour caused by their roots as a proprietary trading firm.

Concluding Remarks

Japan's financial deregulation can be explained by three drivers over time. (1) In the late 1960s and the early 1970s, the liberalization of capital movement caused an administrative shift from Japan's extant rigid regulatory system. (2) From the mid-1970s, fiscal reasons were the catalyst for commencement of removing the barriers between the banking and the securities businesses. (3) From the mid-1980s, the pressure from the US, as well as from domestic depositors and banks, urged the Japanese financial authorities to liberalize the financial market.

Until the 1980s financial deregulation in Japan are summarized as the mixture of the following two patterns. The first pattern is that financial globalization and international politics (pressure) triggered the debate on financial deregulation of the targeted financial market and institutions. Interests of domestic financial institutions between several types were carefully coordinated by the financial authority on moderating financial regulation. The second pattern is in relation to domestic politics. Specifically, increase of the national government bonds offered an opportunity of underwriting business to commercial banks, while such securities business had been monopolized by the securities companies in the postwar period. Following the deliberate coordination processes, the barriers between the banking and securities businesses were reduced and finally removed.

It is clearly evident that not only pressure from abroad but also domestic fiscal reasons were important drivers of financial deregulation in Japan. The famed 'gradualism' was caused by the difficulty in coordinating the domestic financial institutions (including the post office savings service). Additionally, the BOJ's prudential (conservative) policy in maintaining the stability of the domestic financial markets contributed to 'gradualism'.

The collapse of Japan's bubble economy from 1990 brought about a significant change in the attitude of the US hardliners on the subject of financial deregulation in Japan. In April 1990, at the US Congress, Alan Greenspan (chairman of the Board of Governors of the Federal Reserve) testified that American financial institutions were still competitive regarding profitability such as return on assets. Greenspan also explained that the Japanese financial market was already '*very substantially open*' since US banks were permitted to engage in the securities business in Japan, (e.g., through subsidiary companies). At the congress, David Mulford expressed opposition to radical options, such as an entry barrier against Japanese financial institutions.[42] Following the Basel Capital Accords of 1988, the international harmonization of financial regulation legitimately began. Probably, these accords might also mitigate the pressure from the US regarding financial deregulation.

It was not until the 1990s that the (domestic) rationale for financial liberalization was identified in the context and contents of financial deregulation. Under the sluggish economy during the 1990s, the financial liberalization was expected to work as a measure of economic recovery and redevelopment. By the time, rigid bank-entry regulation as well as inefficient financial regulations such as a uniform fixed transaction fee undermined the interests of competitive financial institutions and domestic customers. Eventually, the Japanese 'financial Big Bang' in the late 1990s provided a substantial benefit for (general) customers of financial institutions as well as for new entrants—e.g. Seven Bank, Rakuten Card Co., Ltd., and Sony Financial Holdings.

From the mid-1990s, the advance of the IT revolution was also an important driver of financial deregulation in Japan. In parallel with the 'e-Japan Priority Policy Program',[43] the 'financial Big Bang' promoted a new type of financial business such as an online banking, and most of the conventional financial regulations were relaxed by 2001. The impact of the IT revolution on the final step of financial deregulation should be examined for further research.

---

[42] Bank of Japan, 'Japanese Banks' International Presence and Financial Conflicts' (17 July 1990), BOJ Archives, No. 41046–7.

[43] The policy programme formulated by the government's IT Strategic Headquarters aimed to improve an Internet infrastructure for promotion of utilizing the Internet. Konosuke Odaka, *Tsūshōsangyōseisakushi* (History of Japan's Trade and Industry Policy 1980–2000), vol. 1 (Tokyo: Research Institute of Economy, Trade and Industry, 2013): pp. 509–12.

5

Removing Obstacles to Integration

The European Way to Deregulation

Alexis Drach

Next to the national pathways to the post Breton Woods changes in the financial regulatory systems in Europe, the European Economic Community (EEC) played a significant role in liberalizing banking and financial markets.[1] The 1980s were a particularly important decade in this perspective, because it marked the relaunch of the integration process. In particular, the 12 EEC member states signed the Single European Act (SEA) in February 1986 which encompassed an ambitious plan for the completion of the common market by 1992. Furthermore, the Commission's move in the financial sector has to be considered in the context of monetary cooperation and integration, since the European Monetary System established in 1979 contributed to provide a new dynamism to the thinking about Economic and Monetary Union (EMU). In the 1980s, the European Commission put forward that progress in the integration of the financial sector had been much slower than in the industrial sector in the Community and called for a serious change in this respect.[2] Two areas were of particular interest for the banking sector: the creation of a common market in banking, meaning the freedom for banks to establish and to provide services within the Community, and the liberalization of capital flows. The Commission also developed plans in other financial sectors, such as insurance and securities activities, in which banks were increasingly active.[3]

Several scholars have already stressed the role of the EEC in liberalizing financial regulation. Abdelal has in particular stressed the role of the European Community, and in particular of the French government, in the advent of liberal rules for the international financial regime, countering the widely held view that

[1] This chapter was written when I was postdoctoral researcher in the project EURECON funded by the European Research Council (ERC) under the European Union's Horizon 2020 research and innovation programme (grant agreement No. 716849).
[2] Bank of France Archives (BFA), 1357200901/94,'Intégration financière (Communication de la Commission au Conseil)', 18 April 1983.
[3] BFA, 1357200901/94,'Communication de la Commission au Conseil sur l'intégration financière. Dossier technique (Note à l'attention du ComitéMonétaire). 1. Liste des directives communautaires en matière d'intégration financière', 6 October 1983.

Alexis Drach, *Removing Obstacles to Integration: The European Way to Deregulation* In: *Financial Deregulation: A Historical Perspective*. Edited by: Alexis Drach and Youssef Cassis, Oxford University Press (2021). © Alexis Drach and Youssef Cassis. DOI: 10.1093/oso/9780198856955.003.0005

the United States was responsible for worldwide liberalization.[4] Bakker has devoted a monograph to the liberalization of capital movements in the EC between 1958 and 1994.[5] However, both of these studies focused on capital movements, leaving aside other areas of banking and financial regulation. This chapter will consider together the various dimensions of liberalization moves in the EEC: the adoption of the mutual recognition principle, the liberalization of capital flows, and the Commission's plans of 'financial integration' more generally. It will also pay more attention to the point of view of commercial bankers on the question. Moreover, this chapter argues that Abdelal downplays the role of the United Kingdom and other countries in financial liberalization in the EEC, and somehow exaggerates the role of France, even if France did play an important role in the liberalization of capital movements. Several studies have already addressed European monetary integration,[6] and financial integration.[7] However, little archival enquiries have been made on banking and financial directives, partly due to the restricted access to the most recent archival material, and few studies have examined the EC regulatory activity through the lenses of deregulation.

By the 1980s, the effort of the Commission in promoting the financial integration of Europe were already quite old. The 1957 Treaty of Rome establishing the European Community initially planned the liberalization of capital movements in its article 67. Two directives in 1960 and 1962 were supposed to implement the principles of the article 67 of the Rome Treaty, but were of limited impact, and authorised various kinds of restrictions, in particular for short-term capital movements.[8] In the following years, capital movement liberalization in the EEC turned into a political deadlock. By the early 1980s, nothing had happened in this area for twenty years. In the area of banking, the Commission envisioned from 1965 the realization of a common market specific to this sector, meaning an environment where banks could freely provide services and establish with comparable competitive conditions, like a national market.[9] This plan implied both harmonization and liberalization measures. However, the European banking systems were very different, and these initial ambitious plans faced considerable

---

[4] Rawi Abdelal, *Capital Rules: The Construction of Global Finance* (Cambridge, Mass.: Harvard University Press, 2007).

[5] Age Bakker, *The Liberalization of Capital Movements in Europe: The Monetary Committee and Financial Integration 1958–1994* (Dordrecht: Kluwer academic, 1996).

[6] Harold James, *Making the European Monetary Union: The Role of the Committee of Central Bank Governors and the Origins of the European Central Bank* (Cambridge, Mass.: Harvard University Press, 2012).

[7] Jonathan Story and Ingo Walter, *Political Economy of Financial Integration in Europe: The Battle of the Systems* (Cambridge, Mass.: MIT Press, 1997); Ivo Maes, *Half a Century of European Financial Integration: From the Rome Treaty to the 21st Century* (Brussels: Mercatorfonds, 2007).

[8] BFA, 1357200901/93, 'Le Marché Commun bancaire', Charles Campet, *Revue du Marché Commun*, no. 137 (October 1970): pp. 441–6.

[9] Ibid. On the history of the common market in banking, see Josette Farges-Cazenove, 'Construire le marché bancaire européen : modalités de gouvernance de la Commission européenne et rôle des comités d'experts (1969–1989)'. Unpublished PhD thesis, University Paris IV Sorbonne, 2017.

challenges and lack of enthusiasm from both banks and authorities from EEC countries in the 1970s.[10] As soon as it joined the EEC in 1973, the United Kingdom was particularly instrumental in watering down the Commission's plans, not least because the UK government did not want to see the UK's traditionally informally regulated system harmonized with the more formal style of continental regulation.[11] The British banks, in particular, saw the harmonization of banking regulation in the European context as an unacceptable increase of regulation.[12] The situation would change in the 1980s as liberalization and mutual recognition would become the cornerstone of progress in European integration.

This chapter deals with the role of the European Commission, and of European integration in general, in the move towards deregulation that swept the 1980s. It concentrates on three cases: the realization of a common market in banking, and the liberalization of capital movements, and the intertwining of banking and other financial areas' regulatory activity of the Commission. It focuses more on banking regulation than on financial regulation, but will analyse in the third section the initiatives of the Commission in the field of insurance and securities regulation. The chapter argues that the European Community played a key role in the deregulation move analysed in this book, even though its motives were specific to its particular political project. In particular, the chapter will argue that the Commission's liberal turn in the 1980s was primarily motivated by a wish to relaunch the integration process, to revive the plans for monetary integration, and to complete the single market. In addition, the European Commission's activity was very representative of the ambiguity of the so-called deregulation move of that period, as analysed in the introduction. The Commission produced an avalanche of regulations as the plans for completion of the single market by 1992 entailed about 300 directives. The Commission sometimes asked member states to *remove* pre-existing regulations such as exchange controls, sometimes sketched the rules of a more liberal area in Europe, through the mutual recognition and freedom to provide services principles, for example, and sometimes introduced new rules in a harmonization perspective. The Commission devoted substantial efforts to harmonization in banking supervision, next to broader forums such as the Basel Committee on Banking Supervision: it had started earlier and had more coercive power, through the directives (which, under EEC law, had direct effect in the EEC member states' legal system), than the Basel Committee recommendations.[13] Harmonization also aimed at removing obstacles to integration

[10] Alexis Drach, 'Reluctant Europeans? British and French Commercial Banks and the Common Market in Banking (1977–1992)'. *Enterprise & Society* 21, no. 3 (September, 2020): pp. 768–98.
[11] Alexis Drach, 'From Gentlemanly Capitalism to Lobbying Capitalism: The City and the EEC, 1972–1992'. *Financial History Review* 27, no. 3 (December 2020): 376–96.
[12] LMA, BBA documents, M 3227B 5, 'A Common Market in Banking in the European Community. A Discussion Paper', Inter-Bank Research Organization, undated but circulated in January 1980.
[13] Alexis Drach, 'A Globalization Laboratory: European Banking Regulation and Global Capitalism in the 1970s and Early 1980s'. *European Review of History: Revue Européenne d'histoire* 26, no. 4 (July 4, 2019): pp. 658–78.

by reducing the regulatory heterogeneity in the Community. As a result, the EEC was an important factor in the post Bretton Woods era change of regulatory regime from a state-led to a market-led financial system and played an important role in pushing member states towards the liberalization of their banking system. The chapter argues that, in this story, monetary concerns and common market concerns played an important role.

The Freedom for Banks to Establish and Provide Services in the Community

The Commission first attempted to put in place the freedom to establish and to provide services within the Community in the field of banking in 1965, when it submitted to the Council of Ministers a directive proposal aiming to suppress restrictions in this area.[14] It took eight years and lengthy discussions for the proposal to become a directive, which was enacted in June 1973.[15] The directive abolished all restrictions which could have a discriminatory character. For example, it required not to apply restrictions against foreigners, when they existed, to other EEC member states nationals.[16] Some countries indeed had specific regulations for foreign subsidiaries or branches on their territory, requesting for instance part of the management to be a national from the host country. In addition, according to the 1973 directive, foreign bankers from other EC member states had to be granted the same rights as locals to allow them to join professional associations. Furthermore, the 1973 directive aimed to foster the freedom to set up foreign establishments in other EEC countries, in particular for branches. The idea was that a bank A from one member state could conduct business in a member state B in the same conditions as other banks from member state B.[17] Likewise, the directive encompassed the same principle for the provision of banking services. The idea was to promote the provision of banking services in one country even when a bank was not physically established in that country. The freedom to provide services proved more difficult to realize than the freedom to establish, in part because of the restrictions that existed at the time for capital movements. The preparation of the directive had been an occasion to realize the

---

[14] BFA, Journal *Banque*, no. 327, 'La libération de l'activité bancaire dans la Communauté Économique Européenne. La directive du 28 juin 1973', Charles Campet, March 1974. See also Emmanuel Mourlon-Druol, 'Banking Union in Historical Perspective: The Initiative of the European Commission in the 1960s–1970s', *JCMS: Journal of Common Market Studies* 54, no. 4 (January 2016): pp. 913–27.

[15] Council Directive 73/183/EEC of 28 June 1973 on the abolition of restrictions on freedom of establishment and freedom to provide services in respect of self-employed activities of banks and other financial institutions.

[16] Ibid.

[17] BFA, Journal *Banque*, no. 327, 'La libération de l'activité bancaire dans la Communauté Économique Européenne. La directive du 28 juin 1973', Charles Campet, March 1974.

serious challenges that the realization of a common market in banking entailed. Eventually, the 1973 directive had very limited impact.

The liberalization objective of the directive soon revealed the necessity to introduce some degree of harmonization within European banking legislations. The vast heterogeneity in this respect hampered the objective of the 1973 directive and could lead to distortions in competitive conditions.[18] For example, the legal status of banks were different in Italy, Germany, and France: would that mean that, since the 1973 directive allowed the free establishment of branches (as opposed to subsidiaries, whose case was simpler as they were established under local regulation), a French or German bank establishing in Italy would have to change its legal status? Likewise, in Italy a branch could be limited to conduct activities in one region only; therefore the Italian branch of a German bank could be limited to one region whereas a German branch of an Italian bank could operate on the entire German territory.[19] This would create competitive distortions running counter the idea of a common market. The problem was even more complex in the case of the provision of banking services, as the bank providing services could be expected to respect the regulations of the country of its client, whereas these regulations had usually been devised for banks physically established in that country.[20] A last issue concerned the scope of the directive, since all member countries had different definition of banks and closely related professions, and that these all had different status. The 1973 directive thus called for more harmonization in the field of banking legislations. The preparation of the directive had in fact highlighted the need for two complementary approaches: liberalization and harmonization.

In order to address the need for better coordination and harmonization in banking regulation in the EEC, the Commission worked on another directive proposal. This proposal faced unfortunate circumstances. First, the UK, which had just joined the EEC, fiercely opposed the Commission's originally ambitious harmonization programme, as the UK saw it as a major threat to its own system. Second, the 1973–74 economic and monetary crisis hampered European efforts in this area.[21] The initially very ambitious plans of the Commission were drastically

---

[18] 'The Development of a European Capital Market.Report of a Group of experts appointed by the EEC Commission, BRUSSELS' (Segré Report), Archive of European Integration, University of Pittsburgh, November 1966, http://aei.pitt.edu/31823/, accessed 17 February 2020.

[19] BFA, Journal Banqu, no. 327, 'La libération de l'activité bancaire dans la Communauté Économique Européenne. La directive du 28 juin 1973', Charles Campet, March 1974.

[20] Ibid.

[21] BFA, 1357200901/98, 'Analyse de la première directive du Conseil de la C.E.E. du 12.12.77, visant à la "coordination des dispositions législatives, réglementaires et administratives concernant l'accès à l'activité des établissements de crédit et son exercice"', Association Française des Banques, 27 February 1978. On the relations between British banks and EC regulatory activities in the 1970s, see Sargent, Jane A. 'Pressure Group Development in the EC: The Role of the British Bankers' Association', JCMS: Journal of Common Market Studies20 (1982): 269–85.

dampened.[22] The directive, called the first banking coordination directive, was eventually enacted in December 1977.[23] The aim of the directive was to coordinate the rules governing the accession to the banking profession so as to improve the efficiency of the 1973 directive. Commercial bankers had followed the regulatory process, but with limited enthusiasm. When the French banks' Association (Association Française des Banques) examined the text, they stated that it reflected the laborious negotiations which the directive had necessitated, and that there were so many compromises that the final text was unclear and would imply almost no change at all in France.[24] However, it formulated plans for the future, and thereby laid the foundations for the EEC banking regulatory exercise. It also created a Banking Advisory Committee, which would have the task to draft the future directives. The Council eventually adopted the directive, which was called the first banking coordination directive, in December 1977. In the United Kingdom it pushed towards the introduction of a licensing requirement, which was done with the 1979 Banking Act. The British Bankers' Association (BBA) had used the European process to introduce regulations preventing access to their professions to what they considered as imprudent 'cowboy' banks responsible for the 1973 secondary banking crisis.[25] Overall, the first banking directive was more a starting point than a regulation introducing major changes.

The 1980s would bring an important change to the rhythm and spirit of EEC banking regulatory activity. The Commission had realized the impossibility of aiming for total harmonization, in banking regulation and elsewhere. Even though plans for a second banking coordination directive, which was conceived as a cornerstone of the common banking market to come, had been discussed with commercial bankers since 1981, the progress in this area was slow. The Commission repeatedly asked commercial bankers, through the European Banking Federation or through national banking associations directly coming to Brussels, what could be done in the banking area.[26] The British banks proved to be the most influential, partly because they hosted a major financial centre and

---

[22] BFA, 1357200901/98, 'Analyse de la première directive du Conseil de la c.e.e. du 12.12.77, visant à la "coordination des dispositions législatives, réglementaires et administratives concernant l'accès à l'activité des établissements de crédit et son exercice"', Association Française des Banques, 27 February 1978.

[23] First Council Directive 77/780/EEC of 12 December 1977 on the coordination of the laws, regulations and administrative provisions relating to the taking up and pursuit of the business of credit institutions.

[24] Ibid.

[25] Sargent, 'Pressure Group', 274. The secondary banking crisis was a crisis affecting financial institutions ('fringe' banks) which had been booming in the City since the late 1950s, and then faced liquidity difficulties which turned into a crisis of confidence in 1973/74. See Capie, *The Bank of England* (New York: Cambridge University Press, 2010), pp. 524–86.

[26] LMA, BBA documents, M 32329/6, 'Report of a Visit by Representatives of the British Bankers' Association to the E.C. Commission and Others in Brussels on 26th and 27th March, 1981', p. 4; 'Report of a Visit to the E.C. Commission and Others in Brussels on 12th and 13th October, 1981—Advisory Committee', p. 1.

took the question more seriously than other countries. Together with the European Banking Federation (EBF), they resisted the harmonization principle which had become central in the European regulatory exercise since the 1970s.[27] They considered that the Commission's plans represented an unfortunate increase in regulation and insisted that the Commission should focus on removing real obstacles to integration.[28] Commercial banks, and the BBA in particular, supported liberalization much more than harmonization, as this internal note from 1982 illustrates: 'The B.B.A. wholeheartedly supports the Commission's avowed long-term aim to establish a common market in banking, with minimal regulation by the home country authority.'[29]

In 1980, the authors of a discussion paper prepared by the Inter Bank Research Organization, an organization close to the BBA, stressed that: 'The Community should take into fuller account the costs of its harmonization policy in terms of the additional regulations and barriers to freedom of entry that it entails for some countries. It might even start to think in terms of harmonization via deregulation in some cases, by levelling regulations downwards rather than upwards.'[30] In 1981, the EBF issued a paper, drafted by the BBA, aiming at showing a more positive attitude of the banking industry towards the European Community. The paper prioritized the reduction of regulation over harmonization, and stated that authorities from each member state should trust the procedures of other member states, so that a bank wishing to establish in that country would not have to go through an additional procedure, other than that of its country of origin.[31]

The mid-1980s were a turning point. The release of the White Paper on the completion of the internal market, followed by the enactment of the Single European Act, entailed an ambitious programme for the realization of a single European financial market by 1992. Commercial banks welcomed this change of attitude from the Commission, even if they did not play a role as important as major industrial companies, for example through the European Roundtable of Industrialists, in its advent.[32] Even before the release of the White Paper, in

---

[27] London Metropolitan Archives (LMA), British Bankers'Association (BBA) documents, M 32329/7, 'Plans for Second Council Directive for Credit Institutions'.

[28] LMA, BBA documents, M 3227B 5, 'A Common Market in Banking in the European Community. A Discussion Paper', Inter-Bank Research Organization, undated but circulated in January 1980.

[29] LMA, BBA documents, M 32329/8, 'Brussels Visit—Suggested Questions', p. 3.

[30] LMA, BBA documents, M 32327b/5, 'A Common Market in Banking in the European Community. A Discussion Paper'. Undated but circulated to the BBA for its 31 January 1980 executive committee meeting, p. 2.

[31] LMA, BBA documents, M 32329/7, 'Development of the Banking System in the European Community' Banking Federation Discussion Paper'. Background paper no. 24 for the visit to Brussels on 9–11 November 1981.

[32] Alexis Drach, 'Reluctant Europeans? British and French Commercial Banks and the Common Market in Banking (1977–1992)'. *Enterprise & Society* 21, no. 3 (September, 2020): pp. 768–98. On the role of the European Roundtable of Industrialist on the Single Market programme, see in particular: Maria Green Cowles, 'Setting the Agenda for a New Europe: The ERT and EC 1992'. *JCMS: Journal of Common Market Studies* 33, no. 4 (1995): pp. 501–26.

February 1985, Robin Hutton from the BBA declared in preparation to a meeting with the British ambassador to the European Communities that: 'The banks should support all efforts of the Commission to reduce barriers to cross-frontier services business, no matter whether the immediate beneficiary is insurance, investment or any other service: all freedom of services directives are valuable building blocks against national protectionism and towards a common market in banking and finance.'[33] The White Paper stated that harmonization was not considered as an end in itself anymore: the mutual recognition principle would be used to circumvent the difficulties raised by harmonization. It meant that authorities from each EEC member state would recognize the authorization procedures of other member states as sufficient for all already authorized EEC banks to conduct business on their territory.

The first draft of the Second banking directive, issued in February 1987, encompassed this change of philosophy from the Commission which enabled liberalization with minimum harmonization.[34] The main subject of controversy was the question of reciprocity. A clause of the directive proposal dealt with the conditions under which non-EEC banks could access the EEC market. The UK government and its banks were fiercely opposed to this principle because they feared it would damage the attractiveness of the City as an international financial centre. In a meeting gathering financial actors from the City around the Bank of England in July 1988, Sir Jeremy Morse, president of the BBA and of Lloyds Bank stated that 'the BBA were at one with the UK Government in seeking clear deregulation of markets and in seeking to avoid the erection of barriers round the European Community'.[35] The French, on the other hand, favoured this principle as they hoped to use it as a leverage in negotiations with non-EEC countries. Eventually the directive entailed a flexible approach to reciprocity, with no strict conditionality for entering the EEC banking market. The Second banking directive was issued in December 1989. Several other directives affecting the banking sector had been adopted earlier or were adopted around the same time: in particular, two directives harmonized the definition and the requirements of own funds in the Community in June and December 1989, while the liberalization of capital flows had been enacted in June 1988. Combined with these other directives, the second banking directive enabled banks to freely establish and provide services throughout the Community, with comparable competitive conditions. The common market in banking, although far from complete because of the remaining differences in national financial systems, now had a legislative

---

[33] LMA, BBA documents, M 32459, letter from Robin Hutton to R.J. Dent, 'Meeting with Sir Michael Butler', 7 February 1985.

[34] Société Générale Archives (SGA), 81084, 'Le contenu de la deuxième directive de coordination bancaire', XV/187(86) Rev. 1, 9 February 1987.

[35] Bank of England Archives (BEA), 6A395/16, 'City Liaison Committee Meeting: 6 July 1988', 8 July 1988, p. 2.

framework, and exemplified the removal of all kind of restrictions to banking in the Community. In particular, the mutual recognition principle was an original way of 'deregulating' without removing existing regulations, simply by facilitating cross-border banking activities and foreign establishment.

The Liberalization of Capital Movements

The liberalization of capital flows in the context of European integration went through several different stages: after some progress and a dynamic role of the Commission in the early 1960s, the tendency to restrict capital movements increased again in several member countries, and the Commission regulatory activity in this area came to a halt until the 1980s. Then from the mid-1980s onwards, the situation totally reversed, and the liberalization of capital movements became the priority of the European Commission and of some member states.[36] Unlike the creation of a common market in banking, which primarily revolved around fostering commercial banks' business activities in the Community, the question of capital movements, and of their potential liberalization, primarily revolved around monetary policies in the Community. The main rationale for the existing controls on capital movements existed for monetary reasons, such as fighting inflation or protecting the currency against speculative attacks.[37] The arguments against capital controls also had a monetary dimension: freedom of capital movement was seen, in particular by Germany, as a healthy constraint on economic policy, and as a way of fighting inflation.[38] In the European Monetary System, the liberalization of capital movements was at times used as a defensive proposal put forward by the German and the Dutch governments against the French government's repeated demands for shifting the burden of adjustment towards their hard currencies: the liberalization of capital movements would shift the burden of adjustment towards weak currency countries.[39] Lastly, all EEC member countries recognized that the liberalization of capital movements was a prerequisite for a possible Economic and Monetary Union. However, the liberalization of capital movements also had other motives: a better allocation of resources, a support to a common industrial policy, and more generally the financial integration of the Community, against the backdrop of slow growth in the 1980s. In the run-up to the liberalization of capital movements, which was enacted by a directive in June 1988, Germany was a vocal supporter of the

---

[36] James, *Making the European Monetary Union*, p. 213.   [37] Bakker, *The Liberalization*, p. 7.
[38] BFA, 1357200901/229, 'Extrait du compte rendu Monétaire des 17 et 18/10/83, IV. Intégration financière'.
[39] Bakker, *The Liberalization*, p. 255.

abolition of all kind of control and a key player in the exercise.[40] The United Kingdom, which had removed exchange controls in 1979, was also a strong supporter, as well as the Netherlands.[41] However, France played a pivotal role, as its change of attitude towards capital controls in 1983 marked an important change for other countries with capital controls too.[42] Throughout the whole period under study, the work on capital movements in the European Community was to a large extent prepared by the Monetary Committee, which had been created by the Treaty of Rome, and gathered officials from national central banks and treasuries and from the Commission.[43] The Committee of Central Bank Governors of the EEC, established in 1964, also played an important role.

Two directives were enacted in the early 1960s to foster the liberalization of capital movements. The first one (11 May 1960) broke down capital movements in four categories: A, B, C, and D and defined rules for each.[44] The list A and B mostly concerned direct and real estate investments, operations in securities normally dealt in on the capital market, or personal capital movements. The directive stated that the exchange operations authorizations, when they were in force, could not be refused. The list C mostly concerned operations in securities not dealt in on the capital market, long-term commercial credits, and issuing of securities.[45] The directive stated that member states should also grant the exchange authorization when necessary, but that they could maintain existing restrictions if they considered it useful for their economic policy. France, Italy, and the Netherlands used this possibility. The list D concerned short-term speculative capital movements. The directive called for no liberation in that case, but these capital movements were regularly examined for potential liberation. The second directive, issued on 18 December 1962, added a few elements to the list A, and refined a few definitions. In April 1964, the Commission submitted to the Council a third directive proposal which aimed at abolishing discriminatory regulations or procedures against foreign actors in the field of issuance, initial public offerings, and securities acquisitions by foreign financial institutions.[46] The member states never reached an agreement on that directive proposal, however. France was reluctant from the beginning, but the main problem was that countries which had abolished or had no exchange restrictions (Germany, Belgium, and

---

[40] BFA, 1357200901/229, 'Extrait du compte rendu Monétaire des 17 et 18/10/83, IV. Intégration financière', BFA, 1357200901/229, 'Extrait du procès-verbal de la 221ᵉ séance du Comité des gouverneurs. 12 janvier 1988'.

[41] BFA, 1357200901/229, 'Extrait du compte rendu Monétaire des 17 et 18/10/83, IV. Intégration financière'.

[42] Bakker, *The Liberalization*, p. 256; Abdelal, *Capital Rules*.

[43] James, *Making the European Monetary Union*, p. 44.

[44] First Directive for the implementation of Article 67 of the Treaty.

[45] BFA, 1357200901/93, 'Le Marché Commun bancaire', Charles Campet, *Revue du Marché Commun*, no. 137 (October 1970): pp. 441–6.

[46] BFA, 1357200901/94, 'Examen du projet révisé de 3e directive pour la mise en oeuvre de l'article 67 du Traité de Rome concernant la libération des mouvements de capitaux', 29 January 1968.

Luxembourg) did not want to make any change in their domestic regulations on capital markets before other member states had abolished their exchange restrictions too. France, on the other hand, did not want to engage in this direction when no plan for a European capital market was yet devised, and not knowing if there would be one at all in the future.[47] These differences between member countries turned into a political deadlock.

In 1965 the Commission charged an experts group chaired by an official from the DG II of the Commission, Claudio Segré, to conduct a study on the European capital markets.[48] The group was mainly composed of commercial bankers, and associated closely people from the European Investment Bank, the Organization for Economic Cooperation and Development (OECD), and the European Coal and Steel Community.[49] The Commission was both trying to give the topic new impetus and to examine the issue a different angle, that of capital markets and not of capital movements. Officials from the DG II of the Commission had soon realized that obstacles to integration in the financial sector were sometimes of regulatory nature, but were also linked to the very structure of national markets, and if they wanted to make progress, some research had to be done in this area.[50] The Segré Report, published in 1966, promoted the removal of regulatory and fiscal obstacles to financial integration, while at the same time being realistic in the pace of possible progress. Commercial banks and associations and other private sector actors often supported liberalization of capital movements. Claudio Segré, who himself left the Commission for the private sector in 1967, explained that they were sometimes useful for mitigating governments' resistance.[51] The Segré Report did not unlock the political deadlock in which the liberation of capital movements was, but was a first in-depth study and roadmap for the development of a European capital market in the context of the European Community.

The end of the 1960s and the 1970s were an adverse period for capital movement liberalization. The French social movements of 1968 and the monetary difficulties of the end of the decade, followed by the crash of the Bretton Woods system and the first oil shock, radically changed the monetary and financial international landscape and the governments' priorities.[52] The priority became

[47] BFA, 1357200901/94, 'La position française sur le projet de 3e directive concernant la libération des mouvements de capitaux', 1 December 1967.

[48] Historical Archives of the European Union (HAEU), 'Interview with Claudio, Segré'. Recorded in 2004, https://archives.eui.eu/en/oral_history/INT734, accessed 25 January 2020.

[49] 'The Development of a European Capital Market. Report of a Group of experts appointed by the EEC Commission, BRUSSELS' (Segré Report), Archive of European Integration, University of Pittsburgh, November 1966, http://aei.pitt.edu/31823/, accessed 22 January 2020.

[50] HAEU, 'Interview with Claudio, Segré'. Recorded in 2004, https://archives.eui.eu/en/oral_history/INT734, accessed 25 January 2020.

[51] HAEU, 'Interview with Claudio, Segré'. Recorded in 2004, https://archives.eui.eu/en/oral_history/INT734, accessed 25 January 2020.

[52] Bakker, The Liberalization.

dealing with short-term capital movements and their destabilizing effects on the monetary situation. In March 1972, the Council adopted a directive requiring member states to have available instruments to control them. If at all, capital movements were actually being more regulated. The major change of the decade came with the advent in 1979 of the European Monetary System (EMS) which, in the face of this international turmoil, aimed at ensuring regional monetary stability.[53] It would prove a key framework within which the liberalization of capital movements would be discussed in the 1980s.

The end of the 1970s and the early 1980s came with major changes. The EMS pushed EEC monetary policies to converge and showed the merits of coordinated action in economic policies, as well as the limited efficiency of exchange controls.[54] At the same time, the financial sector was sharply growing and internationalizing, in particular through the petrodollar recycling mechanism, which was pushing countries to follow the worldwide trend towards liberalization.[55] In March 1982, the Dutch finance minister, van der Stee, irritated that some countries were regularly asking for EMS amendments while not respecting the capital liberalization normally included in the Treaty of Rome, suggested the EEC member states to reconsider the question of the liberalization of capital movements.[56] Moreover, the 1983 change of French economic policies, from expansionary policies to stability-oriented policies, played a critical role in unlocking the political deadlock of capital movements, as it pushed other countries which still had controls to follow suit. The French government's change of orientation towards a market-oriented economy, although not as radical as often suggested, had both domestic and international reasons, among which a European one: the choice to keep the expansionary orientation would have led to an inextricable clash with the EMS, a choice that Mitterand was not ready to make.[57] A 'franc fort' was meant to help France negotiating with Germany.[58]

The Commission was also preparing a change of position, through a renewed activism in the area of capital liberalization. As mentioned above, it was already discussing with commercial bankers a project of a second banking directive in

[53] Emmanuel Mourlon-Druol, *A Europe Made of Money: The Emergence of the European Monetary System*, Cornell Studies in Money (Ithaca, NY: Cornell University Press, 2012).

[54] Jean-Pierre Baché, 'La Libération Des Mouvements de Capitaux: Bilan et Échéances', *Revue d'économie Financière* 8, no. 9 (1989): p. 107.

[55] On the internationalization of European banks in the wake of the oil crisis, see for instance : Edoardo Altamura, *European Banks and the Rise of International Finance : The Post-Bretton Woods Era* (London, New York: Routledge, 2017).

[56] Bakker, *The Liberalization*, p. 150.

[57] Marion Gaillard, *France-Europe* (Bruxelles: De Boeck Supérieur, 2010), 121–42; Laurent Warlouzet, 'Le spectre de la crise financière française de 1983', *Vingtième Siècle. Revue d'histoire* 138, no. 2 (April 2018): pp. 93–107. For an analysis of the domestic reasons for the liberalization of the financial sector in France, see Chapter 7, this volume.

[58] Laure Quennouëlle-Corre, 'Les réformes financières de 1982 à 1985', *Vingtième Siècle. Revue d'histoire*138, no. 2 (April 2018): pp. 65–78.

1981. At the same time, the European Parliament criticized the Commission for its permissive attitude on the restrictions on capital movements.[59] In April 1983, the Commission issued an ambitious discussion paper entitled 'Financial Integration' which marked the beginning of the renewed activism of the Commission in the area of capital flows.[60] The document did not focus only on the liberalization of capital flows, but stressed that financial integration concerned different but connected areas, and mentioned the first banking directive, the Commission's plans to go further in this direction, or the work of the Commission on banking supervision.[61] The liberalization of capital flows was thus part of a broader plan linked to two main concerns: the deepening of the Common Market, in which the better allocation of resources was often mentioned, and the consolidation of the EEC monetary identity.

The reception of the paper by commercial banks was overall positive. The European Banking Federation welcomed the paper's objective, particularly the proposals for examining whether the restrictions of capital flows should be allowed to continue.[62] The Commission paper was giving satisfaction on several recommendations which had been given by the European Banking Federation in its 1981 paper previously mentioned. The EBF considered that the Commission should go further in its plans: 'The eventual aim should be to dispense with all exchange controls rather than re-impose them albeit at a lower level in those countries where they have already been abolished.'[63] The Banking Federation was however much less enthusiastic when it came to harmonization and was opposed to the emergence of common ratios in banking supervision throughout the Community.[64] National banking associations were not necessarily willing to change their existing national systems. The EBF also criticized the negative view that the Commission had on the Eurodollar market, and stated that international banking was already very competitive, disputing the Commission paper's view that increased competition would lower borrowing costs.[65] For commercial banks, the Eurodollar market compensated the poorly integrated European capital and markets.[66]

The major change came with the June 1985 White Paper and the ensuing Single European Act of 1986. The White Paper gave to full liberalization of capital flows

---

[59]   Bakker, *The Liberalization*, p. 154.

[60]   BFA, 1357200901/94, 'Intégration financière (Communication de la Commission au Conseil)', 18 April 1983.

[61]   BFA, 1357200901/94, 'Intégration financière (Communication de la Commission au Conseil)', 18 April 1983.

[62]   LMA, BBA documents, M 32423, 'Comments of the E.C. Banking Federation on the "Communication from the Commission to the Council Concerning 'Financial Integration'", draft, 12 August 1983, p. 2.

[63]   Ibid., p. 2.   [64]   Ibid.   [65]   Ibid., p. 5.

[66]   LMA, BBA documents, M 3227B 5, 'A Common Market in Banking in the European Community. A Discussion Paper', Inter-Bank Research Organization, undated but circulated in January 1980.

a central place in the completion of the internal market. In the meantime, the Commission and member states had accepted the idea of full liberalization, although with a gradual approach, as countries which still had controls on capital movements wanted a transitional period to remove them. Once again, the Commission stated in the White Paper that the liberalization of capital movements would play a critical role in the integration of national financial markets, which would in return improve the allocation of savings within the Community.[67] In addition, it would strengthen the EMS by exerting a 'greater discipline in the conduct of economic policies'.[68] The timing of the planned changes was ambitious: the single market was to be achieved by the end of 1992.

After some negotiation about how the Commission would proceed, the Commission issued in May 1986 a communication to the Council setting two phases for the liberalization of capital flows. The first implied the abolition of all the safeguards that had been used by several countries, thereby implementing fully the 1960 and 1962 directives.[69] The Commission quickly proposed a directive on this matter, amending the first 1960 directive, which the Council adopted on 17 November 1986. This directive extended liberalization of capital movements to long-term commercial credits and to all transactions in securities, including non-listed securities as well as admission on a national market of securities issued by an issuer from another member state.[70] However, short-term capital movements were still excluded from liberalization, and the directive did not represent a major move towards liberalization, but just an important first step.[71] The second phase was more critical, as it aimed to full liberalization. Next to Germany and the United Kingdom who were both pushing for liberalization, the Commission and in particular its president Jacques Delors were giving this topic priority because they considered it would create a critical impulse for other areas of economic, financial, and monetary integration.[72] As Bakker puts it, three groups of countries existed in the Community: one group with full liberalization already in place (Germany, Belgium, Luxembourg, the Netherlands, the United Kingdom, and Denmark), another group with controls still in place and a weaker economic situation (Spain, Portugal, Ireland, and Greece), and a last group, made of France and Italy, 'which could seek allies on either side'.[73]

---

[67] Completing the Internal Market. White Paper from the Commission to the European Council (Milan, 28–9 June 1985), COM/85/0310 FINAL, 14 June 1985.

[68] Ibid., p. 33.

[69] 'Communication from the Commission to the Council. Programme for the Liberalization of Capital Movements in the Community'. COM(86) 292 final, 23 May 1986, Archive of European Integration, University of Pittsburgh, http://aei.pitt.edu/4029/, accessed 20 February 2020.

[70] Baché, 'La Libération', p. 108.

[71] BFA, 1357200901/229, 'Communication de la Commission au Conseil.Création d'un espace financier européen', 4 November 1987.

[72] Baché, 'La Libération', pp. 108–9.   [73] Bakker, The Liberalization, p. 180.

The European Banking Federation supported the move towards liberalization, but internal divisions existed. They somehow mirrored that of their governments. At its October 1986 meeting, members of the EBF stated that, in the White Paper programme in general, three things had to be stressed: they had divisions about the rhythm of planned changes, those countries where controls were still in place considering that 1992 was too close; the planned changes should guarantee fair competitive conditions; and priority should be given to the liberalization of capital movements and to some degree of fiscal harmonization.[74] Some members (from Germany, Belgium, and Portugal) stressed that the need for harmonization should not be exaggerated, while others (from Ireland, Spain, Italy) stressed that liberalization and harmonization should go along. The British delegate also stressed that the use of directives was the least adequate regulatory tool of all to achieve the single market, compared to mutual recognition. He considered that liberalization should not be a bureaucrats' concern, but should be done by bankers, and therefore called for intensifying contacts with the Commission.[75]

The second phase of the capital movement liberalization programme was still to be realized. However, 1987 came with serious monetary and financial turmoil. Indeed, during the 1980s the growth of financial markets had been considerable, and central banks' reserves had not grown in the same proportions. The rise of the dollar had been a constant problem since the beginning of the 1980s. This had caused much discussion among central bankers from the G7 countries about cooperation and had led to a first concerted action to make the dollar fall in February 1985.[76] This first action was followed by the Plaza agreement in September of the same year, where major central banks agreed to coordinate to organize a decline of the dollar which would not make the Deutschemark rise so as to preserve the EMS stability. However, the cooperation experience quickly receded, and the fall of the dollar became problematic as well. In September 1987, the Finance ministers (in Nyborg) and the governor of central bankers of the EEC (in Basel) agreed on a series of measures to reinforce the European Monetary System so as to face speculative pressures.[77] On 19 October 1987 the New York market crashed, the Dow Jones lost about 22% and the shock immediately propagated to other international financial centres.[78] This financial crisis, although with limited consequence on the real economy, made regulators realize how intertwined the financials systems were now. It had put to the fore the failure of monetary cooperation, which for some observers were one of the causes the

---

[74] SGA, 81084, European Banking Federation, 'Minutes of the 58th Board meeting (Madrid, 31 October 1986)', 24 November 1986.

[75] Ibid., p. 4.

[76] Olivier Feiertag, 'La France, le dollar et l'Europe (1981-1989). Aux origins globales de l'euro', Histoire@Politique 19, no. 1 (January 2013), pp. 128–42.

[77] James, Making the European Monetary Union, pp. 222–3.   [78] Feiertag, 'La France'.

crisis.[79] In November 1987, the Finance ministers of the EEC declared that the October financial crisis had confirmed that the steps taken in September to reinforce the EMS were right and urged central bankers to work on full liberalization of capital flows in December.[80]

The directive implementing full liberalization of capital movements was relatively quickly drafted and adopted. Pushed in particular by Germany and the United Kingdom, and having gained the support of France, the Commission could seize the opportunity to go for full liberalization. It submitted to the Council a communication and a directive proposal in November 1987. On 10 November 1987, the governors of central banks of the EEC created an expert group to study the implications of the proposed liberalization of capital movements for the EMS and the conduct of monetary policy.[81] The group was chaired by Dalgaard, assistant governor of the Danish central bank, who was also chairing, since 1983, the group on foreign exchange policy, a subcommittee of the EEC governors committee.[82] In its November 1987 Communication to the Council, the Commission stated that three questions had emerged in its reflexion on the liberation of capital movements: how this programme of liberalization matched that of harmonization in the field of financial supervision? Which measures could be necessary to limit the possible tax evasion which could result from the liberation of capital flows? And what were the links between European financial integration and the participation to the EMS?[83] The Commission did not consider these questions as necessary preconditions for capital movements liberalization, however. Even if the French criticized the March 1988 report of the Dalgaard group on the grounds that it was more 'German' than 'European' because it did not insist enough on coordination, they did not want to be seen as slowing down progress.[84] Most discussions and reports from that period show that governors and experts had some concerns that liberalization could increase difficulties for the EMS. The 1992–93 monetary crisis proved that these concerns were not misplaced.[85] Other points included the challenge that the United Kingdom was not a member of the EMS, in particular for Ireland whose economy

---

[79] Ibid.

[80] BFA, 1357200901/229, 'Les pays de la Communautéexamineront, début de 1988, les propositions de la Commission, concernant la libération des mouvements de capitaux', *La Correspondance Economique*, 17 November 1988.

[81] BFA, 1357200901/229, 'Groupe d'expert présidé par M. Dalgaard. No 63. Annexe 1. Mandat', 29 February 1988.

[82] James, *Making the European Monetary Union*, p. 480.

[83] BFA, 1357200901/229, 'Communication de la Commission au Conseil. Création d'un espace financier européen', 4 November 1987.

[84] BFA, 1357200901/229, 'Trois brefs commentaires sur le Rapport n°63 du groupe Dalgaard', 3 March 1988; BFA, 1357200901/229, 'Projet de rapport final du Comité des gouverneurs sur les propositions de la Commission de Libération complète des capitaux dans la communauté', 28 March 1988.

[85] Olivier Feiertag, 'Les banques centrales et les Etats dans la crise de change de 1992–1993. Le Baptême de la monnaie unique', in *Les banques centrals et l'État-nation*, edited by Olivier Feiertag and Michel Margairaz (Paris: Presses de Sciences Po, 2016), ch. 24, pp. 617–44.

was closely linked to that of the United Kingdom, and the fact that some countries would have to choose priority between joining the EMS or liberalizing capital movements.[86] The Commission had initially proposed, supported by France and Italy, to amend the 1972 directive so as to preserve means of coordinated control of capital movement with non-EEC countries.[87] Faced with strong opposition of Germany and of the United Kingdom who did not want to erect barriers around the Community, this proposal was abandoned. In June 1988, the Council of Ministers adopted the final version of the directive: full liberalization of capital flows was enacted, with transitory period for some countries, and with no barrier to capital movements between EEC and non-EEC countries.

Financial Deregulation

In November 1986, an article from the *Financial Times* affirmed, shortly after the Big Bang introduced by Margaret Thatcher in the financial markets: 'But the real Big Bang may not be the one which took place in London the other day. The true Big Bang may yet to be produced in Brussels, in a year or two.'[88] The author described the new approach of the Commission based on mutual recognition as a Copernican revolution which would enable British building societies to freely provide their services in the rest of Europe, particularly where retired British nationals liked to go, or to German insurance companies and French mutual funds to provide their product in the UK. A few years later, commenting on the on-going changes in EEC securities regulation, the legal scholar Manning Warren stated in 1990 that 'in this age of worldwide deregulation, regulatory barriers have begun to fall. Nowhere has this regulatory evolution been more dynamic than in the European Communities (EC), where, by the year 1992, a single common market is to be achieved.'[89] The liberalization of capital flows, as well as the second banking directive implementing the mutual recognition principle and the freedom to establish and provide services throughout the Community, were not considered as self-sufficient regulations. They were part of a programme aiming to foster financial integration in Europe, which the Commission saw as lagging behind commercial integration. The Commission also saw financial integration as a crucial element to the completion of the single market, for the possibility of an Economic and Monetary Union, and for the relaunch of economic growth and

---

[86] BFA, 1357200901/229, 'Rapport n° 63 du groupe Dalgaard. Implications pour la politique de change et la politique monétaire de la libéralisation totale des mouvements de capitaux', 3 March 1988.

[87] Bakker, *The Liberalization*, p. 198.

[88] 'Now for Europe's bigger bang', Olivier Pastré, *Financial Times*, 5 November 1986, p. 29. Financial Times Historical Archive, https://link.gale.com/apps/doc/HS2304963955/FTHA?u=glasuni&sid=FTHA&xid=e1c8eed2, accessed 21 January 2020.

[89] Manning Gilbert III Warren, 'Global Harmonization of Securities Laws: The Achievements of European Communities', *Harvard International Law Journal* 31, no. 1 (1990): p. 187.

of the European integration process in general. However, financial integration did not concern only banks, but also stock exchanges, insurance companies, and other institutional investors. Although this chapter primarily focuses on banks, analysing the sectors of insurance and securities helps to highlight two things: first, that a similar approach to that of banking was used for these sectors; second, that the regulatory and deregulatory moves to foster financial integration in Europe followed the same international trend that was blurring the boundaries between insurance, banking, and securities activities.

The blurring of the traditional boundaries between insurance, banking, and securities activities resulted from both innovation and deregulatory measures in all three areas. In April 1986, the Bank for International Settlements Cross report, presented in the introduction to this volume, was documenting the 'massive shift from international bank credit to international securities markets', relating this evolution to deregulation, technological changes, growing competition. It also pointed to circumstantial issues of the financial markets in the early 1980s such as a decline of long-term interest rates, international debt problems, and weakening of some banks' balance sheets.[90] In the EEC context, financial integration had long been conceived as concerning various areas of the financial sector and not just capital movements liberalization: the 1966 Segré report already devoted considerable attention to stock exchanges, insurance activities and securities activities.[91] Even if European financial systems were often bank based,[92] various financial activities became increasingly connected by the 1980s.

The Commission followed this trend carefully. In September 1984, a member of the Directorate General XV in charge of financial institutions at the Commission, wrote to a member from the British Bankers' Association about recent evolutions in banking and financial markets.[93] He wanted to know to what extent banking activities conducted by non-banks and the blurring of limitations between commercial banking, insurance and investment banking, was progressing in Europe. As banks' involvement in securities business and as the Commission's efforts to foster financial integration progressed, the British Bankers' Association became more active in supporting the Commission's exercise. In a February 1985 letter, a member of the BBA stated: 'British banks are, in many cases, becoming much more heavily involved in the securities business, with the intend of making London more of a centre of international investment

[90] Recent innovations in international banking (Cross Report), http://www.bis.org/publ/ecsc01. htm, April 1986, p. 13, also pp. 8 and 12.

[91] 'The Development of a European Capital Market. Report of a Group of experts appointed by the EEC Commission, BRUSSELS' (Segré Report), Archive of European Integration, University of Pittsburgh, November 1966, http://aei.pitt.edu/31823/, accessed 17 February 2020.

[92] Michel Lescure, 'Banking and Finance,' in The Oxford Handbook of Business History, edited by Geoffrey Jones and Jonathan Zeitlin (Oxford: Oxford University Press, 2007), pp. 319–45.

[93] LMA, BBA documents, MS 32459, Letter from Peter Troberg to J.M. Evans, British Bankers' Association, 7 September 1984.

and fund management. The BBA is therefore wholly supportive of the Commission's efforts to break down the barriers to international private and public capital flows, and to open up the investment markets of the EEC to allow investors a freer choice of homes for their savings. This is as true for equity and bond markets as it is for house purchase or the finance of factories or commercial trade.'[94] In 1985, the DG XV of the Commission set up a special unit on 'financial supermarkets', relating to the integration of banking, insurance and securities markets, and programmed a colloquium on 'Financial Services in the Year 2000' for October 1986.[95]

As the 1992 horizon approached, the issues of the increasing intertwining of banking, securities and other financial activities became more pressing. In a June 1988 speech on Barclays' European strategy for 1992, Norrington, executive director of overseas operations, connected this trend to the EEC legislative programme: 'Technology, economies of scale and the 1992 legislative programme are all encouraging a shift away from traditional branch banking, insurance and investment services networks to centralised delivery systems with minimal investment in bricks and mortar.'[96] During the preparation of the second banking directive, securities activities became a contested topic. In 1987, a new proposal of the Commission for the second banking directive excluded securities business from the list of activities associated with banking and subject to mutual recognition.[97] This move triggered a vivid protest of the European Banking Federation because banks' securities business was sharply growing at that time, and regulation in the area tended to be lagging behind and incoherent at the EEC level. The Federation pressed the Commission to include securities business in the mutual recognition list of the banking directive, which was eventually accepted.

In the field of insurance, the Commission adopted comparable principles to the approach used in banking, involving a degree of harmonization and an effort to insure the freedom to establish and to provide services throughout the Community. A first directive on non-life insurances, adopted in 1973, aimed at facilitating the freedom of establishment of insurance companies. Another directive, adopted by the Council in May 1978, regulated co-insurance, when various insurers were involved in sharing a risk. It aimed at preventing distortion of competition in insurance activities and to promote the freedom to provide

---

[94] LMA, BBA documents, M 32459, letter from Robin Hutton to R.J. Dent, 'Meeting with Sir Michael Butler', 7 February 1985, p. 2.

[95] BEA, 6A404/30, 'City/EEC Committee: recent developments', 17 July 1985.

[96] Barclays archives, 0391–0153, 'BRI Conference—30th June 1988. "EC 1992: The Changing Face of Banking"'. Speech: 'A UK Bank Planning for the Internal Market', p. 9.

[97] Lloyds Banking Group Archives (LBGA), HO/Ch/Mor/154, 'Minutes of the 60th Meeting of the Board—Athens, 30th October 1987', 24 November 1987.

insurance services in the specific area of co-insurance.[98] The freedom to provide services proved more difficult to establish: the Commission submitted in 1976 to the Council a proposed second directive in this area, but it was only adopted in June 1988.[99] This was the result of long negotiations.

An important step was the four judgements of the European Court of Justice of December 1986, which ruled in favour of the Commission against Germany, France, Denmark, and Ireland. In all four cases the United Kingdom and the Netherlands supported the Commission, while the defendants where supported by Belgium, Italy, and the other countries which were defendants in the other cases.[100] The cases aimed at declaring illegal existing national regulations blocking cross-border provision of insurance services.[101] In the four defendant countries, the rulings ended the protective national regulations which required the lead insurer to be established in the member state where the risk was situated and imposed restrictive thresholds on the minimum and maximum risks covered by co-insurance deals.[102] The four cases helped unlocking the negotiation of the second non-life insurance directive in June 1988. The UK was particularly instrumental in supporting the Commission, in particular because insurers complained that the 1978 directive on co-insurance had not resulted in any commercial benefit to the UK because of national restrictions existing in other states.[103]

In the July 1988 meeting of the City Liaison Committee, an organization created by the Bank of England to formulate and defend the interest of the City, the governor celebrated this achievement of the second insurance directive, which had 'long ranked high on our list of desirable measures', while regretting it had taken so long to accomplish.[104] The governor however noted that the contrast was sharp between this long process for the non-life insurance directive and the fast (eight months) adoption of the directive on capital movements liberalization, recently adopted by the Council.[105] His remarks forcefully illustrate the change of attitude between the 1970s and the 1980s in the European context. By the 1980s, member states had actually embraced, or for some of them, reluctantly accepted,

---

[98] Council Directive 78/473/EEC of 30 May 1978 on the coordination of laws, regulations, and administrative provisions relating to Community co-insurance.

[99] Second Council Directive 88/357/EEC of 22 June 1988 on the coordination of laws, regulations, and administrative provisions relating to direct insurance other than life assurance and laying down provisions to facilitate the effective exercise of freedom to provide services and amending Directive 73/239/EEC.

[100] Valerie Pease, 'Commission v. Germany', *The International Lawyer* 22, no. 2 (1988): pp. 543–54.

[101] BEA, 6A404/32, 'City EEC Committee Background Note', April 1986, p. 11.   [102] Ibid.

[103] BEA, 6A404/32, 'Record of a meeting of the City EEC Committee held in the Oak Room, Bank of England, on Friday 18 April 1986', p. 5.

[104] BEA, 6A395/16, 'City Liaison Committee: 6 July 1988. Speaking note', draft, 1 July 1988, p. 2. See also Alexis Drach, 'From Gentlemanly Capitalism to Lobbying Capitalism: The City and the EEC, 1972–1992'. *Financial History Review* 27, no. 3 (December 2020): 376–96.

[105] Ibid.

a liberalization approach to financial regulation, which had unlocked the Commission's possibilities in the field, and accentuated the pressure for liberalization in return. Two other directives adopted in 1979 and 1990 dealt with life insurances in the same way, insuring first the freedom of establishment and then the freedom to provide services.[106]

The EEC regulatory activity in the field of securities activities also followed an evolution from a focus on harmonization to a focus on mutual recognition. Three so-called 'Stock Exchange Directives' were adopted in 1979, 1980, and 1982.[107] They set up minimal requirements for listing securities on the stock exchange of EEC member states, in particular in terms of disclosure, and requirements for financial firms to publish semi-annual reports on their activities. But a major change came with the 1985 directive on the undertaking for collective investment in transferable securities (UCITS).[108] It enabled financial institutions such as unit trusts and other kinds of open ended investment funds to market their units (close to shares but with legal and pricing differences) throughout the Community, as long as they were authorized by one member state.[109] It thereby promoted the circulation of transferable securities in the Community.[110] It was the first directive in the financial sector using the mutual recognition principle.[111] Another directive was adopted on the same day to liberalize the movements of capital associated with the operations of unit trusts.[112] Even if it was confined to unit trust type operations, the Bank of England described it as a 'the first specific move to liberalise capital movements in the Community for some 23 years, and is seen as a major step towards the creation of a capital market within the Community'.[113]

A second step was taken in 1988 when the Commission issued a proposal for a directive on investment services. It was presented in a press communiqué as 'a logical follow up to the Commission's proposal for a second banking Directive as it provides for a parallel regime for non-bank investment firms'.[114] The aim was to enable all investment firms already authorized in their home country to operate

---

[106] First Council Directive 79/267/EEC of 5 March 1979 on the coordination of laws, regulations and administrative provisions relating to the taking up and pursuit of the business of direct life assurance; Council Directive of 8 November 1990 on the coordination of laws, regulations and administrative provisions relating to direct life assurance, laying down provisions to facilitate the effective exercise of freedom to provide services and amending Directive 79/267/EEC.

[107] Warren, 'Global Harmonization'.

[108] Council Directive of 20 December 1985 on the coordination of laws, regulations and administrative provisions relating to undertakings for collective investment in transferable securities (UCITS).

[109] BEA, 6A404/32, 'City EEC Committee Background Note', April 1986, p. 17.

[110] Warren, 'Global Harmonization', p. 218.

[111] Amir N. Licht, 'Stock Market Integration in Europe', *Harvard Institute for International Development, CAER II Discussion Paper*, no. 15 (1997): p. 74.

[112] BEA, 6A404/31, 'Speaking notes for the City EEC Committee meeting – 15 November 1985', Farrow, 14 November 1985; Council Directive 85/583/EEC of 20 December 1985 amending the Directive of 11 May 1960 on the implementation of Article 67 of the Treaty.

[113] BEA, 6A404/31, 'City EEC Committee – November 1985', p. 10.

[114] 'Proposal for a Directive on Investment Services', Press release, 16 December 1988, https://ec.europa.eu/commission/presscorner/detail/en/IP_88_817, accessed 25 January 2020.

throughout the Community without further authorization. The proposed directive proved much more difficult to be adopted, however, because member states disagreed on the question of market structure.[115] The 1988 proposal focused on investment firms and did not address the question of market structure, meaning firms could have chosen between different market structures in the Community. In 1989, the French government officially opposed this approach and asked to distinguish between regulated markets (with post-trade publications of publications details and formal listing of securities) and over-the-counter markets.[116] They considered that member states should be allowed to ask that domestic securities could only be traded on regulated markets. This move was also an attempt from the French government to improve the status of Paris as an international financial centre, forcing 'the repatriation of French share trading from London back to Paris'.[117] As for liberalization of capital flows, two coalitions opposed, although slightly different: the United Kingdom, Germany, Ireland, Luxembourg and the Netherlands opposed France, Italy, Spain, Portugal, Greece, and Belgium.[118] Determined to defend the status of the City in international financial centres competition, the United Kingdom usually opposed projects which were not based on the London Stock Exchange.[119] The investment services directive was finally adopted in May 1993.[120] It created a single passport for investment firms and banks to access stock exchange and conduct business in all European Union (EU) member states. The common minimum regulatory standards were minimal.[121] Described as the 'constitution' of the EU's securities market, it had an important impact on the market structure in the EU.[122]

An important characteristic of the European capital markets was the large number of stock exchanges compared to more integrated countries like the United States. The 1966 Segré report already recommended to develop links between EEC stock exchanges for the creation of a European securities market.[123] In early 1980, Tugendhat, the British Commissioner for Budget and Financial Control, Financial Institutions and Taxation, who himself had been a consultant for Wood MacKenzie & Co, a stockbroker company,[124] declared that there was a need for the European Commission to make progress towards greater integration

---

[115] Licht, 'Stock Market'.   [116] Ibid., p. 24.   [117] Ibid.   [118] Ibid.
[119] Oral archives of the French Ministry of Finance, Interview with Ives Le Portz, tape no. 35, 1992.
[120] Council Directive 93/22/EEC of 10 May 1993 on investment services in the securities field.
[121] Manning Gilbert III Warren, 'The Harmonization of European Securities Law Symposium: International Company and Securities Law', *International Lawyer (ABA)* 37, no. 1 (2003): p. 213; Warren, 'Global Harmonization', pp. 228–9.
[122] Warren, 'European Securities Law', pp. 213–14.
[123] 'The Development of a European Capital Market. Report of a Group of experts appointed by the EEC Commission, BRUSSELS' (Segré Report), Archive of European Integration, University of Pittsburgh, November 1966, http://aei.pitt.edu/31823/, accessed 22 January 2020, p. 241.
[124] Royal Bank of Scotland Archives (RBSA), National Westminster Bank material, NWB/2533, 'Christopher Samuel Tugendhat', undated but in preparation for a meeting with Tugendhat on 9 February 1978.

of European securities markets.[125] A Symposium was organized by the Commission in November 1980 on the theme 'Towards a European Stock Exchange', which gathered representatives of financial institutions, including the banks, and examined possibilities of the future, such as free movement of capital and the abolition of fiscal and other restrictions.[126] The main idea coming out of the Symposium was that participants favoured a better integration of national stock exchanges over the establishment of a separate European stock exchange. The April 1983 financial integration paper of the Commission also mentioned the need to work on a better connexion between national stock exchanges.[127] The subject was further explored at the October 1983 meeting of the Monetary Committee.[128] A Committee of European Stock Exchanges, chaired in 1984 by Yves Flornoy, existed, but its aims, in the mid 1980s, were modest, and focused on technical cooperation in order to prevent the transfer the market for European stocks to New York.[129] The success of integration plans between European stock exchanges was limited. Even though many projects were devised in this area in the 1990s, they often failed because of the competition existing between these stock exchanges.[130]

Like for banking activities, the activity of the Commission in other fields of the financial sector, such as insurance and securities activities, adopted in the mid-1980s the principle of mutual recognition, debated on the degree of openness vis-à-vis non-EEC countries (and chose an open door approach after much debate), and standardized some procedures either to ensure fair competition or to facilitate cross-border activities. Even though the amount of regulatory activity implied in the process was substantial, the actual aim was the removal of obstacles to integration, be it legal, administrative, or else. Harmonization in some areas, such as the agreement on common minimum standards for banks' solvency ratios, was also meant to foster integration. Integration was thus the common good behind what was, to some extent, a deregulatory process, and at the same time an extraordinary complex regulatory process. The rationale guiding the Commission's activity was the development of a liberal, modern, and competitive capital market, and in that perspective, it was following the spirit of the time.

The European regulators and bankers were aware that an important change was going on in the regulatory and political spheres, even though most of the archival material analysed in this chapter put forward issues and arguments

[125] LMA, BBA documents, M 32329/6, 'Development of European Securities Markets Systems', briefing paper 2 for the BBA visit to the EEC Commission of 27–28 April 1981.
[126] Ibid.
[127] BFA, 1357200901/94, 'Intégration financière (Communication de la Commission au Conseil)', 18 April 1983.
[128] BFA, 1357200901/229, 'Conseil Eco-Fin du 24 octobre 1983', 26 October 1983.
[129] BEA, 6A404/29, 'Record of a meeting of the City EEC Committee held at the Bank of England on Monday 26 March 1984 at 2.30 PM'.
[130] Licht, 'Stock Market', p. 65.

which were more technical than political. This awareness was more apparent in the late 1980s and early 1990s than at the beginning of the decade, however. In January 1991, when delegates from the French Banks Association were preparing a lunch with the British commissioner in charge of financial institutions, Leon Brittan, they declared that with him, Thatcherite liberalism and the City's interests were well represented in Brussels.[131] Likewise, the vice-director of the French Banking Commission, Thoraval, wrote in 1993 that a trend towards much more 'liberal economic philosophy' was undeniable in Western countries' financial systems, even though this was not strictly speaking deregulation.[132]

Conclusion

In his book on capital liberalization at the global level, Abdelal gives an important role to Europe, and within Europe, to France. In contrast, this chapter shows two things. First, that financial integration and capital liberalization was not only about capital movements, but that there were many other areas addressed by the Commission: freedom to establish and to provide services for various financial institutions, mutual recognition of other member states' regulations, harmonization of prudential supervisory rules. Each of these areas implied several directives, where France was not particularly pushing for liberalization. This leads to a second point. Abdelal's account downplays the role of the United Kingdom in financial liberalization in Europe. If he is right in stressing the importance of the French 1983 turn to more liberal financial policies, the United Kingdom was instrumental in almost all the areas of financial regulation in the EEC in the 1980s. The City played a particularly important role, and the British Bankers' Association and the Bank of England were particularly active in defending its interests and in ensuring that London would stay the leading financial centre of the EEC. Likewise, Abdelal somehow minimizes the work done at the EEC level, by the Commission but also by various experts committees, as well as the numerous initiatives the Commission took in the field of banking and insurance in the 1970s.

Partly for single market reasons, partly for monetary coordination/integration reasons, the European integration process played an important role in liberalizing banking and financial markets. The Commission's activity and the integration process was of course also intertwined with national economic and political history of each member state and of their relationship to the rest of the world, which are dealt with in the other chapters of this book. Even though the

---

[131] BNP-Paribas archives (BNPA), CB 289, 'Déjeuner avec Sir Leon Brittan', January 1991.
[132] Pierre-Yves Thoraval, 'La déréglementation du système bancaire français est-elle optimale?', *Revue d'économie financière* 27, no. 4 (1993): p. 223.

Commission's effort to build an integrated financial market can be traced back to the beginnings of the European Community, a major change occurred in the 1980s, particularly with the 1983 Financial Integration paper. But the political impetus came with the 1985 White Paper and the numerous ensuing directives fostering the emergence of an integrated European financial market. This new dynamic gives further weight to the importance of the 1980s in the deregulatory trend. The mutual recognition principle appeared as a very liberal tool for integration. In the European integration context, 'deregulation' served integration purposes. The extent to which the monetary constraints exerted by the EMS and the European commitment to develop integration through the completion of the single market forced member states to deregulate financial markets depends on each country and should not be considered in isolation from domestic and global forces.[133] However, the EEC was an important actor in this global trend, with both specificities linked to the uniqueness of the European process, and similarities with other European and non-European countries.

---

[133] On this question, see also Eric Monnet, *Controlling Credit: Central Banking and the Planned Economy in Postwar France, 1948–1973* (Cambridge: Cambridge University Press, 2018).

6

Fifty Years of Financial Regulation in Germany

Christoph Kaserer

Introduction

German financial regulation, including banking regulation, has been significantly shaped over the last 50 years. In this section I try to give an overview on major developments and their impact on the German financial landscape. Interestingly, for some decades after World War II German banking regulation was quite contained and capital market regulation almost non-existent, at least compared with nowadays' standards.

It should be noted in this regard that the so-called *Grundsatz I*, which was the rule determining the required own funds of a bank, in its first version of the year 1962 contained only three sentences.[1] More importantly, banking activities at that time were restricted by a rule—the so-called *Zinsverordnung*—setting ceilings on borrowing and lending rates. This rule was abolished in 1967. Moreover, up to the 1980s there were rules restricting the securities issuance activities of banks giving thereby the Bundesbank extensive control over the German money market.[2] This is an example that before modern banking regulation started in Germany with the implementation of the Basel I accord of 1988, banking regulation in its narrow sense was quite contained. In a broader sense it was somehow affected by monetary policy goals.

Over time, however, this situation changed significantly. At a very general level it could be said that two major developments were driving financial regulation since the 1970s. First, over time the country became economically more integrated with its European partners. As a consequence, it was also more exposed to economic shocks. This is why it might not have happened by chance that the history of modern banking regulation in Germany started in the 1970s, when the country experienced its first serious banking crisis after World War II.

---

[1] ChristophKaserer, 'Trends in der Bankenaufsichtals Motor der Überregulierung des Bankensektors – Anmerkungenauseiner politökonomischen Perspektive,' *Perspektiven der Wirtschaftspolitik* 7, no. 1 (2006): p. 68.

[2] More details on this will be given in the section 'Capital Market Regulations in Germany: Milestones' in this chapter.

Christoph Kaserer, *Fifty Years of Financial Regulation in Germany* In: *Financial Deregulation: A Historical Perspective.*
Edited by: Alexis Drach and Youssef Cassis, Oxford University Press (2021). © Alexis Drach and Youssef Cassis.
DOI: 10.1093/oso/9780198856955.003.0006

Secondly, the political integration of Germany with its European partners came along with the necessity to further adapt its regulatory landscape. As far as banking regulation is concerned, this process started with the implementation of the Basel I rules in 1988. With respect to capital market regulation in a broader sense the driving force was the establishment of the single market with the Maastricht Treaty signed in 1992 being one of the major pillars.

It should be noted that at the time when Germany entered into this financial regulation process the country could be considered as a relatively liberal economy. As I already mentioned, financial regulation at the beginning of the 1970s was quite contained. For instance, control of capital flows has already been abolished in the 1960s, regulations regarding the interest rates paid on bank deposits were abolished in 1967, and the German banking regulation contained a rather small set of specific rules. Hence, one might expect that the European integration process led to a substantial increase in regulation. However, while this is true for banking regulation as I will show in the following, the picture with respect to capital market regulation is more complex. In fact, the 1990s were a period with a strong focus on liberalizing and modernizing the capital market. As I will argue in this chapter, the underlying reason might be related to the fact that because of the nature of the business, depositor protection almost automatically transforms into controlling the business activities of banks. As opposed to that, capital market regulation is focused on investor protection, which deals with protection from fraud and misrepresentation. These goals can be achieved without any far-reaching interference in the business activities of market participants.

This difference is important, because it has implications with respect to the political and economic forces driving the regulatory process. And this, actually, might be a fundamental reason why in Germany we observed a strong increase in banking regulation tightness and complexity over the last 50 years, while for capital market regulation we have also seen some deregulation.

Some Thoughts on Public Choice and Financial Regulation

It is a matter of fact that financial services, especially banking services, belong to the most regulated markets.[3] A comparable degree of government intervention regularly can only be observed in infrastructure markets. Most likely, this has not happened by chance. Rather it might be a consequence of specific market characteristics enhancing government intervention and rent-seeking activities.

---

[3] A more general overview can be found in Ekkehard Wenger and Christoph Kaserer, 'The Political Economy of Banking Regulation and Its Impact on Competition – Some Considerations Regarding Germany's Banking System', in *European Monetary Union Banking Issues: Historical and Contemporary Perspectives*, edited by Irene Finel-Honigman (Stamford, CT: Jai Press, 1999): pp. 163–87.

As far as the banking sector is concerned, it is important to understand the interplay of two different public choice mechanisms that in this case are reinforcing each other.[4] First, one should remind the large size of the market and the fact that banking services are relevant for everyone. As these services are often tight to payment services and deposits, consumers typically have claims against the banks' balance sheets. The risks associated with potential bankruptcy is therefore a direct threat to consumers creating a political demand for being sheltered from these risks. This is a simple explanation why deposit insurance schemes are so widespread and often offer very large coverage. Interestingly, from an economic perspective deposit insurance was first proposed as a mechanism to reduce systemic risk in the banking sector.[5] However, the political support for deposit insurance is highly related to consumer protection arguments.

This simple example can be generalized to a more fundamental issue in banking regulation. From an economic perspective the most important argument for banking supervision is the systemic risk caused by the liquidity and/or maturity transformation inherent in banks' balance sheets.[6] However, banking regulation before the financial crisis in 2008 evolved in a way where risk management supervision of single credit institutions became the central focus of supervision authorities. This so-called micro-prudential regulation aimed at preventing the failure of single banks subordinating them to a tight set of risk mitigation and solvency rules. In some sense it could be said that in banking regulation, especially before the financial crisis, there was a primacy of consumer protection goals over systemic risk mitigation, i.e. macroprudential regulation. From a political economy perspective this is not surprising.

The second important component in understanding banking regulation is the incentives governing the behaviour of supervision authorities. As was already pointed out by Niskanen in 1971, bureaucrats have a strong incentive for budget

---

[4] Seminal papers on the public choice perspective on regulation have been written, among others, by: Mancur Olson, *The Logic of Collective Action* (Cambridge, Mass.: Harbard University Press, 1965); George J. Stigler, 'The Theory of Economic Regulation', *The Bell Journal of Economics and Management Science* 2, no. 1 (1971): pp. 3–21; Sam Peltzman, 'Toward a More General Theory of Regulation', *The Journal of Law and Economics* 19, no. 2 (1976): pp. 211–40. In their view the driving force behind government regulation is not the 'public interest' but rather the economic interest of different groups, which include also the policymakers and bureaucrats.

[5] There is a large literature why a deposit insurance might help to reduce the systemic risks caused by a banking system prone to bank-runs; as a seminal paper in this regard see: Douglas W. Diamond and Philip H. Dybvig, 'Bank Runs, Deposit Insurance, and Liquidity',*Journal of Political Economy* 91, no. 3 (1983), pp. 401–19.

[6] For a broader overview on the economic foundation of banking regulation cf. among others Sudipto Bhattacharya, Arnoud W.A. Boot, and Anjan V. Thakor, 'The Economics of Bank Regulation', *Journal of Money, Credit and Banking* 30, no. 4 (1998): pp. 745–70; Stuart I. Greenbaum and Anjan V. Thakor, *Contemporary Financial Intermediation* (Orlando: Dryden Press, 1995). A historical perspective can be found in Kevin Dowd, *The Experience of Free Banking* (London and New York: Routledge, 1992), while an empirical based discussion is given in Charles W. Calomiris and Gary Gorton, 'The Origins of Banking Panics: Models, Facts, and Bank Regulation,' in *Financial Markets and Financial Crises*, edited by R. Glenn Hubbard (Chicago: Chicago University Press, 1991): pp. 109–72.

increasing activities.[7] This is due to the fact that regularly perquisites are highly correlated with budget volume. Moreover, the incentive to undertake costly activities in order to get a budget increase is higher the longer the expected office period is. The rationale behind this behaviour is the fact that a budget increase— once granted—is very unlikely to be withdrawn. Moreover, career concerns are biasing the behaviour of supervision authorities strongly towards tightening regulation regardless of the associated economic costs.

There are two simple reasons for that. First, in case of banking regulation the supervision authority will be blamed for any failure that might occur. But there is almost no benefit the authorities can reap, if regulatory behaviour creates a positive economic impact. Moreover, in the context of the German system, where regulatory capture in the sense of Stigler is hard to implement, as job rotation between supervision authorities and the regulated industry is rather unusual, the incentive for industry friendly behaviour by bureaucrats is even smaller.[8] And finally one should not forget that also cost considerations do not matter much, as regulatory expenses have to be covered by the regulated industry.

This very general remarks lead to the expectation that banking regulation might have tightened over time. Actually, we will show in the following pages that this has indeed happened in Germany.

Under this public choice perspective one might also understand why regulation developed differently with respect to capital markets. First, in a German context exposure of the population against capital market risk is by far smaller than against the liquidity risk of the banking sector. This is even more true as capital markets did not play a significant role in retirement savings up the more recent years. Second, consumer protection on capital markets is shaped differently as consumers typically do not have a claim against the balance sheet of a financial intermediary (as it is the case with banks). Losses incurred because of a drop in capital market valuations are socially accepted, as the intermediary, e.g. the investment or pension fund, cannot be blamed for changes in interest rates or price earnings ratios. In the capital market context consumer protection is much more focused on protection from fraud and misrepresentation, which calls for different regulatory interventions. Actually, microprudential regulation as implemented with banks does not make that much sense in a capital market context. Third, the systemic risk of capital markets is small or even negligible as compared to the banking sector, making the economic rationale for regulatory interventions much less convincing.

As a side remark, I would like to point out that these arguments also explain why insurance regulation has evolved more along the lines of banking regulation rather than capital market regulation. Similarly to banks, consumers have a claim

---

[7] William A. Niskanen, *Bureaucracy and Representative Government* (Chicago: Aldine Atherton, 1971).
[8] Stigler, 'The Theory of Economic Regulation'.

against the balance sheets of insurance companies, making these companies subject to political interventions. However, there is also an important difference with respect to banks, which is related to the fact that insurances do not offer liquidity transformation. This makes them being much less prone to systemic risk events, reducing the awareness against the supervision of these companies. In fact, it could be said the insurance regulation in terms of increasing regulatory tightness is somehow in between banking and capital market regulation. In this chapter, however, I will not touch on insurance regulation.

Features of the German Banking System

In order to understand the evolvement of banking regulation in Germany, it is important to have a broad sense of what this system looks like. From a very general perspective, I think three aspects have to be mentioned when describing the German banking system. First, it is a universal banking system which by and large preserved its special three pillar structure for more than a century. So, still today we have the Savings Banks (*Sparkassen/Landesbanken*), the Credit Unions (*Kreditgenossenschaften*) as well as commercial banks. The latter are a rather heterogeneous group consisting of the well-known large universal banks (*Großbanken*), some smaller regional banks (*Regionalbanken*), some small private banks (*Privatbankiers*), and other more specialized institutions (*Spezialkreditinstitute*). The market share of these three groups, measured on the basis of loans extended to non-financial institutions, has been remarkably stable over the last decades.

In fact, Savings Banks, the Credit Unions as well as the large universal banks account for about 65% of all loans to non-financial institutions. Today these market shares are split-up into a market share of 33% for Savings Banks (including the *Landesbanken*), 17% for Credit Unions and 15% for large private universal banks. As can be seen in Figure 6.1, Credit Unions have gained market share significantly since the financial crisis, while Savings Banks, even though they profited from the financial crisis as well, recently have lost market share. It should be noted in this regard that while the normal Savings Banks are sheltered from any takeover threats up to now, the German *Landesbanken* have significantly shaped their profile since the financial crisis. The most important reason for this is the fact that due to antitrust concerns raised by the European Commission Germany at the beginning of the 2000s abolished the unlimited guarantor's liability for publicly owned savings banks. Without going here into the details, this ruling mislead some *Landesbanken* into increasing their balance sheets and investing the money in asset-backed securities related to the US housing market. This caused huge losses in the financial crisis that had to be covered by the German taxpayer. Due to that, some of these *Landesbanken* today no longer exist (as the *Westdeutsche Landesbank*) or have undergone a comprehensive restructuring.

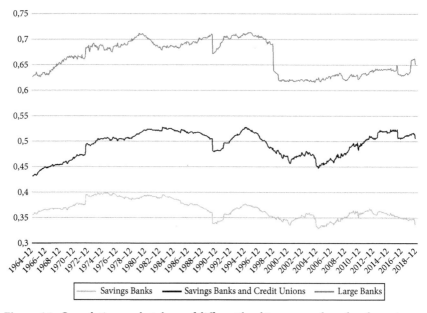

Figure 6.1 Cumulative market share of different banking groups based on loans to non-financial corporations.

Source: Deutsche Bundesbank

For the large universal banks it seems that there is a long-term downward trend. However, more recently they started to regain market share which to some extent might be related to recent regulatory and technological development. Actually, one should not forget that regulatory costs to some extent are fixed, making it harder for small institutions to cover these costs in their business. Similar is true for the ongoing digitization of banking services. As this implies that services are transferred to some platform technologies with the value of these platforms being dependent on how many users are there, economies of scale will arise.

Second, the German banking system is quite large. At current levels, total assets of German banks amount to about 2.5 times the country's GDP.[9] The underlying reason for this is related to the fact that Germany has a bank-based system of corporate finance. By international standards, German firms are quite reluctant to tap the capital market in order to fulfill their financing needs. This is reflected in a relatively small capital market, especially in a relatively small stock market. In fact, the market capitalization of the German stock market is in the range of 40–50% of GDP, while the OECD average is more than 80%.[10] Hence,

---

[9] It should be noted that this ratio by the end of the last decade was even above 3.

[10] A more detailed description of the German system of corporate finance can be found in Thorsten Beck, Christoph Kaserer, and Marc Steffen Rapp, 'Christoph Kaserer, Beteiligungs- und

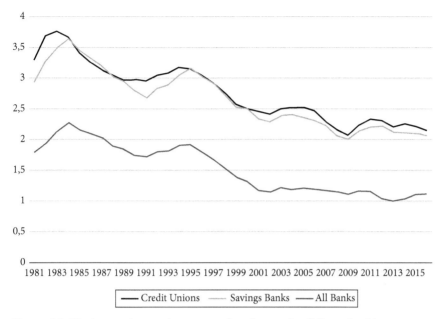

Figure 6.2 Net interest income in percent of total assets for different banking groups.
Source: Deutsche Bundesbank

banking regulation is a critical issue as a large part of the corporate sector heavily depends on it. This is not true for capital market regulation, especially when we talk about the period before the year 2002.

Third, there is an ongoing debate whether Germany is overbanked. It is not the place here to open this debate. However, given that about a third of the banking sector is controlled by publicly owned banks, i.e. the Savings Banks, the question arises whether this might generate any allocational problems as these banks tend to operate at a by far lower cost of equity.[11] Most likely, this has an impact on the competitive landscape and, therefore, also on the prices being charged for banking services. Actually, the lack of profitability is a fundamental problem of the German banking system. Even though there is no clear evidence on that, it cannot be ruled out that overbanking to some extent is responsible for this development. One interesting finding in this regard relates to the fact that there is a long-term downward trend in interest margins, as can be seen in Figure 6.2. Of course, this problem has been further amplified by the recent monetary policy of the ECB, as many people claim. However, it should be noted that there must be

Kapitalmarktfinanzierung im Deutschen Finanzsystem: Zustand und Entwicklungsperspektiven', Report to the German Federal Ministry for Economic Affairs and Energy (2015), chapter 3.
[11] A lengthy discussion of this problem can be found in: Hans-Werner Sinn, *The German State Banks: Global Players in the International Financial Markets* (Cheltenham; Northampton (MA): Edward Elgar Publishing, 1999).

more fundamental problems negatively impacting the profitability of German banks, as the downward trend in the interest rate margin is a long-term phenomenon.

Banking Regulation in Germany

Milestones

As already mentioned, banking regulation in Germany was quite contained in the post-World War II period. Things, however, started to change with the first serious banking crisis Germany experienced at the beginning of the 1970s. This crisis culminated on 26 June 1974, when the supervision authority closed the Herstatt bank, a well-known privately held bank at that time. The Herstatt case is interesting because it led to a first regulatory push on the German banking sector.[12]

It should be noted that this failure was a combination of an adverse macroeconomic environment combined with flawed risk management in the bank. In fact, when currency risk started to explode because of the collapse of the Bretton Woods system, the bank, which had a significant currency trading desk, got into serious problems. To some extent these problems were caused by flawed risk management systems, which evidently were not able to limit the currency risk positions to an amount which could have been supported by the bank. Moreover, it seems that also flawed auditing was going on in the bank. In any case, as market rumours about the difficulties of the bank started to spread, it run out of liquidity. This finally led to its failure. Because at that time deposits were only insured to a relatively small amount, retail depositors suffered significant losses.

The Herstatt crisis is interesting because it is an example how political economy mechanics work. The losses incurred by retail depositors lead to a tempestuous public debate about the potential failures of the supervision authority and deficiencies in banking regulations. As a consequence, soon after the crisis the German parliament amended banking regulation in order to improve the efficacy of the supervision authority and introduced additional risk mitigation rules. Also, the supervision authority revised its approach to control currency risk. And finally, the crisis was the starting point to introduce a deposit insurance scheme with broad coverage.

The next important milestone in the development of banking regulation in Germany was the implementation of the so-called Basel I regulation. In some

---

[12] For a detailed description of this case cf. Christoph Kaserer, 'Der Fall Herstatt 25 Jahredanach – Überlegungenzur Rationalität Regulierungs Politischer Reaktionen unter Besonderer Berücksichtigung der Einlagensicherung,' *Vierteljahrschr Soz Wirtschaftsgesch* 87, no. 2 (2000): pp. 166–92.

sense these recommendations can be seen as the long-term consequence of the problems of the banking sector that we have seen all over the world during the 1970s up to the beginning of the 1980s.[13] The Basel Committee of Banking Regulation approved its recommendations in the year 1988; they were adopted by the appropriate EU directives in 1989 and transformed into national German law in 1993. These directives where further amended in the year 1996, in order to take also market risk into account. Germany amended its rules accordingly in 1998.

It should be noted that the introduction of the Basel I recommendations was the first important step in harmonizing banking regulation among EU member states. Evidently, the EU has gone a very long way since then. For Germany the introduction of the Basel I rules implied a significant shift in its banking regulation approach as up to that time solvency regulation was based on a simple leverage ratio. Since then, Germany moved to a risk-weighted asset approach, which was then further refined in the Basel II and Basel III recommendations.

There is no doubt that with the implementation of the Basel I accord and the shift from a leverage based to a risk based solvency regulation banking regulation became significantly more complex. A more detailed analysis of this point will follow in the next section. Nevertheless, a discussion could be started as to whether capital adequacy rules became more or less restrictive due to the implementation of the Basel I or II accord. In fact, according to the German rules—laid down in the so-called *Grundsatz I*—before the Basel I accord was implemented banks were not allowed to hold loans and participations of more than 18 times their recognized equity. After the implementation of Basel I this was reduced to 12.5 times, which clearly is a more restrictive rule. However, at the same time the definition of what would be recognized as equity became more lax, especially by introducing the notion of Tier 1 and Tier 2 capital. In principle, it was sufficient to hold half of the recognized equity as Tier 1 capital. For instance, revaluation reserves or certain long-term subordinated loans could now be recognized as Tier 2 capital.

When implementing the Basel I accord—based on the own funds directive 89/299/EEC—the German lawmaker, advised by the Bundesbank and the banking supervision authority, took a relative conservative stand with respect to the definition of Tier 2 capital and to the extent at which revaluation reserves could be recognized. German banks heavily complained about that pointing out that this is hampering their competitive position.[14] A similar discussion could also be started with respect to the implementation of the Basel II accord, as giving

---

[13] The Savings and Loan crisis in the USA is probably the most relevant example of the problems the world-wide banking sector experienced during that period; cf. among others Lawrence J. White, *The S&L Debacle: Public Policy Lessons for Bank and Thrift Regulation* (NewYork: Oxford University Press, 1991).

[14] For a discussion of this issue cf.Bernd Rudolph, *Das Effektive Bankeigenkapital—Zur Bankaufsichtlichen Beurteilung Stiller Neubewertungsreserven* (Frankfurt a. M.: Fritz Knapp Verlag, 1991).

banks the opportunity to determine their required capital on the basis of their own models introduced some discretion which banks most likely have used in their own interest.

To sum up, it is an open question whether the implementation of the Basel I and II accords made the capital adequancy rules more restrictive or not. However, what can safely be said is that these regulations made banking supervision much more complex and gave the supervision authorities more power in the supervisory process.

In terms of extending the regulatory perimeter, the Capital Adequacy Directive of 1993 was another important intermediate step. Because of this directive a large number of formerly unregulated financial services, especially related to investment advice, became subject to banking regulation. When the directive entered into force in Germany the number of supervised institutions increased by about 7500.[15]

As a side remark it should be noted that with the Second Banking Directive 89/646/EEC entering into force in 1993 European passporting of banking services was introduced. In some sense one could argue that this was a step of liberalizing the European banking system. In fact, up to that time offering banking services in another European country was only possible under the requirement of having a banking licence granted by the competent national authority. The relatively small number of foreign banks being active in Germany, for instance, most likely was due to the fact that the administrative burden of getting a banking licence was not negligible.[16] Hence, this European passporting was an important precondition for the significant increase in European cross-border banking activities. However, while international activities, at least as far as the European Economic Area is concerned, have become much easier since then, the regulatory burden banks were facing in their home countries significantly increased.

In fact, an even more significant step in the direction of enlarging and tightening the regulatory perimeter was the introduction of Basel II. The Basel Committee finalized its rules in 2004, in 2007 they entered into force in the EU. As opposed to Basel I—and also Basel III—this reform came without public pressure caused by any significant banking crisis. It was driven by the regulators themselves, and for sure, also by industry representatives. Most importantly, Basel II made standard risk models for market and credit risk much more sophisticated and defined precise rules under which banks can calculate risk-weights based on their own models (IRB approach). The supervisory power was strengthened, among others, by explicitly giving the authorities the responsibility of controlling the risk-management processes of banks. In some sense it could be said that Basel

---

[15] Kaserer, 'Trends in der Bankenaufsicht'.
[16] Cf. among others Georg Brüker, *Probleme Der Einlagensicherung Inländischer Filialen Ausländischer Kreditinstitute* (Bonn: Duncker und Humboldt, 1995), p. 11.

II implemented micro-prudential regulation in the narrow sense. It is evident that this increase in the regulatory perimeter and complexity also caused a significant growth in the resources allocated to banking supervision in Germany. I will say more on that in the next section.

While there is no doubt that Basel II has increased and tightened the regulatory perimeter, it should also be said that the standard was somewhat lax with respect to minimum equity ratios. For instance, in Germany for a long time the minimum equity ratio was 5.6% applied as a leverage ratio.[17] Under Basel I the ratio was increased to a risk-weighted 8%. This continued to be the minimum equity ratio also under Basel II. However, this ratio was now applied to risk-weighted assets with risk-weights being calculated in a much more sophisticated way. Moreover, banks were continued to be allowed to fulfil half of this equity requirement with so-called Tier II capital. One pertinent example for Tier II capital, for instance, is revaluation reserves which are unrealized capital gains. It can easily be seen that in times of crisis such reserves might evaporate. Hence, even though Basel II tightened regulatory standards substantially, it did not tighten equity standards for banks. This was one element contributing to the financial crisis in 2008/09.

Finally, a further tightening of regulatory standards was implemented after the financial crisis. The EU transformed the Basel III proposals into law in 2014. This time, not only risk measurement rules, especially as far as market and derivatives risks are concerned, were further tightened. Most importantly, now equity standards were significantly increased by tripling Tier I ratios and re-introducing a leverage ratio. Also, common liquidity standards were introduced for the first time. However, even though some macroprudential supervisory instruments were introduced as well, the character of banking supervision did not change as it is still focused on microprudential supervision.

From a more general perspective Basel III can be regarded as the finalization of a development in German banking regulation that started more than 25 years before. As mentioned above, Basel I was the first step in harmonizing banking regulation in the EU, and on an international level as well. Now, with the implementation of the Basel III reforms, it could be said that the banking regulation has been entirely transferred at the EU level. Because of the so-called single-rule book, i.e. the codification of supervisory rules in the Capital Requirements Regulation (CRR),[18] no headroom for national lawmakers is left any more. Banking regulation now is a core competency of the EU lawmakers.

---

[17] It should be said, however, that there were also some exceptions, for instance of bank and Government loans as well as for covered bonds.

[18] Regulation (EU) No 575/2013 of the European Parliament and the Council of 26 June 2013. It should be said that this regulation is accompanied by the Capital Requirements Directive (CRD IV) 2013/36/EU of 26 June 2013. For this reason there are still some national competencies left, as for instance the rules under which banks are permitted to start operations.

The Tightening of the Regulatory Perimeter

According to the overview on the regulatory development in Germany outlined in the preceding section, one should expect that the regulatory perimeter as well as its tightness substantially increased over time. The interesting question is, however, whether we can see this also empirically. Of course, measuring regulatory tightness or the regulatory perimeter directly is almost impossible.[19] Banking supervision is a combination of legal rules and supervisory technical standards and practices. Moreover, all of these rules have to adapt to a changing world, which in the case of financial services has tremendously increased in complexity over the last decades. And on top of that one should note that if the size of a supervised sector increases it is clear that independently of regulatory standards the size of the supervisory body must increase as well. Therefore, even if we would somehow count and evaluate all of these rules and standards, it would not really be clear whether the result indicates an increasing regulatory tightness or just an adaption to the regulated business becoming larger and more complex.

An alternative indirect way to measure regulatory tightness and the length of the regulatory perimeter would be to measure the increase in the supervisory budget or personnel expenses relative to the increase in total assets or personnel expenses of the banking sector. The main advantage of this approach is that by measuring supervisory budget relative to the banking sector we take account for the increase in size and complexity of the overall banking industry. Of course, regulatory budget is not a perfect measure either, for instance because not all supervisory tasks are allocated within the national supervision authority. Most importantly, in Germany the Bundesbank has an important supporting role for the banking supervision authority. Unfortunately, there is no way to observe how much of its budget the Bundesbank is spending on micro-prudential supervisory tasks.

Therefore, the picture I will draw here rests on the assumption that the micro-prudential supervisory budget of the Bundesbank is growing at the same rate as that of the national supervisory authority, at least. Even though I cannot prove this claim, according to my experience I think this assumption is somehow acceptable.

In measuring the banking supervisory budget additional problems arise. Most importantly, one has to remember that there was an important restructuring of the financial supervision authorities in Germany in 2002. Up to that year, financial supervision was distributed among three different authorities being either responsible for the banking sector, the insurance sector, or the capital market. The authority responsible for the banking sector was the *Bundesaufsichtsamt für das*

---

[19] For the following analysis cf. also Kaserer, 'Trends in der Bankenaufsicht'.

Kreditwesen (BaKred). In the year 2002 these three authorities were merged into one being labeled the *Bundesanstalt für Finanzdienstleistungsaufsicht* (BaFin). Therefore, while the budget of the banking supervision authority could easily be observed up to the year 2001, this is not true since 2002 any more.

However, the BaFin besides its overall budget discloses the share of personnel expenses as well as the revenues coming from the banking sector. It should be noted in this regard that financial supervision in Germany is financed via a contribution that has to be paid by all supervised entities. As this contribution is collected on a cost basis, we can safely assume that the contributions paid by the supervised banks cover the costs for supervising these banks. In this way, at least an estimation of the budget being available for the banking supervision authority is available.[20]

Now, based on these assumptions the development of the overall budget of the banking supervision authority as well as their personnel budget could be calculated. In order to correct for inflation, the growth in the size and the complexity of the regulated industry, I am expressing the budget per million euro of the total assets of the banking sector or per million euro of the total personnel expenses of the banking sector, respectively. The results are given in Figure 6.3.

Interestingly, up to year 1988 there was almost no budget growth beyond any growth proportional to the growth in total assets or personnel expenses of the German banking sector. However, starting with the implementation of Basel I this picture changes significantly. And it can be seen that along with the preparation for the Basel II implementation this growth accelerated significantly. As a consequence, between 1988 and 2011 the banking supervision authority increased its average five year budget twice as much as the banking sector its total assets. Moreover, it should be noted that by looking at five year averages the actual growth is underestimated because of this acceleration towards the end of the observation period. In fact, when looking at the yearly numbers one could see that the total assets of the banking sector more than quadrupled over the period 1988–2011, while the estimated budget of the supervision authority was 16 times its budget in the year 1988. Expressing this as an average compounded annual growth rate translates into a 6% growth rate of the banking sector's total asset versus a 13% yearly growth rate of the supervisory budget.

When using personnel expenses as a measure for supervisory tightness, the picture is even more pronounced. In fact, personnel expenses of the supervision authority over the period 1988–2011 have grown at a rate more than three times as large as the growth rate of personnel expenses in the banking sector. While the

---

[20] It should be noted that the data available for the year 2002, the year of the establishment of the new authority, seems to be somehow biased as the BaFin started its operation on 1 May. Therefore, for the year 2002 I am using averages of the years 2001 and 2003. Moreover, for the years 2002 and 2003 I do not have the revenue ratio of the contributions paid by the banks. Therefore, I am using the same ratio as for the year 2004.

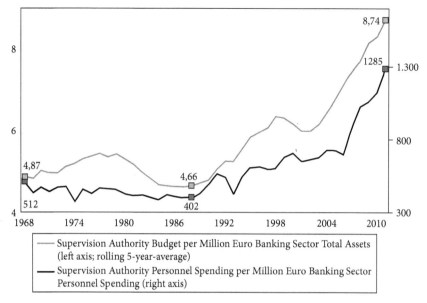

Figure 6.3   Budget of the German banking supervision authority relative to the size of the banking sector.

Source: BaKred, BaFin, Deutsche Bundesbank, own calculations

latter more than doubled over the observation period, the personnel expenses of the banking supervision authority were more than 13 times higher in 2011 as compared to 1988. In terms of compounded growth rates this translates into a yearly 3% versus 12%.

Most likely, Germany is not an exception in this regard. Presumably, also in other countries, especially as far as the EU member states are concerned, similar things might have happened. Unfortunately, with one exception we do not have comparable numbers on other countries. The exception is the UK, for which Haldane reports a pretty similar picture.[21] According to his numbers in 1980 in the UK there was one employee at the financial supervision authority for 11,000 people employed in the financial sector. By 2011 this number decreased by a factor of 37, i.e. per 300 employees in the financial sector there was one financial supervision employee (see Chapter 3 by Capie in this volume). Also for the US a similar development is depicted by Haldane.[22] According to his numbers in 1935 there was one regulatory employee for every three supervised banks. In 2011 this ratio inverted into three to one. Roughly spoken, the number of regulatory employees increased 10 times as fast as the number of regulated institutions.

---

[21] Andrew G. Haldane, 'The Dog and the Frisbee' (speech at the Federal Reserve Bank of Kansas City's 336th economic policy symposium, 'The Changing Policy Landscape', Jackson Hole, USA, 31 August 2012).

[22] Haldane, 'The Dog and the Frisbee'.

It should be noted that these numbers are just an indication that regulatory tightness has significantly increased over the last 30 years. As far as the increase in the cost of regulatory compliance is concerned, most likely, this is only a lower limit. The reason why regulatory bodies have grown so much is related to the increase in regulatory standards, rules, reporting requirements, auditing, etc. Hence, it can safely be assumed that along with the growth in the budget of the supervision authorities, there was also a significant growth of the compliance expenses at the side of the supervised institutions.

Overall, I conclude from this picture that banking regulation in Germany over the last 50 years was characterized by a significant increase in the regulatory perimeter as well as regulatory tightness. Hence, this evidence is not in accordance with the picture that financial deregulation lead to the financial crisis, even though there might have been a very few areas where deregulation actually has happened. However, the picture up to now only relates to banking regulation. I will show in the following that for capital market regulations things are different.

Capital Market Regulation in Germany

Milestones

As mentioned above German securities market regulation was very soft up to the 1980s. From today's perspective it is almost unbelievable that at that time there were no rules banning market abuse or insider trading. Also, takeovers of listed firms were unregulated and firms only had a very limited set of disclosure obligations, making corporate control very flawed.[23] In line with this also the German capital market was kind of sleeping. IPOs happened infrequently, stock market liquidity was very limited and a money market in a modern sense did not exist.

Taking a closer look at how the money market evolved since the 1980s delivers an interesting picture on how deeply the German securities market was shaken-up. In fact, up to the 1980s this market was completely under the control of the Bundesbank. The major reasons were the following. From a supply-side perspective, international investors were hardly interested in buying money market papers because of a 30% withholding tax they had to pay on coupons paid by German bond issuers.[24] In theory this withholding tax could have easily

---

[23] For a critical overview on the German system of corporate governance at that time cf. Ekkerhard Wenger and Christoph Kaserer, 'The German System of Corporate Governance – A Model Which Should Not Be Imitated', in *Competition and Convergence in Financial Markets—The German and Anglo-American Models*, edited by: Stanley W. Black and Mathias Moersch (Amsterdam: Elsevier Science, 1998): pp. 41–78.

[24] This tax was abolished in 1984.

avoided by buying money market papers denominated in Deutsche Mark, but issued offshore, e.g. by foreign subsidiaries of German banks. However, in a Gentlemen's Agreement with the Bundesbank signed in 1968 the German banking industry accepted to issue Deutsche Mark bonds only in Germany.[25] A second important element on the supply side was the fact that at that time money market funds were not allowed according to German investment law.[26]

On the demand side it should be noted that the Bundesbank in 1980 issued a list of financial innovations banks were asked not to sell to the public. Among these financial innovations were floating rate notes, zero-coupon bonds, and double currency bonds. It is not surprising that in this situation also large German industrial companies shy away from issuing money market papers. Actually, it was commonly accepted that up to the 1990s the German capital market was rather tiny by international standards.[27]

However, starting with the year 1990 things changed. Several steps were undertaken by the Government, the Parliament as well as by the Bundesbank in order to promote and develop the German capital market. A brief overview on the most important events can be found in Figure 6.4. Most importantly, the First Financial Market Promotion Act (*Erstes Finanzmarktförderungsgesetz*) in 1990 abolished, among others, the stock duty tax and liberalized investment funds given them more discretion when investing in bond market products and derivatives. With the Prospectus Act investor protection rules in IPOs and on the primary market in general was substantially improved. At the same time, the Bundesbank changed its policy in order to stimulate the money market. Together with the establishment of the first derivatives exchange (*Deutsche Terminbörse*) and with the liberalization of capital movements within the EU member states (and beyond), the German capital market started quickly modernizing and grew substantially over the upcoming years.

The next important steps followed in the year 1994, when the Second Financial Market Promotion Act mandated the establishment of the Federal Supervisory Office for Securities Trading (*Bundesaufsichtsamt für den Wertpapierhandel*). For the first time Germany had an authority supervising the capital market participants. This came along with the Securities Trading Act, which, among others, implemented an insider trading ban and a set of mandatory disclosure rules for listed firms.

What was still missing at that time was a takeover law as well as clear rules regarding market abuse and, of course, many other details with respect to investor protection, disclosure rules, the institutional setting of securities trading, etc.

---

[25] Cf. Monatsbericht der Deutschen Bundesbank, July 1985, p. 14 n.

[26] This changed with the so-called First Financial Promotion Act (Erstes Finanzmarktförderungsgesetz), BGBl. I 266, 22 February 1990.

[27] A description of the impressively small size of the German money market can be found in Monatsbericht der Deutschen Bundesbank, October 1997, p. 45 n.

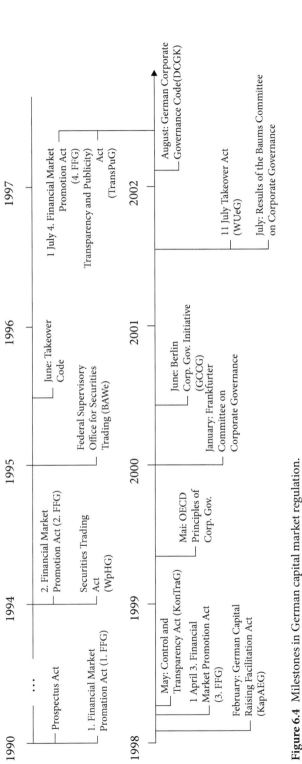

Figure 6.4 Milestones in German capital market regulation.

Source: Own graph based on Kaserer/Bress, Neuere Entwicklungen der Corporate Governance auf dem Prüfstand—Eine ökonomische Perspektive. In: Wollmert P, Schönbrunn N, Jung U, et al. (eds.), *Wirtschaftsprüfung Und Unternehmensüberwachung* (Düsseldorf: IDW-Verlag, Düsseldorf, 2003), pp. 77–99.

Over time, these gaps were closed as can be seen in Figure 6.4. However, especially the introduction of a takeover law as well as a modern corporate governance code were highly opposed by the German corporate sector.[28] This is why it took a relatively long time to implement these rules. It should be emphasized that an important driver in implementing these rules and in the modernization and liberalization of capital market regulation in general was the EU integration process, which slowly started with the single market mandated by the Maastricht Treaty in 1992. This process gained much more speed after the burst of the so-called internet bubble in 2002.

Of course, the modernization of German capital markets did not stop in 2002. I am just reminding here that this was the period were Germany laid the foundations for transforming its capital market from a somehow underdeveloped and sleepy neighbourhood to a dynamic and timely shaped centre as it is today. As already mentioned, while back in the 1990s the need for modernizing the capital market was recognized by the domestic institutions and politicians, the modernization process after the year 2002 was heavily driven by EU institutions. In fact, big legal projects like MiFID I and II, the Prospectus Directive or the Market Abuse Directive, have been driven by the European Commission.

Forces in Shaping Capital Market Regulation

Based on the exposition in the preceding section it could safely be said that capital market regulation in Germany was governed by liberalizing the market environment and improving investor protection. This, at least, is true for the first wave of reforms implemented over the period 1990–2002. Hence, the picture is quite different from what Germany has experienced in the banking regulation area.

Coming back to the public choice perspective on regulation presented in the second section of this chapter this is not so surprising. Capital market institutions typically do not offer liquidity or maturity transformation services making them much less prone to systemic risks. Often it is even the case that these institutions do not promise any fixed repayments, as it is the case with investment funds, for instance, making the whole notion of systemic runs almost meaningless. It is true that these institutions will suffer from systemic crises, as their holdings will lose value. However, shareholders do not have an incentive to withdraw their money as soon as possible in order to profit from a first-come-first-served principle, as it

---

[28] For more details cf. Wenger and Kaserer, 'The German System'; and Ekkehard Wenger and Christoph Kaserer, 'German Banks and Corporate Governance: A Critical View', in *Comparative Corporate Governance—The State of the Art and Emerging Research*, Klaus J. Hopt et al. (New York: Oxford University Press, 1998), pp. 499–536.

is the case with banks. And even if shareholders withdraw their money, the fund will simply sell its holdings, even if this happens at depressed prices.

Of course, once again reality is a little bit more complex in the sense that there might also be some capital market institutions which, at least to some extent, offer liquidity or maturity transformation. A prominent example popped-up during the financial crisis where some money market funds, especially in the US, promised to repay at least the money the investor has paid in. This was an important force in accelerating the institutional run on banks during the financial crisis. Also, open-ended real estate funds in Germany or life insurance companies to some degree offer liquidity or maturity transformation. However, these institutional arrangements could be regarded as being somehow exceptional. In general, the economic rational of capital market institutions does not consist in any kind of liquidity or maturity transformation. They exist because of transaction cost savings and superior information processing.

Therefore, there is much less demand from the (retail) investor audience to be protected against market risks as it is the case with bank deposits. Of course, investors demand for being protected against fraud and misrepresentation. This is why investor protection rules are an important element in capital market regulation. But the whole notion of microprudential regulation, as we know it from the banking sector, does not make much sense for capital market institutions.

A second important element, in my perspective, is the fact that capital markets back in the 1990s played a secondary role in corporate finance and in the retirement system in Germany. For that reason, this regulation area for a long time was neither in the focus of industry associations nor the single retail investors. Even life insurance companies, which already at that time had a significant size in Germany, did not care that much about capital markets as only a tiny fraction of their assets were invested in stocks.

Today this picture is different. Private retirement savings have significantly grown in importance and, along with that, we have institutional investors of significant size also in Germany. From this perspective we might expect capital market regulation to develop in a different direction in the future as it did over the last 50 years.

Conclusion

In this chapter I have tried to give a stringent overview on how financial market regulation evolved in Germany since the 1970s. The picture that emerged was somehow contradicting, as it seems that banking regulation and capital market regulation evolved in a quite different way with a totally different dynamic. This is true even though both regulatory areas nowadays to a very large extent are core competencies of EU lawmakers. However, going back to the 1970s the driving forces behind these regulatory processes were domestic decision makers making the contradictions uncovered here even more interesting.

As far as banking regulation is concerned, I have shown that starting with the Herstatt crisis in 1974 there was a clear trend towards tightening and increasing the regulatory perimeter. I have shown that beyond the pure description of how banking regulation evolved there is also empirical evidence supporting this claim. By looking at the budget of the German banking supervision authority I was able to show that between 1988 and 2011 the banking supervision authority increased its average five year budget twice as much as the banking sector its total assets. And this picture is even more pronounced, if the personnel expenses are used as a measure of regulatory tightness. In terms of regulatory quality it should be said, however, that even though regulatory tightness increased, equity standards did not before the implementation of Basel III. From a hindsight we know that this was one of the reasons why the banking system suffered from a lack of resilience during the financial crisis.

The picture with respect to capital market regulation is quite different. Here, the regulatory process started back in the year 1990 and, at least for the first decade, it was focused towards liberalizing and modernizing the German capital market.

What might have been a reason why we have seen such a different development in two adjacent areas of financial market regulation? To answer this question I laid down some of the public choice principles governing the evolution of regulatory systems. The important difference between the banking and the capital market sector, in this perspective, is a unique characteristic of the former one. This consist in the systemic risk caused by the liquidity and maturity transformation of the banking sector, which comes along with individual claims of a broad public audience against the balance sheets of the banks. This makes the banking sector prone to political interventions, as the risk of these claims is borne by almost everyone.

A similar public choice dynamic does not arise in the capital market. This is even more true as in countries like Germany 30 years ago the capital market was neither an important source of corporate finance nor an important area for retirement savings. Given that this has somewhat changed over the last decade, it might well be that the political dynamics of capital market regulation will be different in the upcoming years then they were in the last 30 years.

7

Financial Deregulation in France

A French 'Big Bang'? (1984–1990)

Olivier Feiertag

The general view of financial deregulation in France has been known for a long time. The second half of the 1980s saw the end of the numerous administrative controls and rules on the money markets inherited from the interwar period and even from World War I. The process of liberalization of the French financial system began with the banking law of January 1984, which guaranteed a level playing field for all banks, and with the creation in December 1984 by Pierre Bérégovoy, the French Ministry of Finances, of certificates of deposit. It ended on 1 January 1990 with the final dismantling of the exchange control in force since 1917. This change is sometimes called the French 'Big Bang' by analogy with the Big Bang of the London Stock Exchange in 1986.[1]

The ways and stages of financial deregulation in France were soon discussed by many scholars.[2] As early as 1991, Henri Bourguinat explained to his students at the university of Bordeaux the process of French financial liberalization through the rule of the 3D: Decompartmentalization, Deregulation, and Disintermediation.[3] There is no doubt that the narrative of the reform of the French financial system is by now precisely established.[4] But, if the 'how' has been abundantly dealt with, the 'why' remains broadly without answers.

The Three Paradoxes of the French Financial Deregulation

The deregulation of the financial system in France in the 1980s and the French commitment to the free movement of capital appears, as recently pointed out by

---

[1] Philip G. Cerny, 'The Little Big Bang in Paris: Financial Market Deregulation in a Dirigist System', *European Journal of Political Research* 17, no. 2 (1989): pp. 169–92.

[2] Joël Métais and Philippe Szymczack, *Les mutations du système financier français (innovations et déréglementation)*, Notes et études documentaires no. 4820 (Paris: La Documentation Française, 1986).

[3] Henri Bourguinat, *Finance internationale*, 3rd ed. (Paris: PUF, 1997): pp. 93–105.

[4] Rémi Pellet, *Droit financier public* (Paris: PUF, 2018), pp. 525–65; Laure Quennouëllle-Corre, 'Les réformes financières de 1982 à 1985', *Vingtième Siècle. Revue d'histoire* 138, no. 2 (April 2018): pp. 65–78.

Olivier Feiertag, *Financial Deregulation in France: A French 'Big Bang'? (1984–1990)* In: *Financial Deregulation: A Historical Perspective*. Edited by: Alexis Drach and Youssef Cassis, Oxford University Press (2021). © Alexis Drach and Youssef Cassis. DOI: 10.1093/oso/9780198856955.003.0007

Rawi Abdelal, 'quite curious'[5] and even triply paradoxical: first, how to understand that the initiative for financial deregulation, as highlighted by Élie Cohen,[6] was taken by the Colbertist State itself and occurred at the peak of the long interventionist cycle of the twentieth century? Second, how to explain that 'the marketing of public finances', to quote Benjamin Lemoine, occurred while the Left was in power?[7] And last but not least, asks Rawi Abdelal, why did France take the lead in favour of financial deregulation at world level and was backed by the main international institutions, feeding the hypothesis of a so-called 'Paris Consensus'?[8]

As usual, the statement of a paradox in history means that the investigation should be carried out further. The issue of the sources is once again crucial. Most of the studies about the French financial deregulation are based on published sources or interviews. Primary archives have not been used. For this article, we use the archives of the secrétariat général de la présidence de la République française. This fund contains the memos of the advisers to President François Mitterrand, the papers produced by the State's main administrative entities, as well as from the Treasury or the Bank of France.[9]

From this perspective, we will try to grasp the economic model of the French financial deregulation in the second half of the 1980s. We argue that the liberalization of the French financial system was not so much a result of the so-called 'neoliberal shift' of the Left, as a financial policy aiming to give leeway to State intervention. We will explore this hypothesis first by depicting the (re)birth of the money market in France triggered by a series of financial innovations which have resulted in very rapid market liberalization. The second section deals with the growth of the French public debt, especially the external debt and its link with the deregulation of money markets. Finally, we will try to analyse the economic model of the Left in power, compared with the model of the 'poor state', which founded the political project of the Right back in power in 1986–88.

[5] Rawi Abdelal, 'Le consensus de Paris: la France et les règles de la finance mondiale', Critique internationale 28, no. 3 (2005): pp. 87–115.

[6] Élie Cohen, 'L'innovation financière et les paradoxes du financement public sur les marchés de capitaux', in L'État, la finance et le social, souveraineté nationale et construction européenne, edited by Bruno Théret (Paris: La Découverte, 1995): pp. 418–31.

[7] Benjamin Lemoine, 'Les valeurs de la dette, l'État à l'épreuve de la dette publique' (PhD dissertation, École nationale supérieure des mines de Paris, 2011).

[8] Abdelal, 'Le consensus de Paris'.

[9] We would like to thank Dominique Bertinotti for giving us access to these archives and the archivists of the French National Archives in Pierrefitte who have greatly facilitated our work. This chapter takes up several elements from two earlier publications: 'Finances publiques, "murd'argent" et genèse de la liberalization financière en France de 1981 à 1984', in Changer la vie, les débuts du premier septennat de François Mitterrand, edited by Pierre Milza and Serge Berstein (Paris: Perrin, 2001): pp. 431–55; and 'Le tournant de la liberalization financière (1984–1988) : Big Bang à la française?', in Mitterand, Les années d'alternance (1984–1988), directed by Georges Saunier (Paris: Nouveau Monde, 2019): pp. 511–36.

Financial Innovations and the (Re)birth of the French Money Market

The deregulation of the money markets in France originates from a series of financial innovations.[10] This is a major difference with the deregulations that took place in the USA, in Canada and the UK. The liberalization of money market in France did not result from the outright removal of existing regulations, as for instance Regulation Q in the US. In France deregulation was based on the introduction of several innovations of products and process. The goal, as mentioned by the research department of the Bank of France, was to 'create one capital market, unified, ranking from very short to long term, open to all economic agents, with spot, futures and option markets'.[11]

In this perspective, the call money market appeared to be the main historical blockage of the French financial system. Only the reform of the money market could cut the Gordian knot. This reform was based on the introduction of new financial products, as far as financing the requirements of both the Treasury and private enterprises was concerned. The most radical innovation aimed to give private enterprises access to the money market. For this purpose, two new financial instruments were created: the certificate of deposit, a short-term negotiable debt security issued by banks, introduced on 5 January 1985; and, especially, the *billets de trésorerie* or commercial paper, also a short-term negotiable debt security but issued by both financial and non-financial companies, introduced on 18 December 1985. These two financial products enjoyed very strong growth from the start. The outstanding market for negotiable debts, 'the largest of this kind in Europe', grew six fold between 1985 and 1994.[12] They led to the privatization and opening of a money market which had been dominated since the 1930s by a small number of operators in the orbit of the Treasury: the Bank of France and the Caisse des Dépôts in close connivance with the big deposit banks' cartel.[13] This relative closeness of the money market was essentially dependent on the central bank's facilities, with a regulation of liquidities through quantity rather than price. From this perspective, the creation of certificate of deposits caused a small earthquake. It amounted to a commodification of the money market, henceforth governed by the law of supply and demand and the principle of free competition.

---

[10] Christian de Boissieu, 'Innovations financières, politique monétaire et financement des déficits publics', in *Government Policies and the Working of Financial Systems in Industrialized Countries*, edited by in Donald E. Fair and F. de Juvigny (Martinus Nijhoff: Dordrecht, 1984), pp. 249–71.

[11] André Icard and Françoise Drumetz, 'Développement des marchés de titres et financement de l'économie française', *Bulletin de la Banque de France* 6 (June 1994): pp. 83–106.

[12] Icard and Drumets, 'Développement des marchés de titres', p. 88.

[13] Olivier Feiertag, 'Le Crédit Lyonnais et le Trésor Public dans l'entre-deux guerres: les ressorts de l'économie d'endettement du XXe siècle', in *Le Crédit Lyonnais, etudes historiques, 1863–1986*, edited by Bernard Desjardins et al. (Genève: Droz, 2003), pp. 805–31.

A similar process transformed the market for Treasury bonds. The decisive innovation was the creation on 27 January 1986 of the *Bon du Trésor négociable* (BTN), a Negotiable Treasury Bond, which replaced and unified all varieties of extant Treasury Bonds.[14] BTNs were accessible to all economic agents and no longer only to banks. They were placed on the market by auction to the highest bidder, and no longer according to an underwriting system reflecting the cartelization of the banking system, with 'the bidders having to compete on the offered price'.[15] The creation of the Negotiable Treasury Bond was at the very heart of the constitution of a genuine monetary market in France. It provided the market with a basic financial instrument, normalized and perfectly liquid, which had been missing since the end of the *Bons de la Défense nationale* in the 1920s. The daily volume of transactions grew threefold between 1986 and 1988.

The new dynamics of the money market contributed to the spectacular rebirth of the Paris financial market, which had been at its lowest since the early 1980s.[16] Here again, the decisive innovation originated from the State. The creation in June 1985 of the *Obligations assimilables du Trésor* (OAT), a new kind of Treasury Bonds, led to the normalization and simplification of the stock of public loans issued in heterogeneous conditions that had segmented the French bond market and slowed its growth. The placing of OAT, like that of BTN, was by auction to the highest bidder. As Jean-François Pons noted: 'The State, as the main issuer on both the market for negotiable short-term debt and the bond market, had a duty, by reforming the conditions in which it managed its debt, to further this upheaval.'[17] Significantly, the first two forward contracts negotiated on the MATIF (Marché à Terme des Instruments Financiers), the Paris derivative market inaugurated on 15 February 1986, dealt with Treasury securities.[18] In the same way, one should not underestimate the role played by the small network of the *Specialistes en Valeurs du Trésor* (Specialists in Treasury Securities), officially established in autumn 1986 under the aegis of the Treasury and originally including 13 'trusted' operators (commercial banks, insurance companies, and stockbrokers).[19]

There is thus little doubt about the revolution that took on the Paris financial markets in the early 1990s. Admittedly, similar changes took place in all advanced economies. However, it must be emphasized that in the French case, these changes were the result of a series of financial innovations; while another French specificity was that these innovations were introduced on the State's initiative. They were part of a financial policy and, so far as can be said on the basis of current archival

---

[14] French National Archives (FNA), AG/5(4)/6154, Hannoun files, press release from the Ministry of Finance, 27 January 1986: 'Le Trésorveillera à privilégier la fongibilité des bons du Trésorencompte courant qu'ilémettra'.

[15] Ibid.   [16] Pierre Balley, *La Bourse: mythes et réalités* (Paris: PUF, 1986).

[17] Jean-François Pons, 'Réforme de la politique d'émission et de gestion de la dette publiqueen France (1985–1987)', *Revue d'économie financière* 4 (1988): p. 89.

[18] Ibid., pp. 93–4.   [19] Ibid.

material, do not appear to have been dictated by financial actors. This raises the question of the interest that the State had in reforming the financial markets. For Jean-François Pons, chief clerk at the Treasury in 1988, the answer is obvious: 'The State has its own interest in this reform, which enables him to turn regularly and at a cheaper cost to the market.'[20] This hypothesis deserves to be more closely examined. This requires to assess the constraints imposed by the public debt during this period and, more importantly, how these constraints were perceived *at the time.*

Facing the Constraints of Sovereign Debt

From October 1985 the Bank of France, through its Governor Michel Camdessus, a former Permanent Secretary to the Treasury, became alarmed: 'A financial innovation that broadens the role of markets and interest rates, and provides economic agents with the latest tools to manage their funds would not fail to get the active support from the central bank. […] However, the monetary facilities that the Treasury could find in this reform for an easier and cheaper financing of the public debt, which keeps growing faster than national wealth, could be seen as opening the way for the State's financial laxity.'[21] This statement throws light on two important points: first, the public debt clearly started becoming a worry in the second half of the 1980s. This reality has tended to be downplayed or even denied in actors' later declarations. This bias can be explained by the huge weight taken by the sovereign debt in recent years, which can retrospectively make look as negligible the debt ratios prevailing at the time. On the other hand, the links between the growth of public debt and the reform of financial markets are clearly stated—at any rate within the State's financial administration. This dimension is hidden to an even greater extent by later testimonies. Against these retrospective illusions, one must resort to what Jean Bouvier called the intersection between 'hot history'—the history of actors' discourses—and 'cold history'—as expressed in figures.[22]

'For the last twenty-five years, the debt of public administrations has been relentlessly growing: between 1980 and 2004, it has grown fivefold […] In effect, for twenty-five years, debt has been a loophole for permanently postponing the adaptation of our public administrations and answering all problems, especially social questions, through new expenses.'[23] The conclusions of the Pébereau report,

[20] Ibid., p. 89.
[21] Bank of France archives (BFA), 1035200103/97, Camdessus files, Note from the governor of the Banque of France, 29 October 1985, pp. 1 and 4.
[22] Jean Bouvier, 'Histoire financière et problème d'analyse des dépenses publiques', *Annales, ESC* 33, no. 2 (mars–avril 1978): p. 211.
[23] 'Rompre avec la facilité de la dettepublique', Official report of the commission chaired by Michel Pébereau, La documentation française, 2005, p. 23.

who was then chairman of BNP Paribas, were clear. Commissioned by Thierry Breton, Economic and Finance Minister in early 2005, the report would nevertheless end up in oblivion, swept away by the financial crisis that broke out in summer 2007. Its principal merit was to perfectly understand the long-term dynamics of public debt. Nevertheless, the report remained very vague on the genesis of the cycle of debt, merely underlining in passing a strong acceleration in the years 1992–97: 'paradoxically, it was during the years immediately following the Maastricht negotiations that it grew at it fastest rate'.[24] On the *terminus a quo* of 1980s, the report remained cautiously silent. On the eve of the Left's accession to power, the situation of public finances was balanced, 'the result of the Barre's austerity', noted Pébereau, was the balance of public accounts in 1980'.[25] Hervé Hannoun made the same observation: 'the strong point of Barre's management was undoubtedly the public debt at less than 30 per cent of GDP'.[26] From this perspective, public debt clearly soared after 1981, whether in absolute terms or as a percentage of GDP (Figures 7.1 and 7.2).

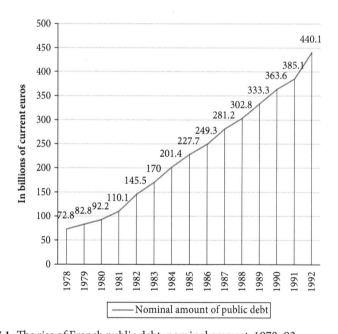

Figure 7.1 The rise of French public debt, nominal amount, 1978–92.

Sources: FNA, AG/5(4)/6154, *La Correspondance économique*, 4 May 1987; AG/5(4)/6153, note from P. Jaffré to the Minister, 7 August 1987; AG/5(4)/6154, note from Hervé Hannoun, 22 April 1988 (OECD data); INSEE.

[24]   Ibid., p. 31.
[25]   Oral archives of the François Mitterrand Institute (FMI), testimony of M. Pébereau, 15 April 2015.
[26]   FMI, testimony of Hervé Hannoun, 15 April 2015.

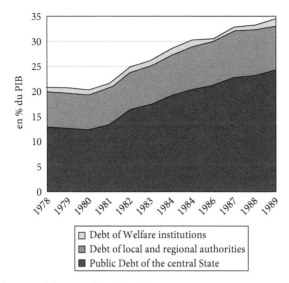

Figure 7.2 The rise of the French public debt ratio, 1978–89.

Sources: FNA, AG/5(4)/6154, *La Correspondance économique*, 4 May 1987; AG/5(4)/6153, note from P. Jaffré to the Minister, 7 August 1987; AG/5(4)/6154, note from Hervé Hannoun, 22 April 1988 (OECD data); INSEE.

It is also obvious that the growth rate of public debt increased during the period 1981–85 and decreased significantly from 1988 (see Table 7.1).

This evolution didn't go unnoticed. Jacques Chirac made it one of the themes of his presidential campaign in April 1988, claiming that: 'The socialists have multiplied the public debt by three.' Hervé Hannoun, at the Élysée, tried to ward off the attack: 'Internal debt is one of the indicators used by M. Chirac to pretend that France has been on the verge of bankruptcy. The French, to whom it has been ceaselessly repeated that the public debt has increased between 1981 and 1986, must know that this phenomenon has been observed nearly everywhere in the large industrialised countries.'[27] The upsurge of the debt was put in perspective but not denied. As Isabelle Bouillon, Deputy Chief of Staff of Jacques Delors cabinet in the Ministry of Finance, emphasized in an internal note: 'it shouldn't be forgotten that *in volume*, our debt is high.'[28] On 14 December 1984, the day after his speech at the HEC Foundation, which really launched France's policy of financial liberalization, Pierre Bérégovoy, who succeeded Jacques Delors as Finance Minister, justified to the Senate the policy of public indebtedness: '[Our debt] has undoubtedly increased since 1981. This has been the result of a necessary choice in order to contain the progress of unemployment. The debt burden is heavy, but bearable.'[29]

---

[27] FNA, AG/5(4)/61545, Hannoun files, note for the president, 23 April 1988.

[28] FNA, AG/5(4)/EG/243, E. Guigou files, handwritten note from Isabelle Bouillot to E. Guigou, November 1983, underlined in the document.

[29] FNA, AG/5(4)/6154, Hannoun files, 'Argumentaire de Pierre Bérégovoy pour discours au Sénat, 14 décembre 1984, transmis à FM envue de son intervention TV du 16 janvier 1985'.

Table 7.1 Annual growth rate of nominal public debt in France (1978–92) (year-over-year percentage)

1979	1980	1981	1982	1983	1984	1985	1986	1987	1988	1989	1990	1991	1992
12	10	16	24	14	16	12	9	11	7	9	8	6	12

Source: J. de Larosière, 'Fiscal Policy: A Challenge for the European Union', Pierre Werner Lecture, Luxembourg, 11 October 2005. I am grateful to J. de Larosière for providing me these statistics, originally prepared by BNP-Paribas, on which his presentation was based.

The foreign press, especially in the English speaking world, took a more alarmist view. The American magazine *Fortune*, in particular, published on 30 April 1980 an article relaying figures from a Morgan Stanley study and entitled 'France Flirts with Third World Debtor Status'.[30] The secretariat of the Élysée took the matter very seriously. Élisabeth Guigou asked Isabelle Bouillot to prepare 'a TTU argument: are the comparisons correctly based?'.[31] The financial adviser at the French embassy in Washington, Gérard de Margerie, was mobilized to check with Morgan Stanley the figures on which the *Fortune*'s article were based!

The impact of this publication was all the bigger as it took place at the very moment when a parliamentary committee 'charged with evaluating the structure and amount of France's external debt' published its own report.[32] The committee had been established on 17 November 1983 on a proposal from Charles Pasqua and was chaired by Jean Colin, a Centrist senator from Essonne. The rapporteur, was Marcel Lucotte, senator mayor of Autun, and president of the *Républicains indépendants* in the Senate. More importantly, the committee's spokesperson was Jacques Fourcade, former Finance minister at the beginning of Valéry Guscard d'Estaing's presidency, from 1974 to 1976. The committee was thus dominated by the Opposition and from January 1984 started auditioning the main financial officials in the State and government: the governor of the Bank of France, but also Laurent Fabius, Jacques Delors, and Edith Cresson. 'The committee's report', warned E. Guigou in a note for François Mitterrand, 'will be exploited for political ends by the Opposition in a very big way'.[33] François Mitterrand admitted that 'I'm afraid that we've been neglectful in this matter'.[34]

The external debt, i.e. the debt denominated in foreign currency and subscribed by non-residents, was indeed the then fastest growing part of the sovereign debt.

---

[30] FNA, AG/5(4)/EG/243, E. Guigou files, 'Comparaison entre l'endettement de la France et celui des autres pays' (file 3), article in *Fortune*, 30 April 1984.

[31] Ibid.

[32] French Senate, repport no. 301, 'fait au nom de la commission d'enquête chargée d'évaluer la structure et le montant de la dette extérieure de la France, ses incidences prévisibles sur l'évolution de la balance des paiements ainsi que la part prise par les enterprises publiques et les banques dans l'évolution de la dette extérieure depuis 1981', annex to the proceedings of the 9 May 1984 session.

[33] FNA, AG/5(4)/EG/243, E. Guigou files, 'Commission d'enquête du Sénatsur la dette extérieure de la France', note from E. Guigou to the President of the French Republic, 17 April 1984.

[34] Ibid.

Hervé Hannoun underlined this fact to François Mitterrand in 1987: 'France's external debt has exploded between 1973 and June 1985.'[35] Jacques Attali concurred: 'No country has been able to escape since the rise of oil prices. France's external debt gew tenfold from 1974 to 1981 and tripled from 1981 to 1985.'[36] From the beginning of 1983, Élisabeth Guigou, sounded the alarm: 'the rise of our foreign indebtedness is too fast. In 1982, new medium and long-term foreign borrowing by public enterprises and the Treasury reached 92 billion francs [...] Sustaining such a rhythm is dangerous for France's credit and threatens our national independence.'[37]

The external debt was clearly perceived in François Mitterrand's close entourage as a sword of Damocles. The threat was especially strong as the external is difficult to quantify. Its servicing, in particular, which depends on the foreign exchanges, is hardly foreseeable. This was the main motivation of the Senate committee of inquiry: 'It is extremely uneasy to quantify in undisputable conditions the amount of the foreign debt', and the report acknowledged that the gaps in statistical information served 'the intention, found in all States, not to disclose figures that might shake the confidence of financial circles'. The main unknown dimension concerned public enterprises' and banks' short-term foreign indebtedness. Published data only included the Treasury's medium and long-term foreign indebtedness. The difference between the two was substantial, underlined É. Guigou, and would no doubt fuel 'the controversy': at the end of 1983, short-term indebtedness in foreign currency could be estimated at 450 billion francs, whereas the Treasury's medium and long-term external debt was only 30 billion francs.[38] In May 1985, Raymond Barre published in his own paper, *Faits & Arguments*, a very pessimistic article estimating that the country's external debt *latosensu* would reach 661 billion francs by 1987: 'In any case, France will have to bear for many years the burden of the debt contracted since 1981 and its refund will significantly cut back into the income of the French people.'[39] Even on the basis of the official figures of Treasury operations published in the *journal officiel*, the explosion of the external debt was obvious (see Figure 7.3).

As a percentage of GDP, the growth of the external debt was even more spectacular, as acknowledged by Hervé Hannoun in a so-called 'in house' note: from 1.1 per cent of GDP at the end of 1974, it jumped to 6 per cent at the end of 1981. It peaked at 12 per cent at the end of 1984 before dropping to 8 per cent at the end of 1986 as a result of the oil counter shock and the fall of the dollar.[40] This

---

[35] FNA, AG/5(4)/6154, note from H. Hannoun to the President of the French Republic, 3 August 1987.
[36] FNA, AG/5(4)/6154, note from J. Attali to the President of the French Republic, 17 September 1987.
[37] FNA, AG/5(4)/EG/243, Note from E. Guigou to François Mitterrand, 25 February 1983.
[38] FNA, AG/5(4)/EG/243, Note from E. Guigou to François Mitterrand, 17 April 1984.
[39] FNA, AG/5(4)/6154, Hannoun files, *Faits& Arguments*, no. 26, May 1985, p. 7.
[40] FNA, AG/5(4)/6154, 'Éléments demandés par le président de la République sur la dette extérieure', note from H. Hannoun, 'maison', 18 March 1988.

Figure 7.3 The explosion of the external pubic debt, 1976–87.

Sources: FNA, AG/5(4)/6154, *La Correspondance économique*, 4 May 1987; AG/5(4)/6154, note from Hervé Hannoun, 22 April 1988 (OECD data).

evolution was considered as very worrying by François Mitterrand's advisers in 1984–85. The 'arguments' destined to feed the President's interventions in the media kept repeating that 'France's foreign indebtedness was entirely under control' and that 'France's signature was one of the best in the world'.[41] It was also recalled that 'foreign indebtedness is not an impoverishment: it has made possible the financing of our country's development'.[42] Off the record, however, the narrative was more circumspect. As É. Guigou and H. Hannoun reminded Jean-Louis Bianco in an internal note: 'in a few weeks the statistics of indebtedness will be published and they will be bad in francs (dollar at 9.50F today as against 8.40F at the end of 1983... in our view we must stay fairly general: we have borrowed to a large extent in order to finance our deficits (and not only the electronuclear programme)'.[43]

In the light of the archives, there is thus little doubt that the public debt, especially its foreign currency component, was a major concern from the end of 1983. The upsurge of the debt was henceforth analysed as a double constraint: as an internal constraint, because of the growing politicization of the debt, which had completely disappeared during the golden age; but also as an external constraint, with the potential of greatly limiting the room for manoeuvre in the conduct of a national economic policy. É. Guigou explained to the President that 'the servicing of the debt can only be controlled if current account operations are balanced in

[41] FNA, AG/5(4)/EG/243, 'Aide-mémoire', E. Guigou and H. Hannoun, 14 December 1984.
[42] FNA, AG/5(4)/EG/243, 'Fiche pour la conférence de presse du président du 21 novembre 1985'.
[43] FNA, AG/5(4)/EG/243, Handwritten note to Jean-Louis Bianco accompanying the 'aide-mémoire' of 14 December 1984.

the next few years and even, as M. Delors has said on several occasion, in surplus. This puts a strong constraint on the government's economic policy; this constraint should be clearly assessed and submitted for your appreciation by the Finance minister and the Prime minister'.[44] In this context, financial liberalization in France appears less as an end in itself, ideological in nature, than an essentially technical tool that could remove the constraint of the sovereign debt.

Public Debt and Financial Deregulation

Since the 1970s, in standard economic theory, in other words, the 'neoliberal' theory, financial liberalization has been based on its ability to generate economic growth by improving the allocation of financial resources.[45] Financial liberalization would reduce the price of money, but would also result in greater financial stability, as risks would be spread between numerous and diverse financial actors. In the second half of the 1980s, this economic model was widely disseminated among French decision-makers in the political and administrative spheres. It reflected, in particular, a political discourse targeting public opinion. Pierre Bérégovoy, the French minister of economy and finance, fully endorsed it in his *White Paper on the Reform of the Financing of the Economy*, published just before the March 1986 legislative elections: 'As soon as September 1984, I said that tax cuts and the lowering of interest rates would be the instruments of a stronger, non-inflationary economic growth.. This policy of financial modernisation did not come about by chance. Observing what was going on elsewhere, I wanted it passionately, knowing that I would run up against powerful interests and disturb many habits. The fact that we were able to implement it, in the main, in less than eighteen months, shows that dynamism exists in France if we encourage it.'[46] Defending his results in March 1988, Edouard Balladur, the conservative minister of Economy, Finance, and Privatisation (1986–88) during the cohabitation, Edouard Balladur also endorsed this model by placing his action under the double banner of 'economic freedom' and 'financial reform'. He stated that 'The economic and financial reforms carried out over the last two years represent, I sincerely believe, considerable progress towards the consolidation of public

---

[44] FNA, AG/5(4)/EG/243, note from É. Guigou to the President of the French Republic, 25 April 1984.

[45] Ronald I. McKinnon, *Money and Capital in Economic Development* (Washington, DC: The Brookings Institution, 1973); Edward S. Shaw, *Financial Deepening in Economic Development* (New York: Oxford University Press, 1973).

[46] French Ministry of Economy and Finance, 'Livre blanc sur la réforme du financement de l'économie', foreword by Pierre Bérégovoy. Report produced by a working group chaired by Jean-Charles Naouri and composed of Thierry Aulagnon, Jérôme Fessard, André Gauron, Bertrand Kramer, Gilles de Margerie, Jean-François Pons, and Jean-François Stoll. Paris, *La Documentation française*, 1986, pp. 6–7.

finances and an effective liberation of the economy, of companies, and of individual energies.' Was this a bright confirmation of the conversion, beyond the changes of political majority, to neoliberalism?

It is difficult to gauge the depth of the socialist left's and the Gaullist right's conversion to economic liberalism. With the benefit of hindsight, however, one observation can be made: the wave of financial liberalization in the 1980s did not lead to sustainable economic growth in France and failed to overcome long-term mass unemployment. The model did not work. Therefore, we have to look elsewhere for an economic model underlying the financial reform of the second half of the 1980s. Another major trend was the tremendous growth in public debt which exceeds 100% of GDP today, an unprecedented level in peacetime. In this perspective, the alternative model proposed by William Silber in 1983 is useful.[47] He assimilates financial innovation, at the microeconomic level of the firm, to a response to a profitability constraint: 'The main hypothesis is quite straightforward: new financial instruments or practices are created to lessen the financial constraints imposed on firms.'[48] This model applies very well to the French Treasury, which can be considered as a bank. The main constraint on the Treasury's balance sheet in the 1980s was the sharp increase in debt service, that is on the sums it had to pay for interest payments and borrowed capital reimbursement.

A worsening of the debt service burden characterized the second half of the 1980s in France. The government debt outstanding doubled between 1978 and 1985, while the burden of public debt was multiplied by 3.6 at the same time. As shown in Figure 7.5, the trend was not unique to France. It related to the rise in real interest rates in the context of the disinflation policy which prevailed in France as in other countries at that time. 'Zero inflation', stated Jean-Baptiste de Foucault, cabinet member of Finance minister Jacques Delors, in April 1986, 'has become for the collectivity what zero defect is for companies' sales capacity: the entry ticket to the world economy'. However, an opposite analysis was also made in the entourage of François Mitterrand. In November 1985, Michel Charasse, advisor to the French president, warned against 'the perverse political effects of the fight against inflation'. He stated that all indebted actors (low-income employees, SMEs, local authorities) 'who had expected a continuation of inflation of 12 to 14%', were now confronted with the rise in real interest rates, 'because of the reduction in the rate of inflation and therefore of the increase in wages'. Michel Charasse, therefore, advised the French president to be pedagogical towards public opinion and to explain that '8% of interest for a 14% inflation yields less than 6% of interest for 5% inflation'. The State did not escape this development. Jean-Claude Trichet, head of the Treasury since September 1987, explained in April 1988 to

---

[47] William B. Silber, 'The Process of Financial Innovation', *The American Economic Review* 73, no. 2 (May 1983): pp. 89–95.
[48] Ibid., p. 89.

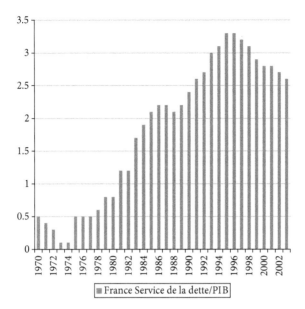

Figure 7.4 French debt service/GDP.

Sources: J. de Larosière, 'Fiscal Policy: a Challenge for the European Union,' Pierre Werner Lecture, Luxembourg, 11 October 2005. I am grateful to J. de Larosière for providing me these statistics, originally prepared by BNP-Paribas, on which his presentation was based.

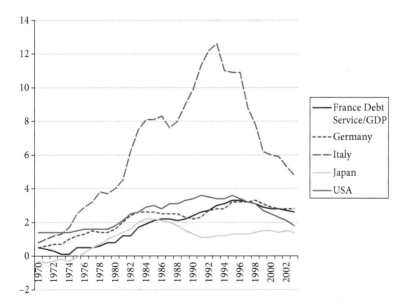

Figure 7.5 French debt service/GDP compared to other countries.

Sources: J. de Larosière, 'Fiscal Policy: a Challenge for the European Union,' Pierre Werner Lecture, Luxembourg, 11 October 2005. I am grateful to J. de Larosière for providing me these statistics, originally prepared by BNP-Paribas, on which his presentation was based.

the minister of finance, Édouard Balladur: 'short and long term rates in France, expressed in real terms, remain the highest among the main industrial countries'. The intersection of the two curves of inflation and real rates, which precisely occurred in 1985, provides a striking representation of this (Figure 7.6).

For the service of the external debt, exchange rate volatility was an additional constraint, on top of interest rates. This was particularly the case in a world now characterized by the floating of currencies, despite the attempts to regulate the international monetary 'non-system', such as the Plaza agreement of 22 September 1985 and the Louvre agreement of 22 February 1987. The fluctuations of the US dollar were the most critical constraint. The exchange rate was four francs for one dollar in July 1980 at the end of Carter's presidency. It peaked at 10 francs in February 1985, after Ronald Reagan's triumphant re-election. The impact of this trend on France's external debt service, 70% of which was denominated in dollars, was considerable. The constraint was particularly strong because most of these

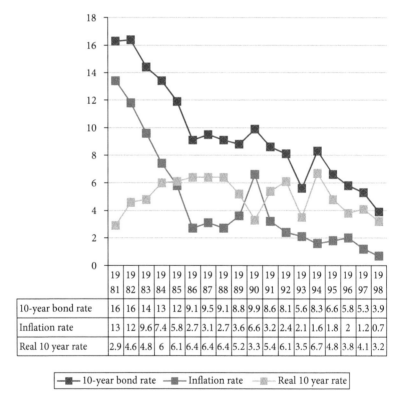

	19 81	19 82	19 83	19 84	19 85	19 86	19 87	19 88	19 89	19 90	19 91	19 92	19 93	19 94	19 95	19 96	19 97	19 98
10-year bond rate	16	16	14	13	12	9.1	9.5	9.1	8.8	9.9	8.6	8.1	5.6	8.3	6.6	5.8	5.3	3.9
Inflation rate	13	12	9.6	7.4	5.8	2.7	3.1	2.7	3.6	6.6	3.2	2.4	2.1	1.6	1.8	2	1.2	0.7
Real 10 year rate	2.9	4.6	4.8	6	6.1	6.4	6.4	6.4	5.2	3.3	5.4	6.1	3.5	6.7	4.8	3.8	4.1	3.2

—■— 10-year bond rate   —■— Inflation rate   —■— Real 10 year rate

Figure 7.6 Disinflation and rise in real interest rates in France, 1981–90, in annual percentages.

Sources: FNA, AG/5(4)/6209, 'Dernières évolutions monétaires', Note from the head of the Treasury to the Minister of Finance, 11 April 1988; INSEE online database; OECD data https://data.oecd.org/interest/long-term-interest-rates.htm (accessed 21 May 2020).

foreign currency credits had been contracted by the Treasury between 1981 and 1983, on expensive terms, while the foreign currency reserves of the Banque de France had been melting away like snow in the sun since the day of the victory of the left (see Table 7.2).

In a similar vein, Daniel Lebègue, who succeeded to Michel Camdessus at the head of the French Treasury in August 1984, declared in April 1985 to Pierre Bérégovoy, as the dollar was beginning to slide: 'the cost of the debt of the French Republic has become relatively high given the evolution of the markets...The French Republic could undoubtedly obtain better conditions today than those which prevailed in 1982–1983.'[49] This statement was another way of putting, once again, 'the Treasury thesis': the placing of the public debt, including the external debt, on the market, which requires the removal of exchange controls, would enable lifting the heavy constraints on the State's financing.

At the end of 1983, François-Xavier Stasse, technical adviser at the Élysée, wrote to his colleagues at the Minister of Finance's cabinet and at the Directorate General of the Treasury. He asked them to explain him once again, 'at the risk of annoying you to always come back on the same subject,' why 'the French public debt has reached a level which it would be dangerous to exceed when it represents half or even a third of that of comparable countries.'[50] François Stasse concluded: 'Thank you for helping me understand' and added in brackets: 'However, I defend with dedication the *Treasury thesis* with the various interlocutors who do not fail to raise this question with me.' The main elements of the 'Treasury thesis' can easily be summarized. Jérôme Vignon, technical advisor to Jacques Delors from

Table 7.2 Foreign currency borrowing by the French Treasury (1982–83)

Date	Terms	Amount	Maturity
October 1982	Eurocrédit (international banking syndicate led by Société Générale)	$4 billions	1992
December 1982	Loan from the Saudi Arabian Monetary Authority	$2 billions	July 1985
16 May 1983	Credit from the EEC	ECU 4 billions	1990
1983	Floating rate Eurobond issue	$1,8 billions	1990
1983	Fixed rate Eurobond issue	$350 millions	1990
1983	Fixed rate Eurobond issue	ECU 150 millions	1990

Source: FNA, AG/5(4)/EG/243, 'Dette de la République françaiseen devises'. Note from Daniel Lebègue, head of the French Treasury, to the Minister of Finance, 9 April 1985.

[49] FNA, AG/5(4)/EG/243, 'Dette de la République françaiseen devises'. Note by Daniel Lebègue, director the French Treasury, to the Minister of Finance, 9 April 1985.
[50] FNA, AG/5(4)/2136, Note by François-Xavier Stasse to Jean-Baptiste de Foucauld, Jérôme Vignon and Daniel Lebègue, 23 December 1983 (emphasis added).

the National Institute of Statistics and Economic Studies (INSEE) and the Plan, formulated the Treasury thesis as follows:

The structural differences in the financing of the entire economy are often put forward to explain the different levels of public debt in France and abroad. Along these lines, a high level of public debt could go hand in hand with a way of financing the economy in which public bond issuance would develop in an important financial market; on the other hand, the relative weakness of the French debt would be linked to the predominant role played by banking intermediation in the financing of companies.[51]

However, the 'Treasury thesis' in no way aimed to diminish fiscal discipline or facilitate a lenient financial state. Jean-Claude Trichet, head of the French Treasury between 1987 and 1993 and governor of the Bank of France between 1993 and 2003, gave in 2015 a retrospective view of the Treasury's perspective: 'The easy choice? I think that the modernisation of the Treasury bonds, the fact of turning Treasury bonds into securities which could be negotiated under the best conditions—like the other (countries), because after all we were only imitating the other (countries)—we did not perceive that at all as the easy choice which would allow us to borrow massively! This was not the idea of Bérégovoy, of Hervé Hannoun, or of Jean-Charles Naouri, nor certainly the idea of the cohabitation government! It is true that this has considerably facilitated the financing of the French State and it is true that, afterwards, we did not conduct the policies of budgetary wisdom that we should have conducted for a long time, and this was here again, alas, a bipartisan phenomenon.'[52] This statement probably expressed the neutrality of the senior civil servant, whose purely technical role stops where politics begins. Nevertheless, the primary archives also confirm that senior Treasury officials explicitly formulated the causal relationship between the reduction in the cost of public debt and the various measures of financial liberalization at the time. Assessing the 'financing of the Treasury in 1987', a note from April 1988 pointed that 'the cost of public debt has been stabilised, despite the rise in rates'.[53] The cost of debt was reduced to 1.7% of GDP in 1987, from 1.9% of GDP in 1984. The note explained this improvement by the 'structural cost reduction permitted by the reform of issuing methods: I estimate that the transition from syndication to bond auction represents a gain of almost 0.5% in the volume of issues, or 500 MF per year'. The note bluntly concluded that 'the results for the year 1987 confirm the benefit that the Treasury derives from the reform of the issuance and management of public debt implemented in recent years'.[54]

[51]   FNA, AG/5(4)/2136, Note by J. Vignon to F. Stasse, 11 January 1984.
[52]   Oral archives of the François Mitterrand Institute (FMI), Testimony of J.C. Trichet, 15 April 2015, 1:10.
[53]   FNA, AG/5(4)/6209, 'Financement du Trésoren 1987'. Note from the monetary and financial affairs service of the Treasury to the Finance Minister, Jean-Claude Trichet, 14 April 1988.
[54]   Ibid.

If financial liberalization was not a sufficient condition for conducting a policy of public indebtedness, it was nevertheless a necessary condition in an increasingly globalized financial world. The 'marketization'[55] of public debt did indeed consist in integrating France to the global financial market, whose advent can be dated to the second half of the 1980s. Michel Camdessus illustrates this in his memoirs: head of the Treasury from March 1982 to August 1984, then governor of the Banque de France, he was elected Managing Director of the IMF in January 1987, 'at a time when the world [was] embarking in a formidable change of era'.[56] ... 'Since November 1984, I [ran] the Banque de France ... I work[ed] in cordial relationships of trust with two successive finance ministers, Pierre Bérégovoy and Édouard Balladur, and obviously with my former comrades in the Treasury department. With my friend Philippe Lagayette, deputy governor, we are starting to tackle the major project of the Bank's renovation. The question is to adapt its instruments to the revolution which, since the British big bang, has shaken the world monetary economy'.[57] Such a statement in hindsight was not retrospective lucidity. Primary sources show that the actors had the feeling of experiencing a historic turn: 'How much has changed in our financial world since I left France in 1978!' said Jacques de Larosière, who returned from a stay of almost ten years at the head of the IMF in Washington when he took office as governor of the Bank of France on 29 January 1987.[58]

The awareness that a global—and no longer just international—money market was now a reality was at the heart of the monetary and financial policies of the second half of the 1980s. In this perspective, the stock market crash of 20 October 1987 was a revealing event. Just after the crash, during the 22 October 1987 meeting of the Bank of France council, the governor Jacques de Larosière declared: 'In a world where markets are closely intertwined, where financial instruments have proliferated, where the possibility of intervening on exchange and interest rates have increased dramatically, where technology and data processing render any speculation or movement possible at any time, where capital movements have almost no limit ... We can no longer, in a global economy whose ebbs and flows are so powerful, be satisfied with insufficient convergence regarding economic and monetary policies'.[59] The analysis of the 1987 crash by Jean-Claude Trichet, director of the Treasury, was even more explicit: 'What happened invites us to be more aware of the fact that there is now one global, completely unified system of markets. We knew that the money markets and the foreign exchange markets formed a system, but we did not realise that the futures markets of financial instruments also formed a system and that all the bond markets were coupled.

---

[55] 'Mise en marché', phrase by Benjamin Lemoine.
[56] Michel Camdessus, *La scène de cedrameest le monde, treizeans à la tête du FMI* (Paris: Éditions des Arènes, 2014).
[57] Ibid., p. XX.   [58] BFA, minutes of the General Council of 29 January 1987, p. 48.
[59] BFA, minutes of the General Council of 22 October 1987, p. 419.

We just abruptly discovered, and this is a fundamental lesson, that all the stock exchanges in the world were virtually coupled. There is one global system, which obviously calls for global collective management.'[60] Taking into account this global scale, the neoliberal turning point in France's financial policy takes a new meaning.

Conclusion

The turning point in financial liberalization, initiated by the left in power in 1984, pursued by the right under cohabitation and completed by the left from 1988 to 1993 was a change of era: the allocation of financial resources was now realized through a financial market freed from the administrative rules and practices which characterized the 'financial repression' inherited from the two world wars and the 1929 crisis.

The Big Bang of the French financial system was, therefore, a significant change. Does it imply, however, the disappearance of the political divide between left and right and a generalized conversion to market values and to a neoliberal view of society? Nothing could be less certain. The history of the financial innovations introduced by the State from 1984 on suggests that financial liberalization was the political response to a series of unprecedented constraints weighing increasingly on government revenue. These constraints were linked to a new context marked, on the one hand, by the increased financial needs of a 'colbertist' State in times of economic crisis, and on the other hand, by the globalization of financial markets.

The evolution of sovereign debt, in particular its external debt component, crystallized these tensions and was in the 1980s an object of major concern. There is no doubt that the increasing cost of public debt has been one of the main motives behind the policy of financial liberalization. The controlled management of the cost of public debt until today, despite its rapid growth since the 1990s and the Global Financial Crisis starting in 2007 with the subprime crisis, shows that this objective was not an illusion. The fact remains that the 1984–88 period, despite the 'bipartisan consensus' (Jean-Claude Trichet) on the need for financial liberalization and efficient debt management, did not abolish the political divide between right and left. In the second half of the 1980s, a dividing line indeed opposed two ideologies: that, for a fraction of the right, of a 'poor' State reduced to conduct a policy of empty coffers to that, on the left, of a 'rich' State, whose preserved financial means, even at the cost of debt, would contribute to the sustainability of the French social model. The rest of the story has since then confirmed the reality of this political debate opposing two choices of society, which hasn't been been settled to this day.

---

[60] Ibid., p. 420.

8

Deregulation, Regulatory Convergence, or Escaping from Inefficiency?

The Italian Financial System in the 1970s–1980s

Giandomenico Piluso

Introduction

Major changes in Western financial systems since the early 1970s offer rather different ways to consider and assess the rationale and objectives as to choices made by legislators and economic policy authorities. The standard approach to the topic is centred upon the twin categories of deregulation and liberalization, quite often coupled with privatizations, whilst the regulatory convergence is a key concept if changes in financial regulation are framed as phenomena interesting one of the components defining the varieties of capitalism.[1] The very diversity of regulatory architectures and regulation extent has been regarded as subject to specific cycles, or pendulum-like swings, over time, substantially affecting macroeconomic movements,[2] from extremely light options to all-encompassing regulations, from free banking to State interventionism.[3] Amongst the commonest purposes and objectives of financial regulation are systemic stability, risk and crisis management, competition against monopolies, client, and customer protection. The main rationale for regulation, anyway, is probably represented by inherent systemic instability: this point assumes a crucial relevance when it comes

The author gratefully acknowledges the generous support provided by the Robert Schuman Centre for Advanced Studies, at the European University Institute in Florence, during his stay as a Jean Monnet Fellow in the academic year 2016–17. He also thanks Francesco Cesarini for his invaluable comments on a previous draft.

[1] See Peter A. Hall and David Soskice, 'An Introduction to Varieties of Capitalism', in *Varieties of Capitalism. The Institutional Foundations of Comparative Advantage*, edited by Peter A. Hall and David Soskice (Oxford: Oxford University Press, 2001): pp. 10–11.

[2] Quite aptly, and just a few years before the last major financial shock (2007–08), some scholars have pointed out why and how a lighter form of regulation, i.e. financial liberalization, tends to be associated with higher degrees of financial fragility which amplify macroeconomic cycles. Cf. Charles A.E. Goodhart, Boris Hofmann, and Miguel Segoviano, 'Bank Regulation and Macroeconomic Fluctuations', *Oxford Review of Economic Policy* 20, no. 4 (2004): pp. 591–615.

[3] James R. Barth, Gerard Caprio Jr., and Ross Levine, *Rethinking Bank Regulation* (Cambridge: Cambridge University Press, 2006).

Giandomenico Piluso, *Deregulation, Regulatory Convergence, or Escaping from Inefficiency? The Italian Financial System in the 1970s–1980s* In: *Financial Deregulation: A Historical Perspective.* Edited by: Alexis Drach and Youssef Cassis, Oxford University Press (2021). © Alexis Drach and Youssef Cassis. DOI: 10.1093/oso/9780198856955.003.0008

to determine why regulation is, or should be, paramount in all financial systems.[4] Yet, on the other hand, usually financial regulation responds to wider monetary constraints or objectives as ultimate factors determining individual instability or inefficiency phenomena amongst intermediaries and markets, a point that appears particularly pertinent when money supply is subject to restrictive conditions.[5] However, financial regulation may significantly vary across countries, owing to their institutional efficiency and their relative degree of economic development, and is largely the product of individual experiences in handling earlier crises, although the emerging of global financial system has been making the case for international coordination since the early 1970s.[6] The international dimension of financial regulation surfaced, by and large, at the same time when a need for a new regulation arose because of a growing allocative inefficiency attributed to the rather strict regulation usually dating back to the 1930s. In this vein, typically, liberalization—as a form of financial deregulation—was meant to restore efficiency in a decade of turbulence and macroeconomic slowdown, although it triggered some major banking crises after decades of prevalent stability. In Europe, as part of the wider regional market integration, financial liberalization was mostly promoted from the late 1970s, with the adoption of the First Banking Directive by the European Economic Community (EEC) in 1977, then accelerating in the ensuing decade after the White Paper of 1985 (see Chapter 5, this volume).[7]

Financial liberalization was basically conceived as a response to an outdated regulation which proved to be increasingly ineffective to foster economic growth, through investments, and productivity improvements, and to deal with macroeconomic turmoil episodes, stagflation and currency instability, after the collapse of the Bretton Woods arrangements.[8] As a result, the 'system of rationed

[4] Charles A.E. Goodhart, Philipp Hartmann, David Llewellyin, Liliana Rojas-Suárez, and Steven Weisbrod, *Financial Regulation: Why, How, and Where Now?* (London and New York: Routledge, 1998): pp. 1–9.

[5] On these fundamental relations see Carmen M. Reinhart and Kenneth S. Rogoff, *This Time is Different. Eight Centuries of Financial Folly* (Princeton: Princeton University Press, 2009); Moritz Schularick and Alan M. Taylor, 'Credit Booms Gone Burst: Monetary Policy, Leverage Cycles and Financial Crises, 1870–2008', *American Economic Review* 102, no. 2 (2012): pp. 1029–61. On the monetary factors determining financial regulation in Italy in the late 1920s and early 1930s see Giandomenico Piluso, 'Adjusting to Financial Instability in the Interwar Period. Italian Financial Elites, International Cooperation and Domestic Regulation, 1919–1939', in *Financial Elites and European Banking: Historical Perspectives*, edited by Youssef Cassis and Giuseppe Telesca (Oxford: Oxford University Press, 2018): pp. 61–91.

[6] Charles A. E. Goodhart, 'Regulation and the Role of Central Banks in an Increasingly Integrated Financial World', in *Multidisciplinary Economics*, edited by Peter de Gijsel and Hans Schenk (Dordrecht: Springer, 2005): pp. 275–7.

[7] Age Bakker, *The Liberalization of Capital Movements in Europe: The Monetary Committee and Financial Integration, 1954–1994* (Dordrecht: Kluwer Academic, 1996): pp. 187–216; Jean Dermine, 'Banking in Europe: Past, Present and Future', in *The Transformation of the European Financial System*, edited by Vítor Gaspar, Philip Hartman, and Olaf Sleijpen (Frankfurt: European Central Bank, 2003): pp. 32–3.

[8] 'The United States and much of the developed world was saddled with a set of outdated regulations that contributed to macroeconomic instability in the 1970s', as stated in Charles A.E. Goodhart,

private sector credit' generally erected in the 1930s—depicted as scarcely innovative, uncompetitive, and essentially unable to assess risks properly—broke down because of emerging unregulated internal competitors and international competition associated to globalization processes. In the 1970s and 1980s declining capital and exchange controls favoured the emergence of a global financial system which imposed international cooperation amongst central authorities to tackle the increasing financial fragility of intermediaries as a consequence of greater risks and lower capital ratios derived from greater competition.[9] Common issues and expected joint benefits may functionally explain the push for international financial harmonization as inaugurated with the Basel I agreements in 1988, even though some scholars highlight asymmetrical implications of such harmonization due to the uneven market and bargaining powers amongst countries and jurisdictions.[10] Thus, in the 1980s also in Europe financial deregulation and regulatory convergence, as a product of gradual international financial harmonization, developed as a reaction to specific national allocative inefficiencies and pressures exerted by external factors, such as globalization and law-making at the EEC level. However, if the overall tendency may actually be plainly framed in such a way, single national cases could show a definitely more complex path to the reorganization of financial structures by deregulating and converging towards common rules and into a shared legal environment during the last decades, both at a global level and within Europe.[11]

This chapter focuses on the rationale and objectives of financial deregulation as it was pursued in Italy in the 1980s and early 1990s. In fact, in the Italian case, deregulation appears as a complex adjustment process to major changes, both within the domestic economy and in the international environment, more than the result of a clear-cut plan explicitly put on the political agenda from its start. If deregulation and liberalization were openly on the political agenda in the US and in some European countries in the 1980s, primarily in Britain, Italy shows a different path to financial liberalization, depending upon difficulties in the manufacturing sector, an external shift in monetary policy and an emerging European legal frame. The (imperfect) regulatory convergence eventually obtained throughout the 1990s emerged as the result of a gradual adjustment

---

Anil K. Kashyap, Dimitrios P. Tsomocos, and Alexandros P. Vardoulakis, 'An Integrated Framework for Analyzing Multiple Financial Regulations', *International Journal of Central Banking* 9, no. 1 (2013): p. 110.

[9] Goodhart, 'Regulation and the Role of Central Banks', pp. 272–3.

[10] Thomas Oatley and Robert Nabors, 'Redistributive Cooperation: Market Failures, Wealth Transfer and the Basle Accord', *International Organisation* 52, no. 1 (1998): pp. 35–54; Daniel W. Drezner, *All Politics Is Global: Explaining International Regulatory Regimes* (Princeton: Princeton University Press, 2007).

[11] See Laurent Warlouzet, *Governing Europe in a Globalizing World. Neoliberalism and its Alternatives following the 1973 Oil Shock* (New York and London: Routledge, 2018), particularly chs 7 and 8.

more than of a regulatory agenda overtly defined as such by policymakers, possibly because of the enduring relative weakness of the Treasury vis-à-vis the Bank of Italy. The adjustment process was largely dependent on the ability of the central bank to provide sounding analyses and to promote internal reforms in accordance with the emerging European regulatory framework. In a way, governments and the Parliament did not constitute the real fulcrum of regulatory changes occurring in Italy throughout the 1980s, at the time when policymakers focused on fostering financial markets in all the major developed economies producing a partial reversal of the relative weights between markets and intermediaries in financial systems around the world.[12]

The Inefficiency Trap of Maturity Matching

As financial deregulation could be assumed as a reaction to outdated regulatory arrangements, it is worth considering how the Italian financial system was organized in the early 1970s, how it worked and what consequences its actual functioning had on the overall allocative efficiency vis-à-vis sectors and firms.[13] In other terms, was it able to provide funds by effectively selecting and monitoring firms and investment projects so to boost productivity improvements? In fact, the allocative efficiency of the Italian banking system—according to a quantitative study on the post WWII period—seems to be evidently decreasing from the early 1970s onwards, in stark contrast to the previous positive performance.[14]

If the falling allocative efficiency of the Italian banking system, particularly acute since the early 1980s, has been essentially ascribed to political factors,[15] basically exogenous to the financial structure, it is to be assessed whether the financial system itself had some responsibility for the poor allocative performance experienced from the early 1970s and throughout the 1980s. In effect, the peculiar

---

[12] As abundantly emphasized in Raghuram G. Rajan and Luigi Zingales, 'The Great Reversals: The Politics of Financial Development in the Twentieth Century', *Journal of Financial Economics* 69, no. 1 (2003): pp. 5–50.

[13] 'Allocative efficiency' is not easy to define and measure. It could be related to investment opportunities in terms of expected marginal productivity or profitability increases, that is the ability to provide funds to more innovative and dynamic firms and sectors by assessing their relative creditworthiness. Actually, banks and markets are subject to varying constraints according to their size, functioning, location, regulation. Providing loans or funds to declining sectors or inefficient firms should mirrored in the worsening quality of the financial assets. Empirical literature tends to observe, for instance, negative correlation between forms of financial repression and relationship banking and allocative efficiency. See, amongst many others, Raghuram G. Rajan and Luigi Zingales, 'Financial Systems, Industrial Structure, and Growth', *Oxford Review of Economic Policy* 17, no. 4 (2001): pp. 467–82.

[14] Stefano Battilossi, Alfredo Gigliobianco, and Giuseppe Marinelli, 'Resource Allocation by the Banking System', in *The Oxford Handbook of the Italian Economy Since Unification*, edited by Gianni Toniolo (Oxford: Oxford University Press, 2013): pp. 485–515.

[15] Battilossi, Gigliobianco, and Marinelli, 'Resource Allocation by the Banking System', pp. 489–92.

way it evolved since the mid-1960s, especially after the breakdown of the Bretton Woods arrangements, had negative effects on its allocative efficiency, with a destructive impact on the largest manufacturing firms burdened by huge levels of indebtedness.[16] Actually, their capital structure had been increasingly relying on the debt component because they had ever more incentives to do so by the accommodating monetary policy adopted by the Bank of Italy since the mid-1960s just to ease liquidity constraints of firms whose profits, on the contrary, were progressively decreasing.[17] Since the 1950s Italian bankers suffered from such a kind of loss of responsibility towards their industrial clientele, with a negative aggregate outcome on the allocative efficiency of the entire financial system as the even more accommodating monetary policy suggested to turn tremendously to short-term credits from the late 1960s.[18]

The relatively hidden but authentic cornerstone of the whole credit system was the State-backed bond market, whose effectiveness, by definition, completely relied upon macroeconomic stability, that is low inflation, interest rates under control and a balance of payments in equilibrium. Such conditions progressively vanished from the mid-1960s, as the Bank of Italy itself had to recognize, when first signs of rising inflation appeared.[19] A progressively pessimistic outlook, in fact, emerged in 1969: mounting inflation, although initially thought as imported, was coupling with a lower investment rate, a decreasing competitiveness of the Italian manufacturing firms, a surge in capital exports and a deteriorating balance of payments.[20] These surfacing major macroeconomic imbalances threatened the very functioning of the financial system even before the first oil shock and the breakdown of the Bretton Woods arrangements.[21] Having to deal with a fast growing public debt, which could dangerously collide with the private capital

---

[16] Leandro Conte and Giandomenico Piluso, 'Financing the Largest Italian Manufacturing Firms. Ownership, Equity, and Debt (1936–2001)', in *Forms of Enterprise in 20th Century Italy: Boundaries, Strategies and Structures*, edited by Andrea Colli and Michelangelo Vasta (Cheltenham: Edward Elgar, 2010): pp. 132–58.

[17] As the Bank of Italy's governor, Guido Carli, unambiguously stated in May 1963: 'the central bank regarded it as its duty to inject sufficient liquidity into the system to finance production at rising prices, so as not to endanger the continuity of growth' (Bank of Italy, *Report for the Year 1962. Concluding Remarks* (Rome: 1963): pp. 32–3). Cf. Leandro Conte, 'L'azione della Banca d'Italia (1948–93)', in *Storia d'Italia, Annali, 23, La Banca*, edited by Alberto Cova, Salvatore La Francesca, Angelo Moioli, and Claudio Bermond (Turin: Einaudi, 2008): pp. 671–2.

[18] On these tendencies see Alfredo Gigliobianco, Giandomenico Piluso, and Gianni Toniolo, 'Il rapporto tra banche e imprese negli anni Cinquanta', in *Stabilità e sviluppo negli anni Cinquanta*, edited by Franco Cotula (Rome-Bari: Laterza, 1999): vol. 2, pp. 225–302.

[19] To this regard, in the summer 1969, Carli first wrote of undesired 'inflationary pressures coming from outside'. See Archives of Bank of Italy (AS BI), Rome, Banca d'Italia, Direttorio Carli, folder 64, file 2, sub-file 12, 'Note sent to the Hon. Emilio Colombo, Minister of Treasury', 10 August 1969, p. 2.

[20] See AS BI, Banca d'Italia, Direttorio Carli, folder 64, file 2, sub-file 24, Letter and notes sent to the Hon. Emilio Colombo, Minister of Treasury, 4 December 1969.

[21] The Bank of Italy's governor pointed out what risks inflationary impulses generated at the international level could have on the Italian economy in his *Concluding Remarks* in May 1971 (Bank of Italy, *Report for the Year 1970. Governor's Concluding Remarks* (Rome: 1971): 3–15). Cf. Barry Eichengreen, *Global Imbalances and the Lessons of Bretton Woods* (Cambridge, MA: MIT Press, 2006).

demand by producing a crowding out effect in the market, in his capacity as governor Carli recognized all the impending inflation-related risks for the Italian economy and her financial system since the early 1970s. In his correspondence with the prime minister and ministers, Carli was adamant as to the impact of printing money to sustain an ailing economy within a deteriorating international context, but, at the same time, he had to come to terms with diversely orientated political preferences.[22]

In the 1970s, as the regulatory architecture was not a matter of discussion, both intermediaries and firms were thus hugely depending on bond-issuing, whilst the stock market had been relinquishing since the early 1960s and literally sank throughout the decade: the stock market capitalization, as a ratio of GDP, decreased from 0.42 in 1960 to 0.14 in 1970, falling down to its lowest point, a mere 0.09, in 1980. If the financial structure designed for a time of macroeconomic stability was to be maintained, the inflationary impulses gravely affected its working harshly distorting the overall resource allocation process.[23] As aforementioned, the Bank of Italy had to sustain actively, as a response, both firms' capital demand and the bond market by adopting a rather lax monetary policy from the early 1960s, almost as soon as Carli stepped in office as governor in 1960. Yet, the Bank of Italy's expansionary strategy had a deeply regressive impact within the whole financial system, essentially reinforcing negative tendencies which further dwarfed the stock market and made bankers less able to screen and monitor their borrowers. In fact, to support the ailing bond market, whose respective demand was negatively affected by high inflation, the Bank of Italy had to impose to commercial banks a string of administrative measures, from credit ceilings to additional compulsory reserves.[24] If the Bank of Italy conceived its expansionary monetary policy primarily to sustain firms' liquidity and industrial investments, the derived inflation reduced investors' preferences for bonds issued by State-owned conglomerates and special credit institutions.

---

[22] See, for instance, AS BI, Banca d'Italia, Direttorio Carli, folder 72, file 7, sub-file 12, 'Note sent to the Hon. Giulio Andreotti, Prime Minister', 15 September 1972, p. 7 (on expected competition between the private demand and public needs in the capital market); Banca d'Italia, Direttorio Carli, folder 72, file 7, sub-file 13, 'Note sent to the Hon. Giulio Andreotti, Prime Minister', 7 December 1972, p. 6 (on decision not to reduce public spending to contain the inflation component depending on internal factors).

[23] In this aspect Italy lacked a proper reform of the banking sector comparable to that introduced in France in 1966 by Michel Debré (cf. Laure Quenouëlle-Corre, 'Les réformes bancaires et financières de 1966–1967', in Michel Debré, un réformateur aux Finances 1966–1968 (Paris: Institut de la gestion publique et du développement économique, 2005): pp. 85–117).

[24] Some episodes are a telling tale of the relevance of the Bank of Italy's lax monetary policy in managing the country's liquidity: for instance, 'the abandonment, in the summer of 1969, of the policy of supporting bond prices, [...] had the effect of depriving the system of second-line liquidity' (Bank of Italy, Report for the Year 1970. Governor's Concluding Remarks, p. 30). At certain moments Carli felt that central monetary authorities had to check high expectations that the Bank of Italy would maintain an accommodating monetary policy (see AS BI, Banca d'Italia, Direttorio Carli, folder 65, file 1, sub-file 3, 'Letter sent to the Hon. Emilio Colombo, Minister of Treasury', 19 January 1970, pp. 6–7).

During the 1970s central monetary authorities, namely the Bank of Italy, reacted to the diminishing demand for bonds by imposing binding administrative measures that further reduced the commercial banks' proper control over their own assets making bankers virtually irresponsible over a vast share of their collected resources.[25]

The resulting inefficiency of this experiment in maturity matching, in a context overwhelmingly characterized by macroeconomic instability (high inflation and volatile exchange rates),[26] had a great impact on allocative efficiency of the whole financial system, comprising bankers and the bond market.

On the whole, undeniably, the Bank of Italy was not really comfortable with such a state of affairs, as Carli admitted on 31 May 1975, when leaving the Bank and considering the conflicting objectives which the central bank had to pursue since the mid-1960s.[27] As governor, whilst countering rising international inflationary impulses, Carli had hardly tried to restrain some regressive tendencies related both to public spending and cost-push inflation.[28] The Bank of Italy, none the less, had definitely too many a target to take into account when acting throughout the decade of stagflation. Macroeconomic stability objectives were in stark contrast with looser economic policies relying upon an inflationary fiscal behaviour by the government, whilst the support of capital formation via liquidity injections, per se, did not help firms to regain competitiveness and on the contrary, and frequently, interfered with episodic, and perhaps erratic, anti-inflationary tightening monetary policy.[29] Actually, the Bank of Italy had to finance public spending by the government, which nevertheless implied rising inflation: the Bank—as Carli argued in May 1974—'could have refused [...] to finance the public sector's deficit by abstaining from exercising the faculty [...] to

---

[25] This was the bitter opinion of one of the managing directors of Banca Commerciale Italiana, Francesco Cingano (see Francesco Cingano, 'La banca: mestiere e professione', *Bancaria* 30, no. 3 (1978): pp. 5–30).

[26] The exchange rate risk was initially underestimated by governor Carli when speculative attacks hit the lira after the British monetary authorities decided to let the sterling fluctuate (see AS BI, Banca d'Italia, Carli, prat. 72, file 7, sub-file 13, 'Note sent to the Hon. Giulio Andreotti, Prime Minister', 7 December 1972, pp. 7–8).

[27] Conte, 'L'azione della Banca d'Italia', 672–5; Alfredo Gigliobianco, *Via Nazionale. Banca d'Italia e classe dirigente* (Rome: Donzelli, 2006): pp. 279–98; Pierluigi Ciocca, 'L'istituzione e l'uomo: Guido Carli a via Nazionale', in *Guido Carli governatore della Banca d'Italia*, edited by Pierluigi Ciocca (Turin: Bollati Boringhieri, 2008): pp. XXVII–XXIX.

[28] On central banks vis-à-vis rising inflation in the 1970s see John Singleton, *Central Banking in the Twentieth Century* (Cambridge: Cambridge University Press, 2011): pp. 184–203.

[29] As recognized in May 1975: in 1974 'Uncertainty as regards anti-inflationary policy and the modification of the policy of bond price support heightened fears of a loss of purchasing power and of a drop in bond prices: capital market disequilibrium reached huge proportions. Despite rationing of new issues and compulsory portfolio investment by the banks, equilibrium could only be restored through a rise in interest rates' (Bank of Italy, *Report for the Year 1974. Governor's Concluding Remarks* (Rome: 1975): p. 18). None the less, administrative measures were not always effective in channelling savings towards investments via special credit institutions, as Carli himself observed in April 1975, just a few months before resigning (AS BI, Banca d'Italia, Direttorio Carli, folder 66, file 2, sub-file 5, 'Note sent to the Hon. Emilio Colombo, Minister of Treasury', 29 April 1975, pp. 2–3).

purchase government securities. Refusal would make it impossible for the Government to pay the salaries of the armed forces, of the judiciary and of civil servants, and the pensions of most citizens. It would give the appearance of being a monetary policy act; in substance it would be a seditious act, which would be followed by a paralysis of the public administration.'[30] Retrospectively, Carli made a bitter assessment of himself as a central banker: the Bank of Italy, by financing the Treasury and sectors chosen by the government, actually exerted an extraordinary role usually attributed to the fiscal system, to which Carli complied with because he interpreted this institutional function as a means to modernize the country and its economy.[31]

A Time to Change: Skyrocketing Debts and High Inflation

Thus, in the 1970s, whilst the overall public debt stock on GDP escalated from 30 per cent to 60 per cent,[32] manufacturing firms' indebtedness became hugely high also because of the lax monetary policy aimed at supporting firms' investments, but, actually, constituting a strong incentive to substitute equity capital with (increasing) external funds. As a result of their heightened financial fragility, industrial firms were more and more prone to failures and liquidity constraints, with growing risks for banking stability itself. As mentioned, a serious problem of allocative efficiency arose throughout the stagflation decade as the hampered the overall ability of banks to screen and monitor effectively borrowers and their investment projects.

As Graph 1 shows, from the mid-1960s to the early 1980s non-financial firms, as a whole, got their financing mostly from debt, massively relying on short-term banking credits. Looking at the capital structure of the Italian non-financial firms, the aggregate picture definitely presents a sour portrait. The non-financial firms' capital structure enormously deteriorated since the mid-1960s and in the middle of the ensuing decade their equity capital component was definitely at its worst, recovering to an acceptable equilibrium only after the mid-1980s. A pair of ratios can help assess their harshly worsening trend. The share to bonds ratio has a net decrease in the early 1960s, abruptly collapsing since 1962–63, whilst the equity

---

[30] Bank of Italy, *Report for the Year 1973. Governor's Concluding Remarks* (Rome: 1974): p. 32.
[31] Guido Carli, *Intervista sul capitalismo italiano*, an interview by Eugenio Scalfari (Rome-Bari: Laterza, 1977): pp. 41–4. See also Giangiacomo Nardozzi, 'Accumulazione di capitale e il punto di vista della Banca d'Italia', in *Scelte politiche e teorie economiche in Italia: 1945–1978, edited by* Giorgio Lunghini (Turin: Einaudi, 1981): pp. 109–23.
[32] This means that Carli's worries about public deficits from the mid-1960s up to his resigning as governor were quite motivated as the public debt stock in terms of gross domestic product actually doubled in less than 15 years (cf. Fabrizio Balassone, Maura Francese, and Angelo Pace, 'Public Debt and Economic Growth: Italy's First 150 Years', in *The Oxford Handbook of the Italian Economy Since Unification*, edited by Toniolo: pp. 516–32).

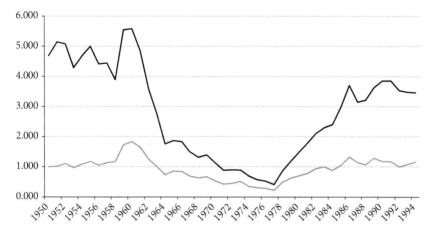

Figure 8.1 The funding sources of non-financial firms, 1950–94. Shares/bonds in navy; shares/debts in brick red (our calculations).

Source: Riccardo De Bonis, 'Ricchezza finanziaria e indebitamento dell'economia italiana dal 1950 al 2004', in I conti finanziari: la storia, i metodi, l'Italia, i confronti internazionali (Rome, 2006).

component, here measured as the ratio between shares and overall debts, constantly fell from that moment until the mid-1980s. Only in the second half of the 1980s non-financial firms recovered from a severe state of indebtedness, after a grave crisis became manifest in the late 1970s when monetary policy had to be reverted to tighter criteria.

Such negative tendencies were noticed by the Bank of Italy, preoccupied with the loss of competitiveness of the largest firms and experiencing difficulties in promoting further productivity improvements. These tendencies had obvious implications as to the overall firms' financial fragility,[33] but they had also a great macroeconomic relevance because the related expansion in monetary aggregates was clearly a sign of a resurgent fiscal dominance,[34] which could ultimately hamper

[33] Such firms' fragility was incompatible with rising wages, whose acceptability could be subordinated only to productivity growth, in turn attainable through investments in more advanced technologies. However, as Carli feared, this was not to be expected, whilst 'nationalizations', that is bail outs by IRI or ENI, were in fact much more likely (cf. AS BI, Banca d'Italia, Direttorio Carli, folder 65, file 1, sub-file 3, letter to Ugo La Malfa, 19 January 1970, p. 3). Carli complained with the Prime Minister Colombo that a 'surreptitious nationalization' was ongoing since 1966 and gearing up in the previous few years (AS BI, Banca d'Italia, Direttorio Carli, folder 65, file 3, sub-file 1, 'Note sent to the Hon. Emilio Colombo, Prime Minister', 13 January 1972, pp. 1–2). In effect, SOEs, within the sample of the top 200 manufacturing firms augmented from 23 in 1960 to 58 in 1981 (see Conte and Piluso, 'Finance and Structure of the State-Owned Enterprise in Italy. IRI from the Golden Age to the Fall', in *Reappraing State-Owned Enterprise: A Comparison of the UK and Italy*, edited by Franco Amatori, Robert Millward, and Pier Angelo Toninelli (New York-London: Routledge, 2011): pp. 126–7).

[34] The Bank of Italy was persuaded that the 'increase in the inherent parasitism of public expenditure' had been eroding 'the area of high productivity' of the Italian economy (Bank of Italy, *Report for the Year 1974. Governor's Concluding Remarks*, p. 22). Cf. Michele Fratianni and Franco Spinelli, 'Fiscal Dominance and Money Growth in Italy: The Long Record', *Explorations in Economic History* 38, no. 2 (2001): pp. 252–72; Roberto Ricciuti, 'The Quest for a Fiscal Rule: Italy, 1861–1998', *Cliometrica* 2, no. 3 (2008): pp. 259–78.

the ability of Italy to take actively part in the current European integration process as it was outlined after the Werner Plan.[35]

The Turnaround: A Different Central Bank

In the mid-1970s the existent financial regulation appeared undoubtedly outdated or, at best, inconsistent with the new domestic and international context. To make it work the Bank of Italy had to introduce a string of administrative constraints which, in the end, produced distortions in resource allocation, much aggravated by widespread soft loans to foster investments in the South and the weaker sectors. Besides, the loose credit policy centred on recurrent liquidity injections collided with macroeconomic targets: a low inflation and a balance of payments in equilibrium. The model of central bank under governor Carli was unfit to manage effectively a sum of inflationary and incoherent requests from a modernizing society (calling for a more generous welfare state),[36] further productivity improvements associated to continuity of capital formation and macroeconomic targets. During the decade prior to 1975, thus, the Bank of Italy had to cumulate such a contradictory lot of objectives and engagements, eventually making governor Carli feel a 'profound melancholy as a central banker'.[37]

The fall of the Bretton Woods system, from August 1971 onwards, forced the Bank of Italy at least to endeavour to adopt consistent monetary policies to avert resource misallocation and convergence policies coherent with the first projects of a European economic and monetary integration.[38] The leaving of the Italian

[35] Even though the Werner Plan, proposed in October 1971, failed, the gradual monetary integration of the EEC appeared as an emerging relevant area for monetary policy, as Carli admitted in January 1972, commenting on the currency realignment attained with the Washington Agreement reached by the Group of Ten (G10) and ratified on 18 December 1971. 'The destructive effects [of floating exchange rates] – he wrote to the Prime Minister – on the unification of the European economies can be avoided only by accelerating the economic and monetary integration [...]. Yet, the economic and monetary unification requires the adoption of common economic policies, not just monetary policies, by the member countries' (AS BI, Banca d'Italia, Direttorio Carli, folder 65, file 3, sub-file 1, 'Note sent to the Hon. Emilio Colombo, Prime Minister', 13 January 1972, p. 11).

[36] As declared on 31 May 1974: 'The sum of the demands made by the social classes on the national product tends to exceed the dimensions of that product: inflation has become the means whereby the sum of demands is brought within those dimensions. Inflation renders all aspirations for income distribution compatible with the real flow of resources' (Bank of Italy, *Report for the Year 1973. Governor's Concluding Remarks*, p. 3).

[37] Carli, *Intervista sul capitalismo*, p. 52. Privately, Carli expressed his gloomy appraisal of the state of the Italian economy and its prospects at least since 1971: 'The year 1971 could be defined as a triumphal year for SOEs. [...]. Could such a success be attributed to the cleverness of SOEs' management? Although there are undeniably cases of clever managers, the real causes of the advance of SOEs are others. The State ask them to invest just for investing regardless of their profitability' (AS BI, Banca d'Italia, Direttorio Carli, folder 65, file 3, sub-file 1, 'Note sent to the Hon. Emilio Colombo, Prime Minister', 13 January 1972, p. 2).

[38] Emmanuel Apel, *European Monetary Integration: 1958–2002* (London and New York: Routledge, 1998): pp. 31–45; Emmanuel Mourlon-Druol, *A Europe Made of Money. The Emergence of the European Monetary System* (Ithaca: Cornell University Press, 2012): pp. 246–8.

lira from the European monetary snake in February 1973 accentuated the weight of external pressures on domestic monetary and credit choices. In the mid-1970s the cumulative effects of inflation-fuelling investments, scarcely conducive to productivity growth, negatively affected the Italian balance of payments making clear that the declining firms' competitiveness was irreconcilable with the emerging external constraints connected with the post-Bretton Woods international monetary system. The central bank model that governor Carli ought to implement in his last years in office was not feasible any more, monetary policy in Italy was at a standstill. The Italian central bank and its monetary policies had to be redefined to manage aggregates more rigorously, in accordance with the uncertain international context, so as to avoid that 'Italy [could] break loose from its European moorings'.[39]

A first proposal to break the deadlock between competing targets was advanced by Carli himself in May 1975 and entailed an implicit subversion of the criteria underpinning the Banking Law as a way to undertake clear economic priorities. Carli proposed to transform the mass of debts cumulated in the banks' portfolios, particularly those representing soft loans, in shares to be sold to the public, directly or through undefined financial vehicles. In a properly working market context, according to governor Carli, 'public and private enterprises should be free to respond to market pointers; managements should be judged according to the economic results achieved'.[40]

In August 1975 Carli resigned and Paolo Baffi stepped in as the new governor.[41] Baffi adopted a radically different approach to monetary and credit policy marking a cleavage in the concept of central banking in Italy.[42] In May 1976 Baffi made it clear by counterposing 'Carli's propensity to exercise his talents in situations abounding in difficulties' against his own different vision of how a central bank had to act as to the relationships between monetary policy and credit policy. 'There is, to my mind – Baffi declared –, something profoundly unsatisfying in

---

[39] As Carli had to accept when explaining the floating of the lira of February 1973: 'our currency was suddenly affected by shortcomings in international and domestic behaviour, the latter cutting across every social group and fostered by the policies carried out over past years. As a result, the process of integrating our economy in the Community has been slowed' (Bank of Italy, *Report for the Year 1972. Governor's Concluding Remarks* (Rome: 1973): p. 18).

[40] Bank of Italy, *Report for the Year 1974. Governor's Concluding Remarks*, p. 23. The transformation of loans in shares is not present in the English version of the governor's *Concluding Remarks* printed by the Bank, but only in the Italian version (cf. Bank of Italy, *Considerazioni finali* (Rome: 1975): pp. 36–7). Carli's conversion proposal was positively commented by Tancredi Bianchi, 'Su talune possibili modificazioni dell'attività bancaria', *Banche e banchieri* 2, no. 8 (1975): pp. 479–80.

[41] For a biographical profile of Baffi see Gigliobianco, *Via Nazionale*, pp. 307–34.

[42] Baffi was not a great admirer of Carli. For instance, in 1986, in a private letter to Cingano, Baffi acidly observed: 'I have been negatively impressed by my predecessor's intervention, as always eager to embrace new ideas, for its form, its inaccuracy as to historical references, the lack of attention to the internal consistency' (AS BI, Banca d'Italia, Carte Baffi, Governatore Onorario, folder 12, file 25, letter to Francesco Cingano, 28 November 1986). Such a temperamental distance was confirmed by Carli himself in his memoirs (cf. Guido Carli, *Cinquant'anni di vita italiana*, with Paolo Peluffo (Rome-Bari: Laterza, 1993), p. 354).

having to direct central bank action in such a way that it suffocates a system that possesses its own valid parameters and mechanisms; in having to constrain the volume of credit potentially expressed by the flow of monetary base because it is not possible to regulate that flow; in having to channel the flow of credit because, in the absence of adequate budget and incomes policies, the free decisions of market operators are distorted by inflationary or exchange rate expectations. This is unsatisfying not only from the point of view of logic but also because the effects tend to be ephemeral since the mobility of credit flows, profit considerations and the adaptability of market operators in the long run bring the flows back into line with basic economic conditions.'[43]

Although Baffi reframed the role of central banker as a matter of adoption of non-inflationary monetary policy and rejection of administrative controls over credit intermediation, times for a profound change were ripe. The Bank of Italy, as Baffi made soon clear, had to tackle macroeconomic instability ('the reciprocal influence between exchange rates and domestic prices is a factor of instability') and unsustainable indebtedness levels of firms, which in turn affected the banks' solvability itself.[44]

Macroeconomic Instability and a Call for Efficiency-Boosting Reforms

Thus, a completely different approach took place amongst central monetary authorities, even though the current regulatory architecture was not considered per se as the ultimate cause of allocative inefficiency. None the less, the accommodating monetary policy deployed to back the weakening bond market since the mid-1960s had contributed to produce alterations within the capital structure of non-financial firms. Moreover, as Baffi noticed, the 'stop and go' monetary policy pursued since the early 1970s was not good enough to counter inflationary impulses and currency devaluation. Thus, macroeconomic instability appeared as a component of cumulating inefficiencies, which hampered both firms' competitiveness and the balance-of-payments equilibrium. As standard counter-cyclical policies proved to be ever more ineffective to re-establish economic growth amongst industrialized economies, in Italy the juncture was even harder and, in a way, at a crossroads, for relatively restrictive policies further hindered an already drifting economy. In this line, under the aegis of Baffi, the Bank of Italy promoted

---

[43]   Bank of Italy, *Report for the Year 1975. Concluding Remarks* (Rome: 1976), p. 8.

[44]   As the governor added by discussing the 'circular' process of currency depreciation and inflation: 'This risk can be avoided by refusing to finance the increase in costs and prices, i.e. by pursuing a restrictive monetary and credit policy; but an ever shorter "stop-go" cycle [that had characterized Carli's policy] has negative repercussions on the long-term growth rate' (Bank of Italy, *Report for the Year 1975. Concluding Remarks*, p. 10).

the idea that market principles were to be adopted as better allocative mechanisms by removing administrative controls that prevented a return to macroeconomic stability.[45] The gloomy picture drawn by Baffi required a bold and, most of all, consistent course of action. Indeed, the Bank of Italy was probably the only credible institutional actor able to react and revert the Italian economy to stability and growth.[46]

The new course was centred on two related main objectives, promoting macroeconomic stability and restructuring industrial firms as a means to foster investments, although it did not necessarily imply a revision of the regulatory architecture by entirely dismantling the mass of administrative controls and constraints built up in the 1960s and early 1970s.[47] To restrain inflationary tendencies and restore market allocative mechanisms, for both the private and public sector, Baffi had, nevertheless, to intervene on the vast array of administrative controls previously adopted as a method to funnel funds to investments. Even though Baffi was not in condition to win his war, because of the steady increasing volume of public spending—and its associated impact on monetary aggregates—and the resulting currency crisis of 1976, during his four years as governor the Bank of Italy redefined basic criteria of allocative mechanisms. A specific working style characterized Baffi's approach as governor, to a certain extent in tune with Carli's modernization of the Bank's organization, services, and personnel, particularly by developing its research activities and recruiting promising economists.[48] Along these lines of action, Baffi entrusted his director general (and successor in 1979), Carlo Azeglio Ciampi, with the engaging task to coordinate the Bank's most qualified economists in devising economic programmes and plans to sort Italy out of the severe state of macroeconomic instability and allocative inefficiency.[49]

In the late 1970s and early 1980s, in official and internal documents as well, the Bank of Italy did not express a negative evaluation of the current financial regulation, if not for the underdevelopment of the stock market and the lack of competition that made it too rigid and therefore inefficient. Yet, the recovery of efficiency by the banking system, in its components, required a preliminary reduction of the large amount of credits given, directly or indirectly, to firms whose financial structure appeared seriously deteriorated. None the less, as it was

---

[45] Conte, 'L'azione della Banca d'Italia', pp. 675–7.
[46] As Beniamino Andreatta, an influent economist, pointed out in November 1975 the present standstill, in the end, was to be ascribed to the very nature of the institutional economic model of the country (cf. Beniamino Andreatta, 'Il banchiere riluttante', *Sole 24 Ore*, 18 November 1975).
[47] To this regard a comparison could be drawn with the French case. France first removed administrative controls, for instance, regarding branch openings by banks since 1966–67 (cf. Laure Quennouëlle-Core, 'Les réformes bancaires et financières', pp. 96–9). See also Eric Monnet, *Controlling Credit. Central Banking and Planned Economy in Postwar France, 1948–1973* (Cambridge: Cambridge University Press, 2018): pp. 88–91.
[48] Gigliobianco, *Via Nazionale*, pp. 292–7.
[49] Conte, 'L'azione della Banca d'Italia', pp. 680–2.

quite clear that the already deep-in-debt Italian firms badly needed further external funds to regain competitiveness and profitability, the Bank of Italy was well aware that their financial reorganization constituted a prerequisite for getting further capital from savers, investors, and shareholders. In other terms, the ultimate solvability (and prospect efficiency) of intermediaries and the deterioration of the firms' financial structure were two sides of the same coin and, even though some economists called for an overall reform of the financial system, the Bank of Italy opted for intervening first on the latter one.[50] To this end, Baffi encouraged collaboration and pieces of advice by bankers and economists alike. Between autumn 1975 and late 1976 Baffi received a series of analyses and notes from the most prominent bankers. In October 1975 Enrico Cuccia, the managing director of Mediobanca, sent to Baffi a long note on the 'problem' of the financial structure of large firms operating in manufacturing sectors and services. Cuccia analysed the current deterioration of the capital structure of the largest firms (a sample of 703 enterprises, representing 79% of the aggregate turnover), whose ability to further obtain money had been progressively 'thinning' whilst the country's productive structure needed investments to positively realign productivity to recent and notable increases in wages. An international comparison with enterprises of similar size and sectors hinted that Italian firms needed a remarkable amount of capital to achieve a suitable industrial restructuring. To this purpose, Cuccia proposed a public-private mechanism of financing selected firms aptly aimed at encouraging responsible nucleuses of controlling shareholders to take serious engagements in such restructuring operations.[51] Even the Bank of Italy's economists commenced to reflect on feasible ways to solve the astonishingly level of undercapitalization induced by a widespread use of soft loans and public funds, often easily available at very low interest rates.[52] The starting point was a note by the economist Beniamino Andreatta, who expressed doubts on merely financial engineering solutions and advocated a series of measures to boost firms' recapitalization as a precondition to get higher productivity levels in the medium term: (1) a reduction in taxation for industrial restructuring and investments; (2) measures to develop the stock market through the support of the banks; (3) encouragements to consortium initiatives to promote larger-sized industrial organizations; (4) and, finally, a

---

[50] Some economists expressed, albeit *en passant*, a different opinion, maintaining that the priority was a reorganization of the whole capital market so that firms could have a better access to equity capital vis-à-vis a mass of debts actually composed by false short-term credits administered by commercial banks (cf. Tancredi Bianchi, 'Il capitale delle imprese', *Corriere della sera*, 3 October 1975).

[51] Cf. AS BI, Banca d'Italia, Carte Baffi, Monte Oppio, folder 62, file 1, letter and a 9-pages note sent by Enrico Cuccia, 1 October 1975 (untitled 'Note', pp. 4, 6–9).

[52] By and large along the same line of reasoning, within the same folder, a report from inside the Bank specified that firms' undercapitalization was largely due to soft loans that had permitted investments with very low levels of equity capital (cf. Bank of Italy, Vigilanza sulle aziende di credito, Sezione credito speciale, 'Appunto per il Signor Governatore e il Signor Direttore Generale. Interventi per la ristrutturazione finanziaria delle imprese', probably October 1975, p. 4).

sort of tentative recombination of the currently fragmented bank functions through agreements and coordination.[53] The Bank's economic research department put some of his best men at work and, in less than a fortnight, Paolo Savona and Tommaso Padoa-Schioppa produced two reports on Andreatta's proposals. In the first report Savona and Padoa-Schioppa were rather critical about the fiscal measures concerning the lowering of interest rates as proposed by Andreatta, but they were adamantly in favour of market mechanisms in interest fixing, whilst in the second one Savona calculated with an econometric model the effects of the high leverage on the investment rate observing that high levels of indebtedness (and a parallel low profitability) exerted a restrain on actual investments, thus hampering any prospect of productivity growth. Yet, it was not entirely clear whether Savona supported the consortium-based means to promote the growth of the stock market.[54]

In October 1976 Francesco Cingano, managing director at Banca Commerciale, sent to Baffi a detailed report written by the economic department of his bank. It addressed the matter, as expected, by the financial side, stressing the importance of giving back to bankers substantial margins of freedom to restore an adequate autonomy of evaluation of their borrowers' creditworthiness. He advocated the removal of all the institutional factors distorting the resource allocation by the financial system, particularly averting the double intermediation.[55] In the following year some other proposals were put forward by other independent economists, such as Francesco Cesarini and Mario Monti, all of them aimed at reducing administrative constraints, at the same time fostering a progressive shift from debts to the equity component within the capital structure of firms. The Bank of Italy took due notice and scrupulously analysed these reports and proposals. In June 1977 Tommaso Padoa-Schioppa, then at the Bank's economic research department, reviewed all the recent proposals on the so-called *planchers*, such as credit ceilings and compulsory reserves, which had been provoking significant distortions in resource allocation, making clear that a removal of the outdated array of administrative constraints was, in the end, a policy decision.[56]

---

[53] AS BI, Banca d'Italia, Carte Baffi, Monte Oppio, folder 62, file 1, Beniamino Andreatta, 'Appunti sui problemi della ristrutturazione finanziaria delle imprese industriali', Rome, 3 October 1975. It is worth observing that this note is overtly much critical towards the disruption of the unity of banking functions associated with the ban of universal banking in Italy as contained in the Banking Laws of 1936 (p. 3).

[54] AS BI, Banca d'Italia, Carte Baffi, Monte Oppio, folder 62, file 1, Bank of Italy, Servizio studi, 'Appunto per il Governatore. Rimunerazione della riserva obbligatoria e tassi bancari', 9 October 1975, signed by Paolo Savona and Tommaso Padoa-Schioppa; Bank of Italy, Servizio studi, Paolo Savona, 'Appunto per il Governatore. Interventi a sostegno dei capitali di rischio', October 1975.

[55] AS BI, Banca d'Italia, Carte Baffi, Governatore Onorario, folder 12, file 25, 'Appunto per il Governatore della Banca d'Italia. Possibili interventi sul sistema bancario', Milan, 25 October 1976, Appendix, pp. 2–3.

[56] AS BI, Banca d'Italia, Carte Baffi, Monte Oppio, folder 62, file 1, Bank of Italy, Servizio studi, Ufficio Mercato Monetario, Tommaso Padoa-Schioppa, '*Planchers* progressivi e vincolo di portafoglio', Rome, 28 June 1977, p. 10. As of May 1978, considering 'credit restrictions', governor Baffi appeared

Actually, from 1977 the Bank of Italy commenced to reduce gradually the measure and the impact that credit restrictions had on commercial banks' assets. It was undoubtedly a partial and soft slackening of the enormous edifice of administrative constraints introduced by Carli, but the Bank's direction appeared now rather distinctly different from the previous approach to liquidity management. This turning point was made even clearer when Baffi specified, on 31 May 1978, that 'the credit restrictions [...] entail ["costs"] in the form of a reduction in market efficiency and an increase in the constraints under which the monetary authorities operate'.[57]

In fact, since late 1977, these constraints on monetary authorities operations were not consistent any more with the objectives that were being imposed by major changes in international markets and in the European community's policy regarding its monetary integration. Unbridled inflation and floating exchange rates had been soliciting a different approach to currency instability and its related difficulties after the failure of the Werner Plan to gain sufficient consensus. The opening of a new phase of European monetary integration from mid-1977, as delineated under the impulse of Roy Jenkins in his quality of president of the European Commission and strongly sponsored by the German chancellor Helmut Schmidt and the French president Valéry Giscard d'Estaing,[58] forced Italy to subordinate her monetary policy to a programme of macroeconomic stabilization more than 'easing the restrictions and adjusting financial flows'.[59] The importance of Europe and its economic and monetary integration drastically re-orientated the central monetary authorities and their choice towards curbing inflation and rebalance the external deficits. As the governor pointed out before the Senate in October 1978, the Bank of Italy had the priority to take control again of monetary aggregates in an anti-inflationary key, even if a tightening policy could have

---

clearly in between noticing 'the costs they entail in the form of a reduction in market efficiency and an increase in the constraints under which the monetary authorities operate' (Bank of Italy, *Report for the Year 1977. Concluding Remarks* (Rome: 1978): p. 34).

[57] Bank of Italy, *Report for the Year 1977. Concluding Remarks* (Rome: 1978): p. 34. In a way, Baffi anticipated a similar move actually made by French authorities, particurlarly Jacques Delors, in 1984 with a new banking law (see Laure Quennouëlle-Core, 'Les réformes financières de 1982 à 1985: un grand saut liberal?', *Vingtième siècle. Revue d'histoire* 138, no. 2 (2018): pp. 67–70). Olivier Feiertag highlights a similar relationship between public debt and banking reforms as observable in the Italian case (cf. Olivier Feiertag, 'Finances publiques, "mur d'argent" et génèse de la liberalisation financière en France de 1981 à 1984', in *François Mitterand, les années du changement, 1981–1984*, edited by Serge Bernstein and Pierre Milza (Paris: Perrin, 2001): pp. 431–55). It is possibly worth noting that between 1979 and 1983, Padoa-Schioppa closely cooperated with Jacques Delors at the European Commission, DGII.

[58] Cf. Peter Ludlow, *The Making of the European Monetary System* (London: Butterworth Scientific, 1982): pp. 37–87; Amaury de Saint Périer, *La France, l'Allemagne et l'Europe monétaire de 1974 à 1981: la perseverance persévérance récompensée* (Paris: Presses de Sciences Po, 2013); N. Piers Ludlow, *Roy Jenkins and the European Commission Presidency, 1976–1980: At the Heart of Europe* (London: Palgrave Macmillan, 2016); N. Piers Ludlow, 'Roy Jenkins and the Importance of Top-Level Politics', in *Architects of the Euro. Intellectuals in the Making of the European Monetary Union*, edited by Kenneth Dyson and Ivo Maes (New York: Oxford University Press, 2016): pp. 117–37.

[59] Bank of Italy, *Report for the Year 1977. Concluding Remarks* (Rome: 1978): p. 28.

undesired effects of credit rationing. In this context, the Bank's priority shifted from abundant liquidity as a means to promote investments to domestic price— and the external exchange rate—stability as the cornerstone of the long-term capital formation.[60]

The Soft Deregulation: Industrial Restructuring and the European Monetary System

In 1978 the Bank of Italy entered into the process of wider policymaking cooperating with the Treasury in defining a programme of monetary stabilization and economic recovery within the European framework which constituted a long-term strategy influencing not only monetary policies but financial regulation as well. Even before succeeding to Baffi in 1979, around summer 1978 Ciampi assumed the lead in top-level policy-making coordinating a group of high-flying economists, amongst whom Padoa-Schioppa would have played a fundamental role in the following decade.[61] In June 1978, believing that Italy had to enter into the European Monetary System in discussion, Ciampi set in motion a soft scheme in persuasion towards the Minister of the Treasury, Filippo Maria Pandolfi, in the wake of their coming back from the Luxemburg ECOFIN meeting. The task to argue in favour of the 'European option' for the weak Italian economy was entrusted to Rainer Masera, the Oxford-trained chief economist of the Bank's research department. Masera was quite clear as to the necessity to free the Italian economy from inflation and stagnation depending on the public sector borrowing requirements and the high cost of labour. In particular, the growing public debt stock required financing through monetization, conducive to high inflation, or the financial market altering the very structure of interest rates severely damaging the private sector investments. The weakness of the economy, high inflation and currency frailties, had the potential to put at risk democracy itself. The recovery of the Italian economy from high inflation and weak growth, accompanied by mounting unemployment levels, was to be pursued within the European community by defining convincing stabilization programmes 'in a global perspective' towards the next-decade objectives of economic and monetary integration.[62]

---

[60] AS BI, Banca d'Italia, Carte Baffi, Monte Oppio, folder 93, file 2, sub-file 3, Servizio studi, 'Materiale per l'intervento del Governatore al Senato', 23 October 1978, pp. 8 and 17. Of course, in such a framework, the main point was cutting the public sector demand for funds and realigning interest rates so to rebalance the overall supply of credit in favour of the private sector.

[61] Fabio Masini, 'Tommaso Padoa-Schioppa: EMU as the Anchor Stone for Building a Federal Europe', in *Architects of the Euro*, edited by Dyson and Maes, pp. 193–211.

[62] AS BI, Direttorio Ciampi, folder 204, file 1, sub-file 32, letter from Ciampi to Pandolfi, Rome, 27 June 1978, and Rainer Masera, 'La opzione europea come momento della sfida italiana', 23 June 1978. The note by Masera preceded the Bremen Council of July 1978, where Italy was represented by Pandolfi, Baffi, Ciampi, Masera himself and Renato Ruggiero from the Ministry of Foreign Affairs (cf. Ludlow, *The Making of the European Monetary System*, pp. 147–8).

The note by Masera on the 'European option' was accompanied by two other notes on firms' recapitalization, the credit system and the recovery from inflation, one of them by Padoa-Schioppa, that completed the strategy sketched out by the Bank of Italy and supported by Pandolfi at the Treasury.[63] The most demanding and encompassing document to support the whole strategy was written by Padoa-Schioppa and adopted by the government as 'Piano Pandolfi' after the Bremen Council, in July 1978. The 'Pandolfi Plan'—formally presented as 'Una proposta per lo sviluppo, una scelta per l'Europa'—made clear that economic stabilization and development were linked to the ability of Italy to comply with the requirements attached to her entering, and staying, into the European Monetary System.[64] The Plan advocated a consistent behaviour over time to stabilize prices and exchange rates, essentially based on intervention on public finance and the cost of labour, as a precondition to get a resurgence in increases in investments and productivity again. As to the financial system the rationale was delineated along the macroeconomic lines motivating the entire analysis and proposal. As Italy had been more and more dependent on a string of financial transfers commanded by the State as the main financial intermediary, allocative efficiency could be resumed, in the end, only by breaking the financial institutions free from the public finance 'coercive' grip.[65]

In the second half of 1978, throughout the negotiations to take part into the European Monetary System, at the Bank of Italy were considered measures to re-establish more balanced capital structure for the enterprises. The issue called for an action meant, on the one hand, to develop the capital market as an alternative channel for external funds and, on the other hand, to promote efficiency improvements within the banking system itself through competition and cost cutting. Such an approach represented a different line of intervention compared with the typical 'public interest' criterion usually adopted in the previous decades.[66] The new market approach was meant to foster efficiency amongst

[63] AS BI, Direttorio Ciampi, folder 204, file 1, sub-file 30 and 31, 'Sistema creditizio e ricapitalizzazione delle imprese', 20 June 1978, and Tommaso Padoa-Schioppa, 'Il "rientro" dall'inflazione e gli indicatori monetari e creditizi', 26 June 1978.

[64] AS BI, Direttorio Ciampi, folder 204, file 1, sub-file Tommaso Padoa-Schioppa, 'Un confronto tra due decenni', note for Minister Pandolfi, 22 July 1978, and 'Una proposta per lo sviluppo, una scelta per l'Europa', 31 August 1978. This point is rather puzzling, as governor Baffi was sceptical about Italy entering the EMS, for he considered the country's economy unprepared. Cf. Peter Ludlow, *The Making of the European Monetary System*, pp. 147–50; Mourlon-Druol, *A Europe Made of Money*, p. 209; Mourlon-Druol, 'A New Monetary System in a Changing Polity. Central Banks, the EEC and the Creation of the European Monetary System', in *Les Banque Centrales et l'État-Nation*, edited by Olivier Feiertag and Michel Margairaz (Paris: Presses de Sciences Po, 2016): pp. 568–9.

[65] AS BI, Direttorio Ciampi, folder 204, file 1, 'Una proposta per lo sviluppo, una scelta per l'Europa', paragraph 40. On a critical history of the so-called 'vincolo esterno' (external tie), and its political implications, see Kenneth Dyson and Kevin Featherstone, *The Road to Maastricht: Negotiating Economic and Monetary Union* (Oxford: Oxford University Press, 1999), pp. 455–80; Kevin Featherstone, 'The Political Dynamics of the Vincolo Esterno: the Emergence of EMU and the Challenge to the European Social Model', *Queen's Papers on Europeanisation*, no. 6, 2001.

[66] AS BI, Direttorio Ciampi, folder 205, file 1, sub-file 21, 'I problemi finanziari delle imprese', 20 December 1978, pp. 3–6.

intermediaries through competition and, after removing credit ceilings in June 1982, to favour a re-functionalization of special credit institutions, together with the development of the stock market.[67] The nature of banks as private profit-making enterprises, positively overcoming the concept of 'public interest', was eventually enshrined in a law in 1985, a presidential decree, that recognized the first European Directive of 1977.[68]

As expected, the EMS introduced further external constraints to the Italian monetary policy and required, at least, a lessening of the fiscal dominance prevailing in the 1970s.[69] The Bank of Italy, under governor Ciampi, succeeded in removing obligations towards the persistent public sector borrowing requirements in 1981 by 'divorcing' from the Treasury. The anti-inflationary policies, in the wake of the Volcker move of October 1979, entailed a robust cutting in public and deficit spending coupled with more efficient allocative market mechanism.[70] The autonomy of the central bank from the Treasury as a prerequisite to get inflation under control by ending public-sector deficit monetization was devised, at last, in March 1981, when the lira was under speculative attacks in currency markets.[71] As agreed, Ciampi wrote to Andreatta at the Treasury confirming that the Bank of Italy would not subscribe any more public securities in contrast with the objectives of its monetary policy.[72]

The soft financial deregulation occurring throughout the 1980s, in substance, had a monetary-led nature, as the gradual liberalization of intermediaries was conceived to serve the return of Italy to macroeconomic stability by curbing the allocative distortions implicit in the prevailing fiscal dominance and adjusting to the emerging monetary paradigm after the deflationary Volcker's move. However, such a soft regulation did not necessarily imply an overall change in the institutional architecture defined in the mid-1930s. The soft deregulation was

[67] Bank of Italy, *Report for the Year 1982. The Governor's Concluding Remarks* (Rome: 1983): p. 19.

[68] In fact, in 1981 the Treasury first 'issued directives on publicly-owned banks that confirmed their freedom from external influence and their nature as enterprises exposed to competition' (Bank of Italy, *Report for the Year 1985. The Governor's Concluding Remarks* (Rome: 1986): p. 21).

[69] See Francesco Giavazzi and Marco Pagano, 'The Advantage of Tying One's Hands: EMS Discipline and Central Bank Credibility', *European Economic Review* 32, no. 5 (1988), pp. 1055–82.

[70] As observed by Ciampi himself in AS BI, Direttorio Ciampi, folder 69, file 1, letter to Beniamino Andreatta, Minister of the Treasury, Rome, 15 January 1981. None the less, as the EEC central bankers conceded in July 1982, a mix of monetary policies was due to avoid an abrupt surge in social unrest related to a too severe reduction in public spending (AS BI, Direttorio Ciampi, folder 266, file 1, sub-file 8, 'Procès verbal de la 168e séance du Comité des Gouverneurs des Banques Centrales des Etats membres de la Communeauté Européenne', Basel, 12 July 1982).

[71] AS BI, Direttorio Ciampi, folder 69, file 1, letters from Ciampi to Beniamino Andreatta, Minister of the Treasury, Rome, 6 March 1981 and 22 March 1981.

[72] Ciampi's letter contained just ten lines. Cf. AS BI, Direttorio Ciampi, folder 69, file 1, letter from Ciampi to Beniamino Andreatta, Minister of the Treasury, Rome, 24 June 1981. Cf. G.A. Epstein and J.B. Schor, 'The Divorce of the Banca d'Italia and the Italian Treasury: A Case Study of Central Bank Independence', *Harvard Institute of Economic Research Discussion Papers*, no. 1269, (1986); Tommaso Padoa-Schioppa, 'Reshaping Monetary Policy', in *Macroeconomics and Finance. Essays in Honor of Franco Modigliani*, edited by Rudiger Dornbusch, Stanley Fischer, and John Bossons (Cambridge, MA: MIT Press, 1987), pp. 265–86.

achieved by the central monetary authorities through gradual interventions, although all of them heading towards the liberalization of financial institutions, more than by lawmakers through an all-encompassing law.[73] This strategy might explain the pivotal role exerted by the Bank of Italy, under governor Ciampi, during the entire decade. As the governor stated in May 1988, the Bank had been creating 'the conditions that would permit the money and financial markets to become broader, more diversified and more efficient. New categories of intermediaries have developed. Competition has intensified.'[74]

The soft deregulation undertaken by the Bank of Italy under governors Baffi and Ciampi, as a broader strategy to help the Italian economy to adjust to major instability factors and resume productivity growth, was centred upon financial market development and banking liberalization. To the former end, in 1984 the Bank of Italy promoted the creation of the Mercato dei Titoli di Stato (MTS), the secondary market specialized in government securities,[75] and in 1985 lawmakers reformed the existent financial authority, the Commissione nazionale per le società e la borsa (Consob) established in 1974, in order to favour the stock market growth. These reforms actually produced a capitalization increase of the stock market, whose listed companies doubled in a few years, from 0.09 per cent of GDP in 1980 to 0.14 per cent of GDP in 1990.[76] On the other hand, the banking sector liberalization actions attenuated the credit disintermediation experienced in the 1970s and early 1980s. The hitherto gradual banking sector liberalization accelerated in the mid-1980s as a consequence of the European integration process. In fact, from 1985 financial deregulation, as promoted by the Bank of Italy, was mainly meant to comply with the European regulatory framework and the programme of progressive liberalization of capital movements. The three main issues were represented by what a bank should be (a profit-making firm or an institution subject to the public interest), which business model to adopt in banking activities (universal banking or banking specialization according to assets and liabilities maturity) and whether public financial institutions should be privatized. The first point was successfully defined with the long-due adoption of

---

[73] Pierluigi Ciocca, *Banca, finanza, mercato. Bilancio di un decennio e nuove prospettive* (Turin: Einaudi, 1991).

[74] Ciampi added a list of specific actions conducted by the Bank: 'the shift from a system of supervision based primarily on the authorization of individual operations to one relying principally on general rules, the easing of restrictions on operations and the segmentation of the institutional categories of intermediary, the reaffirmation of the entrepreneurial concept of banking in contrast with others that curtailed banks' autonomy, the introduction of forms of supervision on a consolidated basis, the application of new regulations for bank branches, the permission for public banks to raise private capital, and the indication of the diversified financial group as the preferred form of organization for credit activities' (Bank of Italy, *Report for the Year 1987. The Governor's Concluding Remarks* (Rome: 1988), pp. 27–8).

[75] Franco Passacantando, 'Building an Institutional Framework for Monetary Stability: The Case of Italy (1979–1994)', *BNL Quarterly Review* 49, no. 196 (1996), pp. 83–132.

[76] Giangiacomo Nardozzi and Giandomenico Piluso, *Il sistema finanziario e la borsa* (Rome-Bari: Laterza, 2010), p. 4, Tab. 1.

the first European Directive on banking activities by the Parliament in 1985, much and wholeheartedly sponsored by the central bank as being the more tuned to the market allocative principles adopted by governor Baffi from 1976 onwards. The second one, instead, was to a certain extent a much more debated point, as the Bank of Italy maintained a particular conviction that functional specialization of intermediaries was to be preferred, at least up to 1986.[77] Yet, as it became more and more evident since 1982,[78] the international regulatory framework endorsed by the Basel Committee on Banking Regulations and Supervisory Practices had been gaining momentum.[79] The international dimension of the evolving regulatory standard and practices, underpinned by the increasing internationalization of capital markets, motivated a different approach to regulation and banking business models, as it emerged with the adoption of the White Paper principles by the European Council in 1985. As a result, the Bank of Italy opted for a partial de-specialization of the intermediaries by sponsoring a 'middle-range' approach to the ongoing tendency to 'universality' recognizable within the European Community.[80] In 1986 the Bank, quite reluctant to renounce to the principles enshrined in the Banking Law of 1936, successfully steered the Italian lawmaker towards the 'banking conglomerate', or group, solution which allowed to preserve some elements of the former institutional framework based on specialization within the universal banking model adopted by the European Community.[81]

Along the same lines, as defined by the European Single Act of 1986, in early 1988 the Bank of Italy steered the debate, and Treasury choices, regarding privatizations in the banking sector, where the public component accounted for around 80 per cent up to then. As the Bank directors motivated when trying to

---

[77] To this regard the Bank of Italy, at least initially, did not unreservedly take the syllogism that the European single market should entail financial deregulation and, thus, universal banking (cf. AS BI, Direttorio Padoa-Schioppa, folder 131, file 4, Note on 'credito fondiario', i.e. bulding society, 2 December 1986).

[78] In 1982 a report drafted by Mario Monti, Francesco Cesarini, and Carlo Scognamiglio suggested the adoption of universal banking and an increase of the equity component in the firms' capital structure. See Ministero del Tesoro, *Il sistema finanziario e creditizio italiano* (Rome: 1982).

[79] Charles A. E. Goodhart, *The Basel Committee on Banking Supervision: A History of the Early Years, 1974–1997* (Cambridge: Cambridge University Press, 2011); Alexis Frédéric Drach, 'Basel Banking Supervisors and the Construction of an International Standard-Setter Institution', in *Financial Elites and European Banking*, edited by Youssef Cassis and Giuseppe Telesca, pp. 220–4. See also AS BI, Direttorio Ciampi, folder 266, file 1, sub-file 4, letter from Michael Dealtry on behalf of Peter Cooke, chairman of the Committee, to Carlo A. Ciampi, Basel, 15 September 1982, and the attached 'Report to the Governors on the supervisory treatment of rescheduled, and other problems, international loans', 25 June 1982.

[80] AS BI, Direttorio Padoa-Schioppa, folder 132, file 1, Tommaso Padoa-Schioppa, Notes on 'Financial Conglomerates' written for the European Commission's Banking Advisory Committee, May 1987.

[81] Dermine, 'Banking in Europe: Past, Present and Future', pp. 34–5. See also Rainer S. Masera, *Intermediari, mercati e finanza d'impresa. Prospettive dell'integrazione finanziaria in Europa e della globalizzazione* (Rome-Bari: Laterza, 1992). On the Basel Committee and the European Community as regulatory convergence factors see Barth, Caprio, and Levine, *Rethinking Bank Regulation*, pp. 63–74 and pp. 161–7.

persuade a high-rank representative from the Treasury, through its ability in moral suasion, the European and international integration of the capital markets required the adoption of a largely shared legal status for banks and intermediaries that could favour a positive evolution of the Italian financial institutions in a certainly more competitive environment.[82] In effect, from the early 1980s the chessboard for financial regulation was ultimately constituted by the European Community multi-governance levels and the Basel Committee on Banking Supervision (BCBS). In these standard-setter institutions the Bank of Italy was convincingly represented by the governor and its deputy director general Padoa-Schioppa, who emerged as one of the architects of euro. In several occasions Padoa-Schioppa aptly highlighted the specific nature and purposes of financial regulation (efficiency and stability) in an international context of 'blurring frontiers'[83] and the risk that an incomplete institutional design—represented by the sheer asymmetry between financial integration and the lack of a single supervisory authority—could pose to the stability of the European financial systems.[84]

In the late 1980s the Bank's constant efforts to create the 'conditions' allowing to eliminate the administrative constraints in favour of market allocative mechanisms proved to be successful, although they did not coincide with a mere financial deregulation. The soft deregulation was not, properly, a form of deregulation, but, rather, an essay in restoring efficient allocative mechanisms whilst seeking to boost economic growth within an inflationary context. The gradual and extremely cautious removal of non-market constraints promoted from Baffi onwards had strong endogenous motivations (a public finance out of control and a growth rate of labour cost higher than productivity increases), at the same time by adjusting to an international alteration of prices (peaking prices of oil and intermediate goods). Thus, in the mid-1970s, the rationale for financial liberalization was essentially constituted by the need to escape inefficiency. Since the mid-1980s the rationale for financial regulation was primarily represented by the European

---

[82] AS BI, Direttorio Padoa-Schioppa, folder 100, file 1, 'Note' concerning the meeting with Maurizio Sacconi, Undersecretary at the Treasury, 12 January 1988, and the attached notes 'Le possibili soluzioni per l'adozione da parte della Banca pubblica della forma della società per azioni', 11 January 1988, pp. 9–10.

[83] See, for instance, his speech at the 'Conference on financial conglomerates' held in Brussels on 14 and 15 March 1988 in AS BI, Direttorio Padoa-Schioppa, folder 133, file 2, Tommaso Padoa-Schioppa, 'The Blurring Financial Frontiers: In Search of an Order'.

[84] 'As we move towards a common market for banking services following the strategy that has been designed (namely by harmonizing only certain essential elements of our legislations and leaving the others to the process of mutual recognition) the banking system of the Community will undergo fundamental and perhaps dramatic changes. [...]. Banks will gradually move to a situation in which it will be *one* banking system for the whole Community. What is more important is that it will be no single supervisory authority for the whole market' (AS BI, Direttorio Padoa-Schioppa, folder 132, file 2, 'Remarks of Mr T. Padoa-Schioppa on the Future Role of the Banking Advisory Committee', September 1987, p. 2, regarding: Commission of the European Communities, Directorate General for Financial Institutions and Company Law, XV/A/1 'Outline of a proposal for the Second Directive on the coordination of banking legislation', July 1987).

integration principles of completion of the single market adopted in 1986 with the Single Act. In a way, the impulse came mostly from regulatory convergence as plainly stated by lawmakers and the central monetary authorities. However, as Padoa-Schioppa made it clear when participating in the policymaking process as the vice-president of the Banking Advisory Committee of the European Commission, the financial integration of Europe required forms of regulation to promote both efficiency *and* stability, more than a simple deregulation meant to unbridle market forces, by definition spontaneously able to guarantee both efficiency and stability in resource allocation.

Conclusions

Financial deregulation is usually presented as a sort of linear process proceeding from failures depending on too high a range of regulatory constraints deemed to prevent innovation and efficiency, rather seldom stability, to liberalization of market forces bound to promote innovation and efficiency. The Italian case may tell a different story. Throughout the 1970s the institutional and regulatory architecture entered into a difficult phase of ineffectiveness and, indirectly, even instability. None the less, financial deregulation as such was hardly on the political agenda whilst some aggregate tendencies were a sign of decreasing efficiency in resource allocation, basically because the ability of bankers to check their borrowers' creditworthiness appeared severely impaired. The regulatory failure, a variant of a State failure, originated from a series of administrative constraints more or less haphazardly built up to make the existent regulation working in a macroeconomic context characterized both by imported inflation (the oil shocks) and endogenously generated inflation (public spending and labour cost). The turning point in the approach to regulation by central monetary authorities coincided, not by chance, with a change of leadership at the Bank of Italy in 1975, when Carli resigned and Baffi stepped in as governor.

Since the mid-1970s the Bank of Italy confirmed its unparalleled ability to intervene in financial regulation directly, by regulating the financial system through technical measures such as credit ceilings or mandatory reserves, or through pieces of 'technical' advice to policy-makers. The new policy course undertaken by the Bank under governor Baffi represented a real sea-change in the way the main national regulator and central monetary authorities intended to address both macroeconomic instability (inflation, government borrowing requirements, exchange rate volatility, and external deficits) and deteriorating industrial competitiveness. At least up to the early 1980s the Bank of Italy's main target was the escape from the inefficiency induced by an institutional trap by adjusting to the volatile international monetary environment emerged with the collapse of the Bretton Woods agreements. In other terms, the strategy was mainly devised as a reaction to domestic institutional flaws (an inefficient bargaining system in the labour market) and economic policy errors (growing public spending sustained by deficit monetization) that dangerously cumulated with external shocks (oil shocks). Since the early 1980s the incipient revival in financial globalization modified the wider picture in which the Bank of Italy as regulator had to make choices. Along the previously defined lines, the strategy was re-tuned to comply with the new emerging European regulatory framework more than merely deregulating the financial system.

In the long regulatory cycle commenced in the mid-1970s the Bank of Italy was undeniably the main actor, whilst the lawmakers had a minor part up to 1990, when a new banking law, jointly arranged by Giuliano Amato and Guido Carli, eventually abolished the Banking Law of 1936 on the basis of the second European Banking Directive. Throughout the entire long regulatory cycle the Bank of Italy had to face a combination of endogenous and exogenous factors pursuing a mix of objectives: (1) efficiency more than stability and differently from the 1930s; (2) monetary policy consistency with the international environment, by and large as in the 1920s; (3) regulatory convergence within the European framework possibly by concurring to define its principles so as to maintain its supervisory prerogatives.

9

EU Bank Regulation after the Great Financial Crisis

Swinging the Regulatory Pendulum into a New Paradigm

Agnieszka Smoleńska

Introduction

The Great Financial Crisis (GFC) of 2008 triggered a regulatory wave across the major global jurisdictions. New rules introduced have built on the pre-existing regulatory foundations such as prudential regulations (e.g. capital requirements), however, they as well created novel tools of improving the stability of the banking sector through limiting moral hazard (e.g. by limiting bank bonuses) and the new *ex* ante approach to crisis management and prevention known as resolution. In the EU the new regulatory framework translated into a highly granular and detailed rulebook, with the proliferation of technical rules ongoing and increasing almost by the day. At first glance, it would seem that the liberal regime of the pre-crisis period has been left behind and regulation now reigns supreme. As this chapter will explore, however, specific features of the rules introduced suggest a more complex reality.

By contrast to the rest of the book, this chapter focuses not on the historical explanations for deregulation in the banking sector, but rather explores the features of the new regime created in the aftermath of the GFC in the EU specifically to gauge the *type* of public intervention approach it espouses. The aim being in particular to identify whether and if so how, the regulatory framework seeks to marry the restrictions of private activity in the public interest (i.e. regulation) with free market principles, such as those of openness in the integrated internal EU market (i.e. liberalism). Such a framing of the puzzle is warranted specifically as the pre-crisis EU regulations created an open market allowing for cross-border banking activity, without duly providing for a governance regime for times of crisis.[1] The rudimentary rules for cooperation between national

---

[1] Rachel Epstein, *Banking on Markets: The Transformation of Bank-State Ties in Europe and Beyond* (Oxford: Oxford University Press, 2017).

Agnieszka Smoleńska, *EU Bank Regulation after the Great Financial Crisis: Swinging the Regulatory Pendulum into a New Paradigm* In: *Financial Deregulation: A Historical Perspective*. Edited by: Alexis Drach and Youssef Cassis, Oxford University Press (2021). © Alexis Drach and Youssef Cassis. DOI: 10.1093/oso/9780198856955.003.0009

authorities and the legal uncertainty which prevailed in the financial markets during the GFC exasperated distrust and ring-fencing within the European Union leading to retrenchment and renationalization of the financial markets. As key figures in EU bank regulation have argued, the post-crisis Balkanization of the financial sector across the EU market occurred as a result of absence of common rules and coordinated supervision, that is regulation governing international cross-border entities.[2] Since an outright prohibition of cross-border banking would have been an anathema to European integration, the response of the EU legislators has been to lay down a specific regime, characterized by rules providing for co-responsibilization of bank management for systemic financial stability, an explicit concern for cross-border structures and far reaching powers of the regulators, in particular the new resolution authorities. In this sense, the approach which prevailed was the EU consensus seeking—on the one hand—to maintain the free market principles of the EU liberal order—and on the other—to put in place tools which would ensure its stability.

This chapter explores therefore how the dilemma between preserving market openness associated with EU integration without compromising financial stability is solved under the new regime wherein the structural and cross-border aspects have become to occupy a central place. To this end, the chapter proceeds as follows. First, it recalls how prior to the GFC EU liberalized banking laws and facilitated the emergence of cross-border banking. The second part provides an overview of the five distinct phases of post-crisis reform, both substantive and institutional, which had a bearing on both the EU and national level. Third, the chapter outlines the main features of the new regime, namely the enlarged scope of regulatory object-ives, the altered nature of bank governance, the broadening of the powers of the regulators and finally—the specific concern for cross-border bank activity. The final section draws conclusion into the nature of such re-regulatory efforts to the extent they seek to strike a balance between maintaining the principles of free market openness in the EU and preventing the negative externalities of failure of cross-border bank groups by seeking to change bank behaviour from within.

Market Openness as Foundation of EU Banking Law

Banking under currently applicable EU rules covers commercial activities engaged in taking deposits from the public and providing credit those who need it.[3] Such an

---

[2] Andrea Enria, 'Fragmentation in Banking Markets: Crisis Legacy and the Challenge of Brexit' (speech, BCBS-FSI High Level Meeting for Europe on Banking Supervision, 17 September 2018), Jacques de Larosière et al., 'The High-Level Group on Financial Supervision in the EU' (report, 2009).

[3] Under the current regime the scope of the EU's banking regulations is limited to 'undertakings the business of which is to take deposits or other repayable funds from the public and to grant credits for its own account' (Art. 4 CRR).

intermediation function has an ever more important role in underpinning EU integration, given the seemingly ever increasing financialization of European economies. Cross-border banking, whether as provision of cross-border services or greenfield operations, enables cross-border payments, better allocation of capital across the European markets, greater diversification, but as well transfer of know-how and technology across the EU. At the same time, given the intimate co-dependencies between banking and the politics and economics of distinct Member States, it is often remarked that cross-border banks are 'international in life, national in death'. However, even in 'life' the EU rulebook for banking integration was not achieved lightly.

The slow progress towards an EU banking market started with a rudimentary mutual recognition in 1980s which allowed for cross-border activity of banks. Subsequently, further minimum substantive harmonization was achieved in the 1980s. The pinnacle of deregulation was achieved from the 1990s and 2000s, where pursuit of competition prevailed. The amalgamation of the different sets of rules increasingly led, however, in the direction of creating a bespoke EU jurisdiction for cross-border banking. Scholars explain the reluctance of Member States to integration in this area (and the concomitant complexity of the regime explored further below) by protectionist policies of governments. Such protectionism results inter alia from the public role of banking, that is the mutual dependence of state economies and banks (i.e. the doom loop). Progress in introducing measures allowing for integration of banking markets was therefore the result of a trade-off achieved between nationalist conception of sovereignty and economically driven arguments for EU-wide opening of markets. In other words, EU banking integration measures struck a balance between the domestic protectionism which emphasized the imperative of national direct control of banking markets and resisted integration, and the single-market making objectives pursued in the light of their superior efficiency and the capacity to better deliver the private and public benefits of that business activity at the European level.[4]

Thus, even while differences between the financial ecosystems across the EU prevailed,[5] the progressive opening of national banking markets was allowed through rules providing that a bank authorized in one Member State could pro-

---

[4] For a historical perspective explaining the approach of the European Communities in the early phases see: Alexis Drach, 'A Globalization Laboratory: European Banking Regulation and Global Capitalism in the 1970s and Early 1980s', *European Review of History: Revue européenned'histoire* 26, no. 4 (2019): pp. 658–78; for a historic account of the different ways through which European law addressed the tension between integration and national protectionism e.g. via legislation, competition, and governance, see: Pedro Gustavo Teixeira, 'The Legal History of the Banking Union', *European Business Organization Law Review*18 (2017): pp. 535–65.

[5] Richard Deeg and Elliot Posner, 'Durability and Change in Financial Systems', in *The Oxford Handbook of Historical Institutionalism* edited by Orfeo Fioretos, Tulia G. Falleti, and Adam Sheingate (Oxford: Oxford University Press, 2012).

vide services across the EU market through branches (this is known as the principle of 'single passporting'). In such cases the overall EU activity of the parent bank and its branches continued to be the responsibility of the Member State where the former was established, including with regard to specific guarantees such as those covering the deposits of ordinary citizens (the principle of home supervision). Basic common rules established by the early banking directives were to ensure that Member States had the same minimum requirements and therefore trust across the distinct national regimes was possible (the principle of minimum harmonization). Such trust was further to be facilitated through greater cooperation between the national regulators in rule-making within the so-called the *Lamfalussy* committees. For cases of bank failure, a very basic regime was put in place governing the mutual recognition of winding-up proceedings.[6]

The regime in place at the outbreak of the Great Financial Crisis in 2007 allowed for cross-border activity but did not regulate it deeply—private autonomy prevailed. The EU rulebook was fragmented as it only really covered integrated banks (operating abroad through branches) and failed to capture the multinational banks operating through distinct legal entities (i.e. subsidiaries) across multiple countries. Once the crisis hit, the absence of laws effectively governing cross-border banking activity at the EU level not only facilitated disintegration of cross-border banking activity, but in fact actively pitted distinct national authorities against each other fuelling distrust between EU governments, many of which resorted to effectively ring-fencing their banking sectors.[7] The crisis, therefore, resuscitated domestic banking protectionism (though not always the concomitant re-regulation) with an emphasis on the direct national control of markets and an increasing resistance to cross-border integration. At the same time, the ex post assessment drew attention to the specific shortcomings of the regime, where it led to moral hazard on the part of the markets via distorted incentives for excessive risk-taking and an absence of both a veritable cost-sharing mechanism and adequate tools on the part of the public authorities to both prevent and manage the crises in the context of highly integrated and financialized markets.

---

[6] Directive 2001/24/EC of the European Parliament and of the Council of 4 April 2001 on the reorganization and winding up of credit institutions OJ L 125, 5.5.2001, pp. 15–23 ('Winding-Up Directive').

[7] Martin Sandbu, *Europe's Orphan: The Future of the Euro and the Politics of Debt* (Princeton: Princeton University Press, 2017); Agnieszka Smoleńska, 'Law and Governance of Cross-border Banks After the Great Financial Crisis'(PhD Dissertation, European University Institute, 2020), Katia D'Hulster and Inci Ötker-Robe, 'Ring-Fencing Cross-Border Banks: An Effective Supervisory Response', *Journal of Banking Regulation* 16 (2015): pp. 169–87. For the specific example of failure in crisis management coordination between Member States and the fragmentation which ensued see Pierre-Henri Thomas, *Dexia: vie et mort d'un monstrebancaire* (Paris: Les Petits matins, 2012).

Five Stages of Post-GFC Regulatory Reform

Since the GFC the EU has been riding the regulatory wave, racing to put in place new rules regulating banking activity. In the flurry of new legislative activity, five distinct stages of reform in EU bank regulation can be identified: (a) the calibration of EU state aid rules to the banking sector (2008–10), (b) the first EU institutional reform (i.a. establishing European Banking Authority) (2010), (c) the first substantive bank regulation reform (CRD IV/BRRD) (2010–14), (d) the creation of the Banking Union and the second institutional reform (2013–18), and (e) the second substantive bank regulation reform (CRD V/BRRD 2) (2016–19).[8]

Once the GFC struck in 2008, both the regulators and the banks themselves were faced with a lack of adequate cross-border instruments to govern the fallout. Specifically, there were no prescribed crisis management procedures and uncertainty as to the respective roles of institutions prevailed—for example as to the extent to which the ECB is the Eurozone's Lender of Last Resort. Among the prevailing uncertainty, EU state aid rules were the only effective instrument at the disposal of European Commission and the Member States to provide for some coordination in crisis management. They required that any bank bailout, which violates the general EU Treaty prohibition to keep alive non-viable companies through state action, be subject to common rules. Since 2009 the European Commission adopted almost 500 ad hoc decisions allowing for aid to over 100 individual banks.[9] In the absence of specialized set of crisis management rules, such as a resolution regime,[10] the European Commission's exercise of state aid control—progressively codified under subsequent 'crisis communications'—was the primary tool of EU crisis response coordination at the time.[11]

In the second phase of reform, marginal adjustments were made to the pre-existing rules and the new EU agencies—the European Banking Authority (EBA) and European Systemic Risk Board (ESRB) in particular—were created to

---

[8] See for overview of EU bank regulation reforms after the Great Financial Crisis, e.g. Matthias Haentjens and Pierre De Gioia-Carabellese, *European Banking and Financial Law* (Abington: Routledge, 2015); David Ramos Muñoz and Marco Lamandini, *EU Financial Law: An Introduction* (Milanofiori: Wolters Kluwer Italia, 2016); John Armour et al., *Principles of Financial Regulation* (Oxford: Oxford University Press, 2016).

[9] Between 2007 and 2015 the European Commission took over 400 individual decisions in the cases of 112 banks. Only between 2007 and 2016 DG Competition approved over 450 decisions in the area of State aid. These included €671 billion in capital and repayable loans and €1288 billion in guarantees. The decisions included restructuring and orderly resolution of 112 European banks, see Guillaume Adamczyk and Bernhard Windisch, 'State Aid to European Banks: Returning to Viability', Competition State Aid Brief, 2015.

[10] François-Charles Laprévote, Joanna Gray, and Francesco De Cecco, *Research Handbook on State Aid in the Banking Sector* (Cheltenham: Edward Elgar Publishing, 2017).

[11] See speech of the European Commissioner at the time on how state aid law operated as the EU resolution law regime: Joaquín Almunia, 'Annual Competition Report for 2011 in the European Parliament' (presentation, 19 June 2012).

facilitate the convergence and exchange of information and practices across the EU internal market by developing the technical standards required by primary legislation. Such agencies remained advisory in nature, however, with virtually no direct powers over banks. Further, they are networked agencies, i.e. they are composed of national regulators and any decisions require the agreement of their majority.

Substantive reform, which introduced into the EU law both new, more stringent capital requirements (Capital Requirements Directive, CRD and Regulation, CRR),[12] as well as the new set of rules for bank crisis prevention and management (Bank Recovery and Resolution Directive, BRRD),[13] was approved by the EU Member States and the European Parliament only in 2013 and 2014 respectively. Such regulatory efforts after the financial crisis have focused predominantly on restoring stability, safety, and soundness of the banking system (in the macro-dimension) and individual institutions (in the micro-dimension). Precisely in the context of the preceding (and subsequent) institutional reform, such regulations had a distinctly EU-twist, that is they were concerned with addressing the problems arising in the context of cross-border activity enabled by the liberalizing EU rules. This being the case even if they were in great measure also implementing into the EU legal order commitments made and frameworks developed at the global level, namely within the Basel Committee for the credit requirement framework and the Financial Stability Board (FSB) for the resolution law. For example, it was only with the BRRD the concept of a 'cross-border bank group' was laid down in EU law for the first time, covering only—and specifically—only those parts of the multinational bank subject to jurisdiction of EU-based national authorities.

The main objectives of prudential rules (CRD and CRR) are to improve the stability and resilience of the banking system and individual institutions, thus creating a level playing field across countries, by strengthening capital regulation, liquidity regulation, and activity restrictions. Further these laws seek to strengthen banks' corporate governance arrangements, to better align incentives of the bank management as well as to regulate bank conduct. These regulations are coupled with strengthened microprudential supervision, that is they enlarge the powers of

---

[12] Directive 2013/36/EU of the European Parliament and of the Council of 26 June 2013 on access to the activity of credit institutions and the prudential supervision of credit institutions and investment firms, amending Directive 2002/87/EC and repealing Directives 2006/48/EC and 2006/49/EC OJ L 176, 27.6.2013, pp. 338–436 ('CRD IV') and Regulation (EU) No. 575/2013 of the European Parliament and of the Council of 26 June 2013 on prudential requirements for credit institutions and investment firms and amending Regulation (EU) No. 648/2012 OJ L 176, 27.6.2013, pp. 1–337 ('CRR').

[13] Directive 2014/59/EU of the European Parliament and of the Council of 15 May 2014 establishing a framework for the recovery and resolution of credit institutions and investment firms and amending Council Directive 82/891/EEC, and Directives 2001/24/EC, 2002/47/EC, 2004/25/EC, 2005/56/EC, 2007/36/EC, 2011/35/EU, 2012/30/EU and 2013/36/EU, and Regulations (EU) No. 1093/2010 and (EU) No. 648/2012, of the European Parliament and of the Council OJ L 173, 12.6.2014, pp. 190–348 ('BRRD').

public authorities to oversee and direct individual bank behaviour, thus addressing idiosyncratic risks thereof. In addition, the new tool of macroprudential policy creates a framework for addressing the stability of the banking sector as whole, the logic being that the instruments needed to tackle failures and risk associated with individual credit institutions might differ from those required when the system as a whole is considered (e.g. in the context of build-up of asset bubbles). To this end, macroprudential policy is tasked with identifying, monitoring, and addressing systemic risk, taking into account the financial cycle as well as the direction and scale of cross-border capital flows. In many jurisdictions these tasks are delegated to the central bank empowered with specific tools such as the power to require banks to implement countercyclical buffers or set loan-to-value ratios for mortgages.[14]

The novel resolution approach in bank regulation is a variant of such a macroprudential, systemic approach. Specifically, legislation such as the BRRS is a completely novel set of rules and procedures for dealing with failing banks, which aims to ensure that crises are prevented and better managed. This approach emerged first in the context of the Asian financial crisis of 1990s, where the lesson drawn from the multiple bank failures was that the regulators need better tools to act countercyclically, that is to prevent the build-up of risks not just in a particular credit institution, but in the system as a whole (i.e. macroprudential policy was needed).[15] The concern with bank's resolvability, that is the *ability* to fail, is one objective in this approach. Resolution is thus a special type of crisis prevention instrument, but as well one which serves crisis containment (management). The rules are needed as an uncontrolled failure of a bank due to—for example— insolvency, wreaks havoc to the entire financial system and comes at a high social cost and with a significant destruction of value in the economy. Resolution laws aim to enable restructuring or liquidation of financial institutions in an orderly manner, limiting contagion effects in the financial system, and decreasing taxpayers' exposure to losses from bailouts, while maintaining continuity of banks' critical economic functions. They work, therefore, to make bank exit 'safe'. To this end, new loss-absorption requirements have been imposed on financial institutions such as bail-in, which require that the creditors of the bank, including in some cases the subordinated creditors, contribute to the costs of bank resolution before other safety nets—including public funds—are resorted to. This is intended to bolster the monitoring of the bank by creditors, in addition to the shareholders. Resolution laws also create specific regulatory tools which seek to build up ex ante resilience of banks through planning, that is the preparation of

---

[14] These include measures such as the countercyclical buffer (Art. 160 CRD IV) and designating a given entity as an 'other systemically important institution' (Art. 131 CRD IV) for the purpose of applying more stringent regulatory measures.

[15] Andrew Crockett, 'The Theory and Practice of Financial Stability', *Essays in International Finance* 203 (1997).

so-called 'living wills' detailing the course of action should a bank be faced with a deteriorating financial situation.[16] Such contingency preparation is considered to already ex ante better align the incentives of bank management which translates into better internationalization of possible systemic costs of failure. Resolution is thus conceived as a set of rules and institutional solutions for bank crisis prevention and resolution.[17]

The BRRD is partially a transposition of the FSB's principles for effective resolution, which establish rules to ensure that the continuity of bank's critical functions after the bank is failing, the protection of insured depositors and a rapid return of segregated clients' assets, an allocation of losses in a way which is not more costly to shareholders and creditors than the alternative of insolvency, the moral hazard related to implicit subsidies is limited and the unnecessary destruction of value is avoided. The rules enacted to this end in individual jurisdictions should allow for the speed, transparency, and predictability of the resolution process. As a result, the regime is intended to allow for the exit of non-viable banks from the market in a way which enhances market discipline and provides incentives for market solutions to be adopted rather than for taxpayer bailouts. Specific procedures are foreseen with regard to cooperation, information exchange, and cooperation with competent authorities in other countries.[18]

A turning point with immediate effect on the operation of the market came in 2013, with the creation of the European Banking Union (EBU) which conferred to the EU level the responsibility for oversight (via the Single Supervisory Mechanism, SSM with the ECB at the helm) and for the crisis prevention and management (via the Single Resolution Mechanism, SRM centred around the new EU agency, the Single Resolution Authority, SRB) of largest and most significant banks across the Eurozone.[19] Such centralized authorities are granted far reaching powers of direction vis-à-vis the supervised banks, even if they apply the rules jointly approved by EU Member States and implemented in national law.

In the final stage of post-crisis reform considered, a revision of the substantive rules was introduced to refine the new framework rather than overhaul it.

---

[16] Article 2(1)(101) BRRD defines these as 'crisis prevention measures', enabling the 'the exercise of powers to direct removal of deficiencies or impediments to recoverability under Article 6(6), the exercise of powers to address or remove impediments to resolvability under Article 17 or 18, the application of an early intervention measure under Article 27, the appointment of a temporary administrator under Article 29 or the exercise of the write down or conversion powers under Article 59'.

[17] Patrick Honohan and Luc Laeven (eds), *Systemic Financial Crises* (Cambridge: Cambridge University Press, 2005).

[18] Financial Stability Board, 'Key Attributes of Effective Resolution Regimes for Financial Institutions', 2014.

[19] Though EU regulations creating the SSM allow for participation by non-Eurozone Member States via a mechanism known as 'close cooperation', so far no non-Eurozone Member States entered into such an arrangement. At the time of writing Bulgaria and Croatia are in the final stages of joining EBU as a prerequisite for adopting the common currency.

Amendments to the CRR 2 and CRD IV)[20] and resolution law (BRRD 2 and SRM 2)[21] rulebook approved in 2019 included new rules concerning risk governance, net stable funding ration, and a leverage ratio (in line with international Basel standards for credit institutions). The reform introduced as well greater proportionality so as to reduce the regulatory burden on small credit institutions in the system. Some novel elements were introduced as part of the reform as well, namely via the regulations concerning the Environmental and Social Governance (ESG) aspects of bank activity, including as a measure of supervisory assessment. Such a shift marks a further step into the regulation of internal governance of bank's operations, which is indeed the principal hallmark of the new regime. Precisely how this has occurred under the new rules is explored below.

Towards a New Regulatory Paradigm: Features of the New Regime

At first glance it may seem that the extensive banking regulation reform introduced at the EU level would be tantamount to financial repression, swinging the regulatory pendulum from the liberalizing era of the pre-crisis period back to the days of heavy restrictions constraining banking activity. The fact of the matter is that a much more nuanced regime has been put in place. The new EU set of rules is oriented towards functionally prioritizing financial stability and securing banks' ability to provide their critical functions in the broader economy (i.e. deposit taking and payment systems operation). New EU regulation pursues these goals through co-responsibilization of the banking sector for public objectives, explicit regulation of structure and operations as well as new far-reaching powers of dedicated new regulators, in particular the resolution authorities. At the same time, banks continue to operate as private actors. The new paradigm is one which not merely regulates the open market transactions, but one which deeply affects

---

[20] Regulation (EU) 2019/876 of the European Parliament and of the Council of 20 May 2019 amending Regulation (EU) No. 575/2013 as regards the leverage ratio, the net stable funding ratio, requirements for own funds and eligible liabilities, counterparty credit risk, market risk, exposures to central counterparties, exposures to collective investment undertakings, large exposures, reporting and disclosure requirements, and Regulation (EU) No. 648/2012, OJ L 150, 7.6.2019, pp. 1–225 ('CRR 2'), Directive (EU) 2019/878 of the European Parliament and of the Council of 20 May 2019 amending Directive 2013/36/EU as regards exempted entities, financial holding companies, mixed financial holding companies, remuneration, supervisory measures and powers and capital conservation measures, OJ L 150, 7.6.2019, pp. 253–95 ('CRD 5').

[21] Regulation (EU) 2019/877 of the European Parliament and of the Council of 20 May 2019 amending Regulation (EU) No. 806/2014 as regards the loss-absorbing and recapitalization capacity of credit institutions and investment firms, OJ L 150, 7.6.2019, pp. 226–52 ('SRM 2'), Directive (EU) 2019/879 of the European Parliament and of the Council of 20 May 2019 amending Directive 2014/59/EU as regards the loss-absorbing and recapitalization capacity of credit institutions and investment firms and Directive 98/26/EC, OJ L 150, 7.6.2019, pp. 296–344 ('BRRD 2').

the governance of banks as corporate entities, in particular in a cross-border context. The individual components are explored below in turn.

Broad Financial and Non-financial Objectives of the New Regime

First, the overall thrust of the post-GFC reform has introduced greater heterogeneity among the objectives of public intervention in the banking sector as well as greater granularity of rules, further detailed harmonization and a strengthening of institutional cooperation in bank oversight both for the Eurozone (with the creation of the Banking Union) and the internal market as a whole (with new powers of EU-wide agencies).[22] In such a legal context, the objectives of the new regulations play a much more prominent under the new rules than previously, specifically with regard to the function of banking they seek to protect, namely the critical functions, to the extent these are essential to the proper operation of the real economy (e.g. financing the real economy, financing SMEs).[23] Previously, the prudential regulations were predominantly concerned with the safety and soundness and generic depositor protection, with an arm's-length approach of the authorities. While this continues to be the case, EU resolution law in particular introduces broader considerations which are not only systemic in nature ('financial stability') but as well look to protect the specific functions of banking as underpinning the economy which are simultaneously those which warrant banking be treated and regulated under a distinct regime (i.e. the intermediation function).[24] Disruption of such services (in addition to possible bank bailouts) comes at a too high societal cost, and hence direct intervention is needed at all stages of bank management. New regulations pursue such broader objectives, in the case of EU resolution law specifically seeking (a) to ensure the continuity of critical functions of the supervised institutions; (b) to avoid a significant adverse effect on the financial system, in particular by preventing contagion, including to market infrastructures, and by maintaining

---

[22] Christos V. Gortsos, 'The Crisis-Based European Union Financial Regulatory Intervention: Are We on the Top of the Prudential Wave?' *ERA Forum* 16 (2015): pp. 89–110; Qaiser Munir, (ed.), *Handbook of Research on Financial and Banking Crisis Prediction through Early Warning Systems* (Hershey, PA: IGI Global, 2016); Christos Gortsos, 'The Evolution of European (EU) Banking Law under the Influence of (Public) International Banking Law: A Comprehensive Overview' (2019) (available at: https://papers.ssrn.com/sol3/papers.cfm?abstract_id=3334493).

[23] Such critical functions emerged over the course of the financial crisis, where in a number of countries bank bailouts were made conditional on specific assurances from the bank regarding its lending behaviour Eugenio Cerutti and Stijn Claessens, 'The Great Cross-Border Bank Deleveraging: Supply Constraints and Intra-Group Frictions', *Review of Finance* 21, no. 1 (2017): pp. 201–36. For earlier accounts of public externalities of bank failure Ben Bernanke, 'Nonmonetary Effects of the Financial Crisis in the Propagation of the Great Depression', *The American Economic Review* 73, no. 3(1983): pp. 257–76.

[24] For a more critical view of the role of finance and economics see e.g. Luigi Zingales, 'Presidential Address: Does Finance Benefit Society?', *The Journal of Finance* 70, no. 4 (2015): pp. 1327–63.

market discipline; (c) to protect public funds by minimizing reliance on extraordinary public financial support; (d) to protect depositors covered by Directive 2014/49/EU and investors covered by Directive 97/9/EC; (e) to protect client funds and client assets.[25]

Concerns about financial stability are of course not new for regulators in the financial sector, while the design of oversight was underpinned by the protection of one stakeholder group—the depositors—since the Great Depression.[26] However, the growing financialization of developed economies as well as the increasing role of private debt in creating value has accentuated the need to refine the thinking about financial regulation, beyond concerns about means of payment and (internal) stability of the financial system purely.[27] While some functions have remained fairly stable over time, as financialization of our economies progresses, new critical functions are likely to be added to the list—including functions relating to public data processing and promotion of sustainability, which are increasingly transversal concerns in EU regulation.[28] The new scope of regulatory objectives has in any case already permeated into the obligations imposed on bank management, which—in the aftermath of the crisis—is required to integrate considerations of systemic impact of their activity in the daily operations of the bank.

Bank Governance and Responsibilization of Bank Management

In addition to the greater integration of public interest concerns by the new framework enforced by the supervisors, new public-like duties are placed on bank management which results in 'co-responsibilization' of the bank for the overall financial stability and the attainment of other regulatory objectives. Such an effect is reinforced by a re-alignment of distribution of losses in the case of

---

[25] Article 32(1) BRRD.

[26] For the financial stability concerns in pre-GFC regulation see: Tommaso Padoa-Schioppa, *Regulating Finance: Balancing Freedom and Risk* (Oxford: Oxford University Press, 2005); Alexander K. Swoboda and Richard Portes, (eds), *Threats to International Financial Stability* (Cambridge: Cambridge University Press, 1987). On the role of deposit guarantees in ensuring stability and preventing crises see seminal work Douglas W. Diamond and Philip H. Dybvig, 'Bank Runs, Deposit Insurance, and Liquidity', *Journal of Political Economy* 91, no. 3 (1983): pp. 401–19.

[27] Robert C. Hockett and Saule T. Omarova, 'Public Actors in Private Markets: Toward a Developmental Finance State', *Washington University Law Review* 93 (2015): pp. 103–75; for a critical view of financialization: Wolfgang Streeck, 'The Crises of Democratic Capitalism', *New Left Review* 71 (2011): pp. 5–29; Douglas W. Arner, *Financial Stability, Economic Growth, and the Role of Law* (Cambridge University Press, 2007).

[28] For the growing body of literature dealing with the climate change obligations of financial regulators and central banks see e.g. Javier Solana, 'The Power of the Eurosystem to Promote Environmental Protection', *European Business Law Review* 30, no. 4 (2019): pp. 547–55; Emanuele Campiglio, 'Climate Change Challenges for Central Banks and Financial Regulators', *Nature Climate Change* 8 (2018): pp. 462–8.

failure, which is another area of regulatory innovation with a significant going concern impact. Where the implicit subsidies distorted banks' risk-taking behaviour before the GFC, the post-crisis framework seeks to ex ante redistribute losses in a more equitable way, thus solving the perennial problem of crisis regulation which is preventing the extraction of private benefits by banking and the shifting costs related to risks when they materialize onto the public purse.[29] To this end, the bail-in—discussed further below—requirement allows for losses of bank failure to be imposed on creditors—incentivizing them to monitor bank behaviour and to price the related risk accordingly. Such regulatory interference with the incentives of various stakeholders is present in the other pillars of the regulatory reform; however, the primary tool through which such re-alignment is achieved is the risk management regulation.[30]

In the context of EU resolution law, the impact on bank management is particularly evident. Specifically, the directors are required to adopt and include consideration of systemic impact of its activities as part of the risk management procedures. Bulk of resolution law deals not only with resolution, but with *safeguarding* financial stability through ex ante preparation of resolution plans, which are inter alia oriented at ensuring the bank's resolvability[31] as well as adequate loss-absorbing capacity (through MREL, that is a minimum level of own funds and eligible liabilities which can be used to restore the bank's capital position). The specific tools oriented at instilling such resilience into banks' operations must be interpreted with the general objectives of EU resolution.

New regulations introduced after the GFC create a distinct bank corporate governance regime further reinforced via redesigning the role of banks' debtors in monitoring the formers' behaviour. Under the pre-crisis rules capital requirements were to sufficiently align the risk-taking within the bank. Now, following the BRRD reform, the new bail-in mechanisms which allows for a part of the losses of bank failure to be absorbed by the creditors, is to ensure that the monitoring by bank's shareholders is supplemented by debt governance as well.

---

[29] For a discussion of the moral hazard related to pre-crisis framework, and in particular the implicit subsidies for excessive risk-taking see Kenichi Ueda and B. Weder di Mauro, 'Quantifying Structural Subsidy Values for Systemically Important Financial Institutions', *Journal of Banking and Finance* 37, no. 10 (2013): pp. 3830–42; Franklin Allen et al, 'Moral Hazard and Government Guarantees in the Banking Industry', *Journal of Financial Regulation* 1, no. 1 (2015): pp. 30–50. On the post-crisis shift in allocation of risk see David Ramos Muñoz and Marco Lamandini, *EU Financial Law: An Introduction* (Milanofiore: Wolters Kluwer Italia, 2016).

[30] E.g. caps on dividends, regulations on remuneration and bonuses. On risk regulation in EU law in general see: Hans-W. Micklitz and Takis Tridimas, *Risk and EU Law* (Cheltenham: Edward Elgar Publishing, 2015); Julia Black, 'Regulatory Styles and Supervisory Strategies', in *The Oxford Handbook of Financial Regulation*, edited by Niamh Moloney, Eilís Ferran and Jennifer Payne (Oxford: Oxford University Press, 2015); Stefan Grundmann, Christy-Ann Petit, and Agnieszka Smoleńska, 'Bank Governance', in *Le traitement des difficultés des établissements bancaires et institutions financières: approche croisée*, edited by François Barrière (Paris: LexisNexis, 2017).

[31] i.e. resolution authorities have the power to require banks to remove impediments to resolvability: such as unclear separation of business lines, or unsustainable funding models.

Though such instruments have pre-dated the crisis (notably as CoCos—contingent convertibles),[32] the additional novelty introduced by the regulation is an obligation to issue sufficient amounts of bail-inable debt, should the need to employ this tool arise. This is the so-called Minimum Requirement for Own Funds and Eligible Liabilities (MREL)[33] The MREL requirement is calculated on the basis of a detailed procedure outlined in the regulation so as to ensure that the bank has sufficient own funds and eligible liabilities to enable its return to viability. To this end MREL is composed on the loss absorption amount and the recapitalization amount, which in practice translate into a new type of bonds which are to be issued by the bank in the market.

The immediate objective of the bail-in tool and the MREL is to ensure the bank has sufficient loss absorption capacity (i.e. resilience) to withstand either an endogenously caused crisis, or one materializing as a result of external factors. Bank's loss absorption guaranteed by the bail-in instrument should thus limit the implicit subsidization of banks' activities by the taxpayer[34] and better align the former's risk-taking appetite with loss absorption capabilities, also by incentivizing additional risk-monitoring (and pricing) by creditors.[35] As a result it has been described in terms of a hybrid public–private governance instrument.

Broadening of Powers of the Authorities

A broadening of regulatory objectives under EU law has allowed for a more invasive role to be played by the authorities including with regard to the power of direction they enjoy vis-à-vis the supervised entity and its management. The new rulebook espouses a logic where the overriding public interest allows for interference with the general right to freedom of business. The post-crisis regulatory framework strengthens prudential rules, that is the solvency regulations in particular, with the aim of increasing bank stability, but as well as to re-align their risk-taking approaches, correcting for the perverse incentives arising from time inconsistency of the pre-crisis rules which have allowed and

---

[32] Biljana Biljanovska, 'Aligning Market Discipline and Financial Stability: A More Gradual Shift from Contingent Convertible Capital to Bail-in Measures', *European Business Organization Law Review* 17 (2016): pp. 105–35.

[33] Art. 45 BRRD and amendments pursuant to BRRD to, now Art.45c. Art.12 SRM.

[34] This is effect is reinforced for the Banking Union countries, where a minimum threshold of 8% bail-in is required in order for the bank to be able to access the Single Resolution Fund, see Recitals 78 and 80 SRM, Article 27(7)(a) SRM Regulation.

[35] For a criticism of bail-in approach from a systemic point of view see Roberta Romano, 'For Diversity in the International Regulation of Financial Institutions: Redesigning the Basel Architecture', *Yale Journal on Regulation* 31, no. 1 (2014): pp. 1–76; for a legal critique see Chris Bates and Simon Gleeson, 'Legal Aspects of Bank Bail-Ins', *Law and Financial Markets Review* 5, no. 4 (2011): pp. 264–75; Emilios Avgouleas and Charles Goodhart, 'Critical Reflections on Bank Bail-Ins', *Journal of Financial Regulation* 1, no. 1 (2015): pp. 3–29.

encouraged excessive risk-taking. New microprudential regulations introduce prudential requirements in the form of quantitative requirements (capital, liquidity, MREL) and specific governance processes (resolution planning, supervisory review) which affect bank behaviour and introduce reflexivity between public authority action and going concern decisions of the management. Supervisors and resolution authorities at EU and national levels after the reform have acquired special discretion to calibrate the requirements to fully take into account the specific banking model and bank structure of the supervised entity.

The powers of resolution authorities, that is the authorities responsible for ensuring banks are resolvable in crisis and for minimizing the costs of one should it occur, are particular in this regard. In the first place, resolution under the BRRD allow for a complete takeover of bank operations in crisis. The new rules, as was mentioned, lay down provisions for administratively managed reorganization procedures for banks, which can lead either to restoration of viability or liquidation, as well as for crisis prevention tools that is ex ante recovery and resolution planning.[36] Resolution proper means that the resolution authority takes over the management of the bank with view of using resolution tools to achieve resolution objectives.[37] Such authorities—once specific triggers of failure are met—have the power to take control of an institution and exercise all the rights and powers of shareholders. They have at their disposal the special bank-funded resources created to ensure there are sufficient resources available to finance this process; in the case of Single Resolution Mechanism of the Banking Union,[38] this is the Single Resolution Fund.[39] Moreover, resolution authorities have competences to intervene and guide the behaviour of cross-border banks through on-going oversight with view of attaining specific objectives, while on the other instilling public-like considerations into the daily management of the bank as duties of its managers. This occurs in the normal bank operations already, when banks must prepare their living wills, and where—in cases where they resolution authorities are not fully happy with bank's decisions—they may impose sanctions for non-compliance with the requirements, such as prohibition on certain distributions, such as dividends.[40]

---

[36] See Jens-Hinrich Binder and Dalvinder Singh, (eds), *Bank Resolution: The European Regime* (Oxford: Oxford University Press, 2016).

[37] See Art. 31(2) BRRD.

[38] Agnieszka Smoleńska, 'SRB: Lost and Found in the Thicket of EU Banking Regulation', in *The European Banking Union and Constitution: Beacon for Advanced Integration or Death-Knell for Democracy*, edited by Stefan Grundmann and Hans Micklitz (Oxford: Hart Publishing, 2019).

[39] Art. 67(3) SRM.

[40] The so-called M-MDA, see recital 24 and new BRRD Article 16a (BRRD 2) Resolution authorities may 'to restrict or prohibit distributions or interest payments by an institution to shareholders, members or holders of Additional Tier 1 instruments where the prohibition does not constitute an event of default of the institution'.

Such a sliding scale of intervention marks the difference between resolution authorities and those of supervisors. The latter may influence bank management, even require it be replaced in the case of early intervention. Resolution law, however, in the light of its public interest and stakeholder protection (as opposed to intrasectoral considerations of supervisors) objectives, to the extent specific requirements are implemented in the shadow of full takeover of bank management *by the resolution authority* should a crisis materialise, has unique bank governance implications. While the interest pursued by crisis *management* measures (that is *in resolution*) is clear to be the public interest, already in the context of crisis *prevention* measures (that is in recovery and resolution *planning*) the powers of direction by resolution authorities are considerable. The overall regime is thus governed by a principle of proportionality and can be conceived as a sliding scale of hybrid (public–private) governance between autonomous corporate governance and bank governance by resolution authorities. The incisiveness of powers of the authorities is a function of the state of the bank, financial system considerations and the pursuit of the BRRD objectives outlined above. It involves a distinct and intense relationship between the supervisor and the supervised entity—including in areas previously considered within the sphere of private autonomy of the bank. Such levels of discretion reflect as well the perceived superiority of flexible and reflexive regulation with an approach oriented at individualization and tailoring the regulatory approach to individual financial institutions, over a strictly rule-based approach.[41]

A Strengthened Cross-Border Dimension

A final feature of the post-crisis EU banking regulation regime considered here is the new concern with the internal organization of banks—including their cross-border activity—as a matter of prudential rules. The primary focus of scholarly debate with regard to the organization of banks has been structural separation, that is requiring that banks do not simultaneously carry out proprietary trading activities and traditional credit intermediation. The so-called Volcker rule—in the EU known as the Liikanen proposal—sought in this sense to further contribute to reducing risk in the banking sector.[42] The reform gained little

[41] Cristie Ford, 'Financial Innovation and Flexible Regulation: Destabilising the Regulatory State', *North Carolina Banking Institute* 18 (2013): pp. 27–38.
[42] Neil Gordon and Wolf-Georg Ringe, 'Bank Resolution in Europe: The Unfinished Agenda of Structural Reform', in *European Banking Union,* edited by Danny Busch and Guido Ferrarini (Oxford: Oxford University Press, 2015); Alexandria Carr, 'Bank Structural Reform: Too Big to Fail, Too Big to Save and Too Complex to Manage, Supervise and Resolve?', in *Research Handbook on Crisis Management in the Banking Sector,* edited by Matthias Haentjens and Bob Wessels (Cheltenham: Edward Elgar Publishing, 2015): pp. 283–307.

traction, however, and did not make it past the legislators' scrutiny, predominantly in the light of ubiquity of the universal bank model in the EU.[43]

The structure and internal organization increasingly nonetheless became the object of detailed bank regulation, albeit in a nuanced way, specifically via a new focus on bank complexity. Since GFC complexity came to be considered as a new risk factor, in particular where insufficient information was available to adequately assess and manage bank's activities which in turn increased the costs of failure.[44] Academic scholarship supported this approach—Carmassi and Herring consider that complexity impedes proper governance of banks' activities where it prevents adequate capitalization, makes supervisory action ineffective in constraining risk-taking (in particular where there are no specific international arrangements, e.g. for exchange of information), while the lack of congruence between business and legal lines prevents salvaging of going-concern value once crisis materializes. In the aftermath of the GFC, EU bank regulation increasingly treats opaqueness in banks' organization as a matter of supervisory concern, and responds to this risk inter alia by increasing the transparency of internal organization through specific reporting requirements. However, complexity in banking is not only just a matter of informational asymmetries between parties. New crisis prevention requirements under EU resolution law increasingly differentiate between integrated (single bank) and (cross-border) bank group situations, prescribing different procedures, as a means to facilitate better governance and cooperation between authorities at national and EU levels.

To this end, the reform strengthened cooperation at EU level by creating new EU agencies (European Supervisory Authorities) and establishing a dedicated structure for cooperation between national authorities ('colleges') for the oversight of cross-border bank groups operating within the EU.[45] Though the colleges have maintained the principle of home country control, as discussed above, the reforms have as well strengthened 'host control'[46]—also by giving more powers to the local authorities, and creating new categories such as 'significant branches', which alter the traditional model of home country control (where supervision of branches was deemed to be the responsibility of the authority responsible

---

[43] European Commission withdrew the proposal for structural reform in July 2018.

[44] Arguing that organizational complexity can even undermine the objectives of financial regulation: Thomas Philippon and Aude Salord, 'Bail-Ins and Bank Resolution in Europe: A Progress Report', report, 2017, p. 26.

[45] See recital 6 Directive 2009/111/EC of the European Parliament and of the Council of 16 September 2009 amending Directives 2006/48/EC, 2006/49/EC and 2007/64/EC as regards banks affiliated to central institutions, certain own funds items, large exposures, supervisory arrangements, and crisis management, OJ L 302, 17.11.2009, pp. 97–119 ('CRD III').

[46] Juan A. Marchetti, 'The International Banking Landscape: Developments, Drivers, and Potential Implications', in *The Future of Large, Internationally Active Banks,* edited by Asli Demirgüç-Kunt, Douglas Evanoff, and George Kaufman (Singapore: World Scientific, 2016), pp. 97–111; Financial Sector Advisory Center (FinSAC) World Bank Group, 'Banking Supervision and Resolution in the EU: Effects on Small Host Countries in CEE and SEE' (Working Paper, April 2019).

for the parent bank). Host countries also acquired new prerogatives towards the parent level authority, for example to the extent they can now enquire about the capacity of the deposit guarantee scheme which ensures the branch active in their jurisdiction.[47] The post-GFC regime above all nuanced the terms of cooperation between relevant competent authorities substantially procedural-izes their cooperation. In so doing it lays down the foundations for a model of cooperation between authorities which seeks to preclude the benefits of ring-fencing within cross-border groups, and therefore to facilitate cross-border bank activity also in crisis.

EU resolution law to this end introduces the concept of a 'cross-border group'. Until 2014 there was no such concept in EU law—the primary notion which allowed EU regulations to see cross-border bank activity was derived from accounting rules, namely the 'consolidated situation'. Such cross-border groups—defined structurally by the fact they have 'a parent undertaking and subsidiaries' and geographically whereas 'group entities established in more than one Member State'—may not necessarily encompass the entire multinational bank—in fact there is now an obligation for the bank to have an intermediate parent undertaking estab-lished in the EU and the CRR refers breezily to 'European groups'. This is as the special 'cross-border group' procedures are implemented in respect of the 'Union parent undertaking', that is the parent entity established in one of the EU's Member States (even when the trail of ownership leads beyond). While on the surface such definitions appear general in nature—and some scholars have criticized this new concept, a closer look at the specifics of the regulation and the specific procedures foreseen for cross-border groups under the risk management and crisis prevention and management procedures introduced under the BRRD suggests not only that EU cross-border bank groups are now unqiue entities governed by EU law, but also that that they are governed by a distinct set of rules as discussed above: namely one prioritizing financial stability and banks' functions in the broader economy, a co-responsibilization of the banking sector for public objectives under the spectre of far-reaching powers granted to public authorities.

A Liberal Governance through Regulation?

This chapter has shown how the post-crisis EU rulebook for banks has sought to fill the lacunae in regulation of cross-border bank groups which became evident over the course of the Great Financial Crisis. The specific regulatory failure addressed was that though the emergence of cross-border bank groups had been

---

[47] Pamela Lintner, 'De/Centralized Decision Making Under the European Resolution Framework: Does Meroni Hamper the Creation of a European Resolution Authority?' *European Business Organization Law Review* 18 (2017): pp. 591–616; De Larosière, 'High-Level Group', p. 138.

the result of the internal market in the first place, the absence of their recognition in EU law amplified the crisis and its costs. As a consequence, renationalization and fragmentation of European markets prevailed with broadly negative consequences, in particular with regard to the real economy and societal costs. To remedy this shortcoming, the post-crisis regulatory framework has very broad objectives which relate to the general operation of the internal market in the EU—in order for these to be met cross-border banking had to be addressed specifically as well, in particular with regard to crisis prevention and management. The granular and detailed regulation which emerged marks both a change in the regulatory paradigm by introducing new forms of dealing with bank failure ex ante, but as well addresses the specific puzzle which emerged in an integrated (and liberalized) internal market, namely that of governance of new forms of bank internationalization.

Such cross-border bank structures, increasingly ubiquitous since the end of financial repression, are now a distinct concern of multiple authorities. This is as in the aftermath of the GFC a new way of thinking about banks' inherent stability developed in the EU. It was no longer only exogenous risk factors, but as well the internal organization of the bank which had destabilizing effects.[48] Such risks warrant that the new regulations interfere and guide the internal organization of the large banks and impose new public-like obligations on the bank's management. For this purpose, multiple authorities are tasked with monitoring various aspects of the operation of the financial system. Their powers differ depending on the time horizons (ongoing supervision, early intervention, crisis prevention or management), but also the scope of their mandates, that is whether their function relates to the financial sector only (e.g. stability of the financial system as aim of supervision) or to the broader economy (e.g. public interest in financial stability as the aim of resolution). Further, the new regime is marked by a functional approach focused on critical bank functions, which require sensitivity to specific concerns of discrete jurisdictions where a cross-border bank may be active,[49] especially as the new regulations are expressly concerned with regulating the sovereign-bank loop. The main features of the new regulatory regime, as discussed in this chapter, are the increased discretionary powers of authorities, the public-like duties imposed on bank management as well as the operational risk concern with the structure of cross-border entities.[50] The protective and functional

---

[48] On the shift of attention from exogenous to endogenous risk see: Michel Aglietta and Laurence Scialom, 'For a Renewal of Financial Regulation', in *The Manufacturing of Markets: Legal, Political and Economic Dynamics,* edited by Eric Brousseau and Michel Glachant (Cambridge: Cambridge University Press, 2014), pp. 333–52. For a general overview of the evolution in economic thinking about financial regulation see Jon Danielsson, (ed.), *Post-Crisis Banking Regulation: Evolution of Economic Thinking as It Happened on Vox* (CEPR report, 2015).

[49] Eva Hüpkes, 'Form Follows Function: A New Architecture for Regulating and Resolving Global Financial Institutions' *European Business Organization Law Review* 10, no. 3 (2009): pp. 369–85.

[50] Grundmann, Petit, and Smoleńska, 'Bank Governance'.

perspective on bank regulation means that more emphasis is now placed by regulators on the ex ante risk-preparedness and resilience, i.e. safeguarding the critical functions even before the crisis materializes, which also brings about greater precision as to why banking warrants special treatment.

The novel elements of the regulatory and supervisory framework affect the autonomy of banks to such an extent and with such specific purpose,[51] so as to blur the lines traditionally drawn between regulation and corporate governance. Such a governance focus differentiates the post-crisis regime from the previous regime, which relied primarily on authorization and basic monitoring of compliance by supervisors, supplemented by partial insurance via the deposit guarantees. The new regime in place is preventive, governance-oriented and highly granular, marking a cognitive shift in terms of how the goals of regulation may be achieved.[52] The liberal market openness which continues to characterize EU regulation could be preserved only by increasing the responsibility of the bank management for attaining the regulatory objectives.

---

[51] Business choice of banks are assessed as a matter of EU law also in the context of state aid cases, e.g. Case-526/14, *Tadej Kotnik and Others v Državnizbor Republike Slovenije* (2016) ECLI:EU:C:2016:570.

[52] Julia Black, 'Restructuring Global and EU Financial Regulation: Character, Capacities and Learning', in *Financial Regulation and Supervision: A Post-Crisis Analysis*, edited by Eddy Wymeersch, Klaus Hopt, and Guido Ferrarini (Oxford: Oxford University Press, 2012), pp. 3–47.

Index